THE
PENNSYLVANIA CONSTITUTION
OF 1776

Da Capo Press Reprints in

AMERICAN CONSTITUTIONAL AND LEGAL HISTORY

GENERAL EDITOR: LEONARD W. LEVY
Claremont Graduate School

THE
PENNSYLVANIA CONSTITUTION
OF 1776

A STUDY IN REVOLUTIONARY DEMOCRACY

By

J. Paul Selsam

DA CAPO PRESS • NEW YORK • 1971

THE
PENNSYLVANIA CONSTITUTION
OF
1776

THE
PENNSYLVANIA CONSTITUTION
OF 1776

A STUDY IN REVOLUTIONARY DEMOCRACY

By

J. Paul Selsam, Ph.D.
The Pennsylvania State College

Philadelphia
UNIVERSITY OF PENNSYLVANIA PRESS
London: Humphrey Milford: Oxford University Press
1936

To My
MOTHER AND FATHER

ACKNOWLEDGMENTS

THE author wishes to express his appreciation to Professors Thomas J. Wertenbaker and Clifton R. Hall of Princeton University for their assistance and counsel in the preparation of this study; also to Professor Edward S. Corwin of Princeton who suggested the study and under whose guidance several phases were investigated; and further to Professor H. H. Shenk of Lebanon Valley College and Dr. Curtis W. Garrison, State Archivist of Pennsylvania, for their helpful suggestions and criticisms. To my wife and to Miss Elsie Beaumont my heartiest thanks are due for their assistance in reading the proof.

J. P. S.

CONTENTS

INTRODUCTION

THE transition from colonies to states—the overthrowing of the old governments and the writing of state constitutions—was an important phase of the revolt of the American Colonies from Great Britain. It was more difficult to accomplish this in Pennsylvania than in the other colonies because of the greater conflict of interests. As a result no colony suffered more from internal strife. The bitter struggle which ensued hindered the progress of the war with England and caused rioting and bloodshed in the once peaceful province founded by William Penn.

All was not tranquil in Pennsylvania itself when the shot was fired "by the rude bridge" at Concord. A study of the Revolutionary period in Pennsylvania's history reveals at once the deep-seated and long-felt grievances of many of its inhabitants. The purpose of this study is to show how the first Constitution of the state was formed as a result of the growth of democratic opinions and beliefs, and to discuss the heated battle fought over it and the effect this had upon the Revolution

The attempt to form a new constitution in Pennsylvania was apparently a part of the general movement to throw off the yoke of Great Britain. But in reality it was far more than that! It was the outgrowth of years of patient suffering and smouldering antagonism; the culmination of class rivalry and sectional strife; the development of the spirit of democracy. The struggle over the first constitution framed in 1776 was caused not merely by political questions—theories of sovereignty, checks and balances, the doctrine of the separation of powers—but also by the clash of economic, ethnic, religious, social, and sectional interests.

Pennsylvania in 1776 presented the striking situation of a revolution within a revolution. The revolt against England afforded a favorable opportunity for the Scotch-Irish and Germans to free themselves from the autocratic rule of the English Quakers. The hardy frontiersmen, too, now could avenge themselves upon the Assembly, controlled by the peace-loving Quakers, for its neglect to provide protection from the Indians.

Religion and race were of particular importance because the Scotch-Irish on the frontier were predominantly Presbyterian, whereas the ruling eastern aristocracy were largely English, either Episcopalian or Quaker. This antagonism was heightened by the conflicting economic interests, for the West was exclusively an agricultural section, while the East and Southeast were primarily engaged in mercantile and financial pursuits.

The political movement in Pennsylvania was similar to that in the colonies as a whole—involving the question of representation. One factor, however, distinguishes the two movements. The western farmers of Pennsylvania had representation in the Provincial Assembly, whereas the colonists had none in the British House of Commons. The frontiersmen were concerned with obtaining more adequate representation for themselves.

The emphasis on the sectional characteristics of the struggle can easily be carried too far, for the same differences already mentioned existed in the city of Philadelphia. Due to property qualifications for the suffrage, the laborers and mechanics of the eastern metropolis were denied the vote. Consequently, like the Westerner they suffered from inadequate representation in the Assembly. The questions of race and religion were likewise prominent here.

Thus it was that the real leadership in the movement for a Constitution came from Philadelphia. The Western counties gave the leaders of the East their devoted support, but even this was not powerful enough to overthrow the old aristocratic and conservative rule. Then it was that the radicals in Pennsylvania turned for aid to the members of Congress who desired independence. This coalition was all-powerful. It carried

everything before it and swept away the old charter government of Pennsylvania.

In the pages which follow we shall trace the combined revolutionary and constitutional movement showing the development of a completely democratic spirit. We shall see the down-
fall of the Proprietary Government, an exceedingly democratic constitution established in its place, and the fierce battle which resulted from the attempt to establish a government
under this constitution of the people.

J. P. S.

I

THE PROPRIETARY GOVERNMENT

1. Racial and Religious Groups

ON THE fourth of March, 1681, William Penn was made the sole proprietor of a grant of land in the new world by King Charles II. This grant was in payment of a debt the King owed to Admiral Penn, the father of William. One of young Penn's desires was to found a commonwealth on the principles of perfect equality and universal religious toleration.[1] But the idea was not merely to establish toleration; there was to be religious liberty and freedom from all state interference.[2] While the colony was to be an asylum for the persecuted Quakers of England, so generous was the policy of the Proprietor that Pennsylvania soon became a haven for the oppressed of all religious sects. This magnificent ideal appealed strongly to the downtrodden peoples of Europe. These classes were encouraged, too, by the liberal grants of land. By 1755 it was estimated that out of a total white population of 220,000 there were 100,000 of non-English birth.[3]

The German immigrants were the first to arrive in any great numbers. Several companies, including the Frankfort Land Company, were formed to encourage their coming. Many pamphlets were distributed by these companies through

---

[1] Thomas F. Gordon, *History of Pennsylvania*, pp. 52-54.

[2] Isaac Sharpless, *A Quaker Experiment in Government*, p. 121. Of course this liberty did not extend to non-Christians. By an act of Assembly in 1705 even Catholics were excluded from all civil offices. However, it must be remembered that the Crown had considerable control over the colony, and much legislation was forced upon it. As Sharpless points out: "Had they been independent of English control, the experiment would have been more conclusive." *Ibid.*, p. 3.

[3] *Documents Relative to the Colonial History of New York*, VI, 993.

the Palatinate and the Rhine Valley.[4] "The German nation," wrote Dr. Schoepf, "forms a considerable part, probably more than a third of the state of Pennsylvania."[5] Benjamin Franklin estimated that the population was about one-third English Quakers, one-third Germans, and one-third a variety of races, chiefly Scotch-Irish Presbyterians.[6] The last came in great numbers as the eighteenth century advanced, and poured into the interior, settling principally in Lancaster, York, and Cumberland counties.[7] They kept moving westward and long preceded the development of counties in that section of the province. They were the hardy, fearless frontiersmen who played an important part in the struggle with England and the fight for a new government in Pennsylvania.[8]

To these racial differences must be added those of a religious nature. The freedom which was assured in Pennsylvania led to a rapid multiplication of denominations and sects. Robert Proud, an early historian of the state, remarked that there was "a greater number of different religious societies in" Pennsylvania than perhaps in any other of the British dominions.[9] The settling of these various sects and nationalities in

---

[4] The Frankfort Land Co. secured 15,000 acres of land in Pennsylvania and sent Francis Daniel Pastorius as their agent and attorney. For a detailed list of pamphlets and works which helped to induce German immigration to Pennsylvania see Julius F. Sachse, "Pennsylvania: The German Influence in its Settlement and Development," The Proceedings of the Pennsylvania German Society, VII (1897), 157-163; 175-197 and Appendix.

[5] Dr. J. D. Schoepf, Travels in the Confederation, I, 102. Robert Proud estimated the number of Germans who came to Pennsylvania from the first settlement to 1776 to be about 39,000, and he remarked that their "internal increase has been very great." History of Pennsylvania, II, 274.

[6] Charles J. Stillé, "Life and Writings of John Dickinson," Memoirs of the Historical Society of Pennsylvania, XIII, 131.

[7] Pennsylvania Magazine of History and Biography, X, 285. Hereafter referred to as Pa. Mag.

[8] For a good account of the spirit of the pioneer and how the frontier was extended, vide "An Account of the Progress of the Population, Agriculture, Manners, and Government in Pennsylvania, in a Letter to a Friend in England." Essays, Benjamin Rush, Philadelphia, 1798. See also "Thoughts on the Situation of the Inhabitants on the Frontier," by James Tilghman, circa 1772. Printed in Pa. Mag., X, 316-17.

[9] History of Pennsylvania, II, 337.

different regions of the province early complicated the political situation. Thus resulted sectional differences and disharmony of interests, at times exceedingly acute.

The English, composed mainly of Quakers and Episcopalians, settled largely in Philadelphia, Chester, and Bucks counties. Engaged in commerce and banking, they were the wealthy and aristocratic element in the province. Consequently they had little in common with the Scotch-Irish Presbyterian farmers in York, Cumberland, and the new western counties.[10] The Germans living in Lancaster, Berks, and Northampton counties were of two main groups, the one the Lutherans and Reformed, and the other the pietistic sects such as the Moravians, Schwenkfelders, Mennonites, and Dunkers.

It was but natural that these various racial and religious groups should form themselves into political parties. The Quakers had early assumed the hegemony and, by uniting with the German pietistic sects, which held beliefs similar to their own, were able to maintain themselves in power. This combination eventually became the anti-proprietary or Quaker party.[11] The Proprietary or Presbyterian party con-

---

[10] *Pa. Mag.*, X, 285.

[11] The Germans, however, were not always loyal to the Quakers and by skilful maneuverings could be brought over to the proprietary side. To the reader unfamiliar with the early history of Pennsylvania it might appear strange that the Quakers formed the anti-proprietary party. With the departure of William Penn three political parties developed. One was the party devoted to proprietary interests and sympathies, and included the more wealthy and highly educated Quakers. The second was the popular party, composed mainly of country Quakers, some Germans, and other liberty-loving people. The third was the opposition non-Quaker party without much influence in the Council or Assembly. Its ultimate object was the change to a Crown colony.

During the long series of wars in which Pennsylvania was involved in the eighteenth century these party alignments changed. The Quakers soon became a minority in the Province, but were practically all on one side. The sons of Penn left the Society of Friends and several joined the Episcopal Church, so that body rallied around them. Since the Proprietors advocated a vigorous war policy they were joined by the Presbyterians. These groups stood together for proprietary rights and interests, and had as their stronghold the Governor and Council. The Friends and the German sectarians maintained their ascendency in the Assembly where they opposed the Proprietary pretensions, favored

sisted of the Presbyterians, the Episcopalians, and the German Reformed and Lutherans. The ties which bound them were very loose. They supported the Proprietors not because of any personal regard but because they held political and religious views with which the Penns were sympathetic.[12] Furthermore, the wealthy and aristocratic Episcopalians in the eastern counties had little in common with the Presbyterians. Their lack of strength compelled them to unite with some other group. Francis Alison,[13] in a letter dated April 15, 1764, to the Reverend Dr. Ezra Stiles, president of Yale, wrote: "The Episcopal Party are very uneasy, that their power here is not equal to what it is in England; . . . Our debates run high in this Province at this time, between the Presbyterians & Quakers, who of all others should unite most heartily in defence of liberty. . . . But I fear the consequences of these squabbles; the mice & Frogs may fight, till ye Kite devours both. . . ."[14]

---

grants to the Indians, and reduced expenses for military operations whenever possible. Even during the régime of the founder the Quakers were aroused against him, for William Penn, being a practical man, did not hesitate to commend force in civil affairs when necessary. He was the feudal lord of the province, liable to be called upon to support Britain's causes by force of arms. This he could not do personally, but if the Deputy Governor had no scruples in the matter, Penn would not interfere to prevent obedience to the commands of the Crown. He selected non-Quaker deputies, and a perpetual strife was thus engendered between the Quaker Assembly and the non-Quaker representatives of the Proprietors. *Vide* Sharpless, *op. cit.*, pp. 87; 103-04; 192; *infra*, p. 29, note 99.

[12] John Penn, although not a regular attendant at Quaker meetings and not a strict observer of their customs, never joined the Church of England. Richard Penn became a communicant of that church in youth, and Thomas Penn became an Episcopalian about 1758. This caused the Friends to be bitter against them. *Vide* William R. Shepherd, *A History of Proprietary Government in Pennsylvania*, pp. 216; 551.

[13] Francis Alison, of Scotch-Irish descent, was the Vice-Provost and Professor of Moral Philosophy at the College of Philadelphia.

[14] Ezra Stiles, *Itineraries and Correspondence*, edited by F. B. Dexter, pp. 425-26. The Episcopalians became more influential as time went on. Alison later remarked that the "College is artfully got into ye hands of Episcopal Trustees." *Ibid.*, p. 428. Samuel Purviance, Jr., a Philadelphia merchant devoted to the Presbyterian Church, in a letter to Ezra Stiles on Nov. 1, 1766, shows the bitter feeling existing among the Presbyterians, Quakers, and

2. *Government*

Though William Penn was an enthusiastic sectarian, the propagation of his religious opinions was of secondary importance. He had evolved a plan of civil government which he desired to submit to the test of experience.[15] The charter of March 4, 1681, empowered the Proprietor to enact laws with the assent of the freemen of the province, to appoint judges and other officers, and to carry out the powers usually invested in an executive. Accordingly, Penn drew up in 1682 the *Proprietary Frame of Government.*

Although this instrument was not democratic in its origin —having been granted or "octroyed" by William Penn—yet its equitable provisions and its general acceptability to the people entitle it to a very high rank. How could it be stamped as anything but democratic when it declared: *"Any government is free to the people under it* (whatever be the frame) *where the laws rule, and the people are a party to those laws, . . ."*[16]

But Penn soon got into many difficulties with the people. One of the main sources of irritation was his double rôle of governor and landowner. Here was an attempt to have liberal popular government and at the same time maintain the Proprietor's rights.

The people were constantly striving to get better terms, never seeming to be satisfied. Many refused to pay the quit-

---

Episcopalians. The Episcopalians had promised the Presbyterians their aid in the complicated and acrid party struggle in the election of 1766, but apparently had deceived them. "They rejoice," says Purviance, "at a Quarrel between us and yᵉ Qu—rs & no doubt expect that in the midst of our Contests theyle one day or other get the upper hand of us both; they are certainly more jealous of us as a growing Body than of the Qu—rs & well know our Spirit to oppose them, for wᵗ Reason they throw their Weight into tother Scale ags. us; . . ." *Ibid.*, p. 554.

[15] Gordon, *op. cit.*, p. 54.

[16] For the origin of the first frame of government and the ideas of Penn and his friends, see the volume of the Penn MSS entitled "Charters and Frames of Government", in the Historical Society of Pennsylvania Library. The above quotation is from the preface to the *Proprietary Frame of Government*, 1682. This document shows the influence of Harrington's *Oceana*.

rents, and showed their resentment by electing representatives opposed to the Proprietor. These men scrutinized every action of the administration and continually sought to lessen its power. What appeared in the first session of the Legislature as good-natured requests for changes in the form of government soon developed into a relentless struggle to embarrass the proprietary officials and to curb their power.

Penn was forced to make many concessions to the growing democratic spirit. In 1701, by and with the consent of the General Assembly, he promulgated his last governmental instrument for Pennsylvania—the *Charter of Privileges*.[17] This recognized the existence of the Assembly, but by it the Council ceased to be a representative body and had no share in legislation other than that of advising the governor.[18] And this was of little importance, for the Assembly was inclined to resent any interference whatever in this field.[19] No trace of the spirit which dominated the earlier frames of government is seen. It shows the extent to which Penn was forced to make concessions. The Assembly was no longer merely a ratifying body. After nearly twenty years of agitation[20] it was given the

---

[17] Besides those already mentioned, frames of government were issued in 1683 and 1696. For the *Charter of Privileges* see Ben. Perley Poore, *Charters and Constitutions*, II, 1538; Francis N. Thorpe, *Constitutions and Charters*, V, 3076-3081.

[18] The Charter makes no mention of the Council. It was constituted by letters patent by William Penn in 1701. Its composition was radically changed, for it was now to consist of ten members, "nominated, appointed and ordained" by Penn to act as his advisers. In his absence or that of the deputy the Council could administer the government. *Vide* Proud, *op. cit.*, I, 451.

[19] *Vide* Evarts B. Greene, *The Provincial Governor*, pp. 83, 145.

[20] The chief spirit in this agitation was David Lloyd, an arch-opponent of the Proprietary. James Logan wrote in Feb., 1726, that the "error of William Penn was in heaping things called privileges on a people who neither knew how to use them nor how to be grateful for them." Penn MSS, *Official Correspondence*, I. In November, 1729, Logan, a man of high intellectual attainments who was brought over in 1699 by Penn as his secretary and agent, and who successively held many posts including that of President of the Council, sincerely faithful to the Proprietor, said that Penn "granted to his friends such privileges as might be suitable to those individuals at that time without considering strangers or what disposition his successors might make. He did not preserve the true balance between liberty and power." *Ibid.*, II. See Samuel Hazard, *Register of Pennsylvania*, XV, 182.

right to initiate legislation and was raised to a position coequal with the governor in legislative power.[21]

Penn disliked this change[22] but he was powerless to act, for his position was very precarious. In 1693 his government was taken away by the Crown and given to Governor Fletcher of New York. While it was restored the next year by letters patent from William and Mary, Penn's situation was by no means secure, for during his absence from England—1699-1701— Parliament tried to obtain possession of his province. This move was supported by a group in Pennsylvania who claimed that the Friends were unfit to govern on account of their unwillingness to fight or contribute for defense.[23] Friction thus developed very early in the life of the Quaker colony. It continued with varying intensity throughout its history, bursting into flame on the eve of the revolt of the colonies from England and finally destroying the government of William Penn.

3. *Control of the Purse*

The causes of friction were numerous and varied. One was the ever-increasing democratic spirit nurtured by the frontier.

---

[21] In Pennsylvania the Crown had reserved to itself a veto on legislation. *Charter to W. Penn*, 1681. Poore, *op. cit.*, II, 1509. Albert S. Bolles, in his *Pennsylvania: Province and State*, writes "that very early and perhaps unconsciously, were the seeds of the revolutionary spirit sown. By its charter the Provincial government had five years to present bills to the privy-council. If they thought a bill might be vetoed it was held back for nearly the entire period before sending it over. Then, if dis-allowed, by being re-enacted with some slight change, it was essentially still kept in force. Thus the Assembly kept within the letter of the charter, and thereby exercised almost absolute legislative powers." I, 216. Sometime prior to 1740 the Assembly secured the concession that the decision of the Lieutenant Governor, approving or disapproving a bill passed by the Assembly should be final and not subject to reversal by the Proprietary. *Pa. Mag.*, X, 286, article by Chas. J. Stillé.

[22] Shepherd, *op. cit.*, p. 293.

[23] Bolles, *op. cit.*, I, 186. Several attempts were made to convert Pennsylvania into a royal or crown colony, the most important being in 1764. *Votes and Proceedings of the House of Representatives of the Province of Pennsylvania*, V, 343-45. Hereafter cited as *Votes*. It was a determined fight and was ended only by the passage of the Stamp Act which caused the factions in Pennsylvania to drop their plans and combat the attempt to levy taxes upon them without their own consent. *Vide infra*, pp. 43-48.

Another was the struggle for the control of the purse, a source of discord in all the colonies.

It is a political axiom that the branch of the government which controls finances inevitably dominates the affairs of state. Very early in the history of Pennsylvania the Assembly voted that the government should be supported by the inhabitants. By having the Assembly pay the salary of the Governor and other officials they were subjected to popular supervision. The power thus gained was guarded ever after with the utmost zeal. It caused much hardship to the Founder during his personal administration. Penn expected a grant to himself, but how different a situation developed! Only small sums were forthcoming,[24] and after his return to England Penn not only got nothing, but even made private grants to his deputies and paid the salaries of the deputy governors, attorneys-general, and chief justices, hoping thereby to keep the government more readily in his grasp. Thus from the financial point of view the venture was not profitable and the Proprietor soon found himself in difficulties. He once wrote: "I am a crucified man between Injustice and Ingratitude there [meaning Pennsylvania], and Extortion and Oppression here."[25] He estimated that during the first twenty-five years of his proprietorship he had lost over £64,000.[26]

The Assembly early stated its position in very emphatic terms. In an answer to the Governor's message of December 24, 1706, it said: " . . . we . . . know that the privileges of the people consist not in divesting the Govr. of power & support, and we hope no such thing can be justly charged upon the people here; But on the other hand, If a Govr. would divest or deprive the Queen's Liege people in her particular Governmts. of the Privileges, that by the Statute Laws which are made for the Publick good, as well as by the Common Law, (which is their Birthright) they ought to enjoy, We are

---

[24] Shepherd, *op. cit.,* p. 204.

[25] *Penn and Logan Correspondence,* II, 71.

[26] *Breviat of Evidence, Penn and Baltimore,* p. 82. Quoted in Shepherd, *op. cit.,* p. 183.

clearly of opinion, That such a Govr. can not expect the people with Chearfulness to support him, . . . "[27] In this statement it is plainly discernible that the Assembly intended to interpret the statutes and laws itself and would oppose any governor who attempted to thwart its will.[28]

The position of the Governor, likewise, is clearly stated in a message of Charles Gookin to the Assembly in May 1715. He said that he was "ready to proceed with the. Assembly to finish the Business depending; but cannot be persuaded but that it is as much a part of the Assembly's Business to provide for a Support for the Governor as for any other exigency of the Country." The old methods, he said, did not "answer the End," and asked the Assembly to think of a more adequate way, "otherwise he will have Reason to think that, while Care is taken of all other the Wants of the Country, it is not intended there should be any Regard had of him, or his Support in the Administration; . . . "[29]

Gookin's remarks had little effect, for two years later the Assembly cynically told Governor William Keith upon his arrival that because it was "Seed Time" it would not discuss "any Business that will require Length of Time." But relying upon "the Governor's Resolves and good Intentions to oblige the People, by concurring with any Thing they can reasonably desire for their Service," it would appropriate £500 for his support.[30] No wonder Keith became subservient to the legislature and was accused of deserting the proprietary interests.[31]

Thus the struggle went on. In 1730 Governor Patrick Gordon, in a message to the Assembly, said that a certain bill was,

---

[27] *Colonial Records*, II, 292. Hereafter referred to as *Col. Rec.*

[28] "Nowhere," says Greene, "was the policy of keeping the governor under control by temporary grants, of granting money in exchange for legislation, more frankly and more cynically avowed than in Pennsylvania." *Op. cit.*, p. 174.

[29] *Votes*, II, 178. Governor Gookin said: "Both the Governor and Country are great Sufferers at present for want of necessary Bills to be passed into Laws; . . ." *Ibid.*

[30] *Votes*, II, 213.

[31] Keith was removed from the governorship on this account. *Vide* Proud, *op. cit.*, II, 177ff; *infra*, p. 21.

in his opinion, of "great Moment" and should be given further consideration "to prevent any ill Consequences." But, he said, "if the House do insist upon having it passed with the other Bills, the Governor will agree to it."[32] The House insisted, and when the Governor affixed the "Great Seal" to it and seven other measures the Speaker then presented him "With an Order on the Provincial Treasurer for One Thousand Pounds for his Support this current year, . . . "[33]

Another striking illustration of the power of the Assembly is seen in the application in 1736 of George Thomas, a wealthy planter of Antigua, for the position of deputy governor. He told John and Thomas Penn, the proprietors, that his independent fortune would raise him above temptation to avarice and corruption.[34] A financial compact was made but was kept secret for fear it might be regarded by the public as disreputable. Disputes soon arose between the Assembly and Governor Thomas and nothing was appropriated for his support. The people regarded it as a dire calamity that they should have a governor whose means raised him above the necessity of submitting to their will.[35]

It became a practice to send a favorite measure to the governor for his approbation with a "rider" appropriating his salary.[36] As time went on the Assembly more firmly estab-

---

[32] *Col. Rec.*, III, 379-80.

[33] *Ibid.*, III, 380.

[34] Penn MSS *Official Correspondence*, III, October 5, 1736.

[35] Shepherd, *op. cit.*, p. 207. Gov. Thomas wrote on October 20, 1740: "And that I, in particular, might feel the weight of their resentments, they adjourned themselves without giving that part of my support which had been for many years given to preceding governors at the session held at that season of the year, and kept it from me for near four months." *Statutes at Large*, IV, 470.

[36] For examples of this see the following: *Votes*, II, 178, 213, 463; III, 72, 343, 377, 380, 384; IV, 35, 106; V, 47, 425. A striking illustration of this is seen in the message sent to Governor Thomas by the Assembly in 1743: "We . . . assure the Governor that we are of the Opinion that Government should be honorably maintained; And whenever he shall be pleased to give his Assent to those Bills we shall cheerfully make . . . Provision for his Support." *Col. Rec.*, IV, 628. The next year the Assembly gave Governor Thomas his annual salary at one time instead of the usual two installments. To the committee of the Assembly which announced this fact to him he replied that "he ever disliked

lished its control over legislation through its relentless hold on the purse. In 1755 Governor Morris charged it with aiming to render itself independent and endeavoring to assume a superiority over the Proprietaries and Governors, a plan which it would "not fail to carry into execution were" its powers equal to its inclinations.[37] A few months before Morris asserted that the House was "grasping at the Disposition of all Publick Money and at the Power of filling all the offices of Government especially those of the Revenue, . . . "[38] A member of the Provincial Council stated in 1757 that "the Powers of Government are almost all taken out of the Hands of the Governor, and lodged in the Assembly; as to what little remains, scarce a bill comes up without an Attempt to lessen them."[39]

A report drawn up in 1757 by Mr. Richard Peters, a member of the Council, said that the "Assembly have of late very much encroached on the Rights of Government in this particular, vizt: That where any Office is created by Act of Assembly, the Officers are inserted in the Bill, with a Clause giving the Assembly the Right of Nomination in case of Death; and they will not suffer Amendments to their Bills in these particulars."[40] A pamphlet written in 1759 stated that every proprietary governor has "two Masters; one who gives him his Commission, and one who gives him his Pay, . . . The Subjects Money is never so well disposed of, as in the Maintenance of Order and Tranquillity, and the purchase of good Laws."[41]

---

bargaining for laws, that confidence naturally begot confidence, that the allowance now made him of the whole support for the current year, so far from obstructing his assent to any reasonable and necessary bills, would rather be an inducement to him to exceed their expectations." Bolles, *op. cit.*, I, 286.

[37] *Col. Rec.*, VI, 544.

[38] *Ibid.*, VI, 387. He told the Representatives that their resolutions "are and have been to take Advantage of your Country's Danger, to aggrandize and render permanent your own Power and Authority, . . . That it is for this Purpose and to promote your Scheme of future Independency You are grasping. . . ." *Ibid.*

[39] *Col. Rec.*, VII, 449.

[40] *Ibid.*, p. 449.

[41] *Historical Review of the Constitution and Government of Pennsylvania* (1759), pp. 72-3. Franklin denied the authorship of this pamphlet, but it is

Such was the power of the Assembly! Because the Quakers knew how to maintain their ascendency many a governor came to hate them. But it was not until the ire of the frontiersmen was aroused that the Quaker dominance came to an end. The victory, however, was not the Proprietors'—it was the people's.[42]

4. Attempts to Tax the Proprietors' Estates

A more serious cause for friction soon developed in the Assembly's attempt to tax the lands of the proprietors. Legally the proprietors were feudal lords; in reality they were private individuals possessing vast estates and holding the position of hereditary governors. The taxing power was given by the charter to the proprietors and the Assembly, with no restrictions as to the objects. Their lands had been expressly exempted from assessment, but as the needs of the country became greater the necessity for an increased revenue arose. If the vast estates of the Penns were exempted, this increase had to be borne solely by the people. This the citizens felt was unjust, and as the democratic spirit developed they demanded that the feudal rights of the proprietors be abolished and that, as owners of private property, they be considered as private individuals. In a message to the Governor in 1755 the Assembly said that it did not "propose to tax the Proprietary as Governor, but as a Fellow-Subject, a Landholder and Possessor of an Estate in *Pennsylvania*."[43] They might not be sub-

---

known that it was given his support. In the Convention which framed the Constitution of the United States Franklin made the following remarks concerning the governor in Pennsylvania: "The negative of the Governor was constantly made use of to extort money. No good law whatever could be passed without a private bargain with him. An increase of his salary, or some donation, was always made a condition; till at last it became the regular practice, to have orders in his favor on the Treasury, presented along with the bills to be signed, so that he might actually receive the former before he should sign the latter." *Documents Illustrative of the Formation of the Union of the American States*, p. 148.

[42] In the meantime the governors and the proprietors came to recognize the supremacy of the Assembly in financial matters and the quarrel gradually subsided as the relations with England became more strained. *Vide infra*, p. 18.

[43] *Votes*, IV, 424.

ject to the legislature in the public management of their property, but as private owners they were, in the minds of many, on a level with the poorest freeholder.[44]

On March 29, 1748, Thomas Penn, in a letter to one of his officers, gives us a statement of the proprietors on this subject. He declared that although they were willing to assist in making full provision for the defense of the province, they could not be compelled to contribute, for the Board of Trade had told them that they were no more liable to taxation than were the royal governors.[45] Three years later the Assembly declared that the estates of the Penns could not be taxed by England,[46] but intimated its own right to do so. Since the proprietors were not obliged, the House said, to bear any part of the expenses of a war in which the British nation is involved on account of their lands in Pennsylvania, "they may with us more freely contribute to the Expence of preserving Peace, especially on the Borders of their own Lands, as the Value of those Lands so much depends upon it."[47] An estimate commenced by Thomas Penn and completed by Benjamin Franklin in 1759, placed the value of the Penn estates at about ten millions of pounds sterling.[48]

The French and Indian raids on the western frontier in 1754 and the increasing distress of the people from the outrages of the Indians after Braddock's defeat reopened the question. The Assembly was now determined to take advantage of the serious situation to carry its point. Governor Morris insisted that the Proprietary estates should be exempted, but a bill was presented in July, 1755, which levied a tax on all estates, real and personal. The Governor amended it to exclude the lands of the Proprietors and the session ended with-

---

[44] Vide "Report on the Proprietaries Answer, &c," Votes, IV, 363. See also the long letter of William Penn to the Assembly, dated London, April 29, 1710, printed in Proud, op. cit., II, 45-52.

[45] Vide "The Representation of the General Assembly to Thomas and Richard Penn" (August, 1751), Votes, IV, 361.

[46] Votes, IV, 362.

[47] Ibid. Vide the answer of the "Proprietaries," ibid., pp. 362-68.

[48] Armor, William C., Lives of the Governors of Pennsylvania, p. 193.

out any action. Upon convening in October, a new bill was presented with a clause stating that the propriety of taxing the Penn estates should be decided by the Crown. Morris continued to oppose the bill, whereupon some citizens of Philadelphia agreed to contribute £500, the estimated tax the Proprietors would be compelled to pay.[49] The wrath of the Assembly was aroused and it went so far as to say that if the Governor persisted in his opposition to the bill it would be forced to make "an immediate Application and Complaint against him to our Sovereign."[50] To end the dispute the Proprietors directed that £5,000—more than ten times the amount which would have been realized by the bill—should be paid into the public treasury from the arrears of the quit-rents. This was to be regarded as a *free gift,* not in lieu of taxation. The Governor then signed the measure (November 27, 1755) which exempted the Proprietary estates.[51]

The exigencies of war compelled the Assembly to give way somewhat. But the continued exemption of such vast lands so aroused that body that it resolved to send the most recent money bill (that of March, 1758) to Benjamin Franklin, then in England,[52] so that he might lay it before the King and Par-

---

[49] *Votes,* IV, 439-40. It seemed to be the opinion of the "Subscribers" that the Penns would not tolerate such a condition, for they said, "and we doubt not but they will honourably acquit every Subscriber of this Expense."

[50] *Votes,* IV, 507. *Vide* "A Message to the Governor from the Assembly," *ibid.,* pp. 500-02. The Assembly told Morris that the matter was urgent and seemed just to them, but to try to convince him that it is reasonable if he has definite instructions to the contrary "will only waste Time." The Governor then said, ". . . in the Proprietary Commission appointing me to this Government, there is a Proviso that nothing therein contained shall extend, or be construed to extend, to give me any Power to do or consent to any Act whereby the Estate or Property of the Proprietors may be hurt or incumbered." *Votes,* IV, 421.

[51] *Votes,* IV, 524-26. Governor Morris grew tired of the controversy with the Assembly and resigned early in 1756. He was succeeded by Captain William Denny.

[52] Early in 1757 Franklin was sent by the Assembly to England for the purpose of obtaining a removal of the grievances caused by the instructions to the governors. He presented a paper called "Heads of Complaints," one section of which said: "That the proprietaries have enjoined their deputy by such instructions to refuse his assent to any law for raising money by tax, though

liament.[53] The hostile attitude of the Assembly caused the Proprietors to request the opinion of the attorney-general and solicitor-general concerning the power of the House in this matter. The opinion of these officers was that the legislature had no right to levy taxes on the Proprietors without their consent.[54] Their decision made little difference to the Assembly, for it controlled the Governor through the payment of his salary.

٠ As the French and Indian War continued, the Assembly gained more power. In 1759 a bill was passed which taxed the Proprietary estates under certain conditions.[55] The Penns objected, but realized that they must submit or else have their lands sold. Thomas Penn wrote to the secretary of the council on August 31, 1759, as follows: "You are no longer to say that we will not submit, but delay by appeal and exceptions as other people do."[56] When Franklin returned from his mission to England in 1762 the Assembly decided that the estates of the Proprietors in Pennsylvania should be taxed in due proportion for the defense of the colony.[57] The Proprietors were thus forced to yield to the demands of a people conscious of their own strength.

5. Sectional Controversies

a. DEFENSE

The question of colonial defense was another factor which led to prolonged quarrels between the Governor and the Assembly and also between the conservative Easterners and the hardy frontiersmen. The Quakers, opposed to bearing arms, controlled the Assembly. The frequent wars in Europe in which England was involved during the eighteenth century

---

ever so necessary for the defense of the country, unless the greater part of their estate is exempted from such a tax. This to the assembly and people of Pennsylvania appears both unjust and cruel." *Votes*, V, 20; see *infra*, p. 28.

[53] *Votes*, IV, 806; see *ibid.*, pp. 804-19.
[54] Shepherd, *op. cit.*, pp. 453-54.
[55] *Ibid.*, pp. 459-62.
[56] Penn MSS, *Penn Letter Book*, VI, to Peters.
[57] Franklin, *Works*, Smyth ed., IV, 226.

had their counterpart here and forced the colonists into struggles for which they were not responsible. The Quakers asked, with some degree of justice, why they should become entangled in wars which did not concern them.

In April 1689, the colonists were notified of the declaration of war against France, known in colonial annals as King William's War. Since Pennsylvania, along with Maryland and the Carolinas, was not under immediate royal control, the Lords of Trade recommended to the Privy Council that the Proprietors should be directed to put their dominions in a state of defense. When Governor Blackwell of Pennsylvania placed this suggestion before the Provincial Council and requested that a militia be established, the replies of the Councilors were significant. One said that he saw "no danger but from the Bears & wolves"; another said that "if we should put ourselves into Armes, The Indians would rise against us, suspecting we intended harm to them"; and a third replied that the English king knew full well "the judgment of Quakers in this case before Governor Penn had his patent."[58] After much discussion the five Quaker members of the Council asked leave to retire for a conference. On their return they announced, "We would not tye others' hands, But we cannot Act. We would not take upon us to hinder any, And do not think the Govr. need to call us together in this matter . . . We say nothing against it, and regard it as a matter of conscience to us. . . ."[59] No action was taken.

In 1701 the War of the Spanish Succession, known in America as Queen Anne's War, broke out. England was fighting both France and Spain, and much excitement was created in the colonies. But Pennsylvania had taken no measures for defense, and the Assembly refused every appeal of Governor Evans to enact a military law.[60] Even the ruse of a threatened

---

[58] *Col. Rec.*, (ed. of 1852), I, 306-07. For a discussion of colonial defense see Winfred T. Root, *The Relations of Pennsylvania with the British Government*, ch. ix.

[59] *Col. Rec.*, I, 310.

[60] Gordon, *op. cit.*, p. 140.

attack failed to arouse the peace-loving Quakers.[61] By 1709 the war was being waged on this continent and seriously threatened the northern provinces. In the plan formed by the English Ministry for the conquest of Canada, Pennsylvania was required to furnish only 150 privates with their officers. The Governor, however, fully realized the difficulty of raising even that number and proposed that the Assembly provide £4,000 to be expended by a committee appointed by it.[62] The Assembly considered the request, but declared that "were it not that the raising money to hire men to fight or kill one another, is matter of Concience [sic.] to us and against our Religious Principles, we should not be wanting, according to our small abilities, to Contribute to those designs."[63]

The Assembly did, however, express its loyalty to the Queen and offered to give £500 of the revenue as a present to her. If she chose to use it for military purposes, that was none of its affair. The Governor insisted on a larger sum and in his message said that "altho' you find a scruple in matters of war, no conscience can be pleaded to prevent you from Dutifully offering to Her Majesty . . . a sum that may become you to give her, as well as be in some measure worthy of Her Royal acceptance."[64] The House pleaded poverty and refused to increase the grant, while the Governor declined to consider any bill until a proper supply was voted. In the bitter fight[65] which ensued William Penn was forced to enter.[66] He won the victory, for the popular leader, David Lloyd, was defeated and

---

[61] Proud, op. cit., I, 469-71.

[62] In his address to the Assembly the Governor said: "Perhaps it may seem difficult to raise that number of men, in a country where most of the inhabitants are obliged, by their principles, not to make use of arms; but if you will raise, for the support of government, the sum demanded, I do not doubt getting the number of men, whose principles allow the use of them, and Commissioners may be appointed for disposal of the country's money; that the people may be satisfied, that the money is applied to no other use, than this expedition. . . ." Quoted in Proud, op. cit., II, 21.

[63] Col. Rec., II, 460.

[64] Ibid., II, 462. June 9, 1709.

[65] Proud, op. cit., II, 28-45.

[66] See the interesting letter of Penn quoted in ibid., pp. 45ff.

an entirely new legislative body elected.[67] Although harmony was restored the Assembly still declined to take any active part in the war. It recognized, nevertheless, that it owed some duties to the Crown, for £2,000 was raised for the Queen's use in lieu of the province's quota of men.[68]

After the Treaty of Utrecht in 1713, which ended Queen Anne's War, there was peace in the British Empire for twenty-six years. This was due to the policies of that great Prime Minister Robert Walpole. During this period the relations between the Governor and the Assembly were more in accord.[69] Although the nine years of Sir William Keith's governorship (1717-1726) were marked by fewer difficulties,[70] the old questions which had troubled the province since its beginning were still important—questions which affected the rights of property, the administration of justice, improvement of the circulating medium, mode of buying, selling, and taxing lands, payment of quit-rents, and measures of public defense. The inhabitants, in general, were apathetic to political affairs, save where they touched some personal interest or property right.[71]

More than anything else, peace was needed to preserve harmony in the government of Pennsylvania. But peace was one thing which was denied. In 1739 war broke out with Spain, the so-called War of Jenkin's Ear. The ensuing year this struggle merged into the general European conflict known as the War of the Austrian Succession, or in the colonies as King

---

[67] *Ibid.*, pp. 53-54.

[68] Bolles, *op. cit.*, I, 209; Proud, II, 56.

[69] Every year, however, drew a greater variety of people into the province. The cosmopolitan population increased the difficulties of governing, and loosened the bonds of affection between the Proprietor and the inhabitants. Penn gradually lost interest in his "Holy experiment" and was on the verge of selling his province to the crown—the agreement having actually been made—when he was stricken with paralysis. Thus the proprietary rule was destined to be continued for sixty years longer. Penn died on July 30, 1718. Bolles, *op. cit.*, I, 210; Proud, II, 117.

[70] Keith, however, as governor was unfaithful to the proprietary interests and was removed. *Vide* Proud, *op. cit.*, II, 177ff, and *supra*, p. 12.

[71] *Vide* Bolles, *op. cit.*, I, 263-67.

George's War. Since England was fighting both France and Spain, each ruler of vast domains in the western hemisphere, her colonies in America became involved. The efforts of Governor Thomas to arouse a war spirit were of no avail. The Assembly made a few grants, but when it refused to take any action against the Spanish privateers in the Delaware, Thomas was so enraged that he sent sharp messages to it. The Assembly, in turn, charged him with overthrowing the liberties of the people. In disgust, he told the Board of Trade that it was hopeless to expect military aid so long as the Quakers had the right to sit in the Assembly and dispose of the public money. He suggested stringent measures for the defense of Pennsylvania, even to the extent of excluding the Quakers from the legislature by an act of Parliament.[72] As a parting word Thomas wrote: "I am too well acquainted with the narrow, bigoted views of the governing sect here not to be convinced that it is impossible for me to serve His Majesty faithfully and please them under the present circumstances of public affairs. . . ."[73]

The Quakers, now alert, were unusually active in the elections of 1741. They succeeded in electing to the Assembly a large majority of their belief. Government almost came to a standstill. No salary was paid the Governor; no laws were approved. To maintain himself the Governor determined to remove from office all whose views differed from his own. This aroused active opposition, and both parties again put forth strenuous efforts at the polls in the elections of 1742. Their strength was about equal in the city, but in the counties the

---

[72] Penn MSS, *Official Correspondence*, III, Gov. Thomas to John Penn, Nov. 5, 1739; to F. J. Paris, May 14, 1741; also Shepherd, *op. cit.*, pp. 535-36. The agent of the Assembly, Richard Partridge, by some underhanded means gained a copy of this letter and sent it to the Assembly. That body was exceedingly indignant and petitions were sent to the King and to the Proprietor requesting the removal of Governor Thomas. When this failed the Quakers "persuaded many of the Germans who had never voted before to cast their ballots for candidates who were known to be opposed to the establishment of a militia and to the expenditure of money for military purposes." Shepherd, *op. cit.*, pp. 525-26; Root, *op. cit.*, p. 282.

[73] Pennsylvania *Statutes at Large*, IV, 477. See his interesting letter dated Oct. 20, 1740. *Ibid.*, pp. 468-77.

Quakers, allied with the pacific Germans, were supreme. The latter were told that a militia would subject them to a bondage to governors as severe as "they were formerly under to their princes in Germany, that the expenses would impoverish them, and that if any other than Quakers should be chosen upon the assembly they would be dragged down from their farms and obliged to build forts as a tribute for their being admitted to settle in the province."[74] The party of the Governor groundlessly feared violence from the Germans, and the situation was apparently very tense. Early on the morning of the election a party of about thirty sailors armed with clubs marched through the streets. Suspecting mischief, the Mayor was requested to take proper measures to preserve the peace. He refused. When the polls opened the sailors joined by others advanced upon the "Election Place" in a threatening manner and a riot broke out. The sailors were driven to the ships. Many were arrested and thrown into prison. The Assembly investigated the cause of the riot and in its "Address" to the Governor said, "it is reasonable to believe" that the sailors "must have been engaged in this wicked and Dangerous Enterprise by some who have had longer residence amongst us."[75]

An understanding was finally reached after much discussion, and the Assembly appropriated, in 1745, £4,000 for "Bread, Beef, Pork, Flour, Wheat or other Grain"[76] for the support of the garrison in Louisburg, recently captured by the English. The Governor, giving a wide interpretation to "other Grain," used part of the fund to buy gunpowder.[77] So

---

[74] *Statutes at Large*, IV, 470-71.

[75] *Col. Rec.*, IV, 620-22. The Assembly asked the Governor to recommend or direct what Courts were to take cognizance of the affair, but Governor Thomas refused, saying that it "may not only be of bad Example to succeeding Governours, but be of the most dangerous Consequence to the Liberties of the People; . . ." *Ibid.*, p. 624.

[76] *Votes*, IV, 14. During the previous year £3,000 was granted "for the use of the King . . . to be applied to such Uses as he, in his Royal Wisdom, shall think fit to direct and appoint." *Historical Review*, etc., p. 94.

[77] Gordon, in his *History of Pennsylvania*, says: "Dr. Franklin assures us, that the words 'other grain' were intended to cover the application of part of the money granted to the purchase of gunpowder, and that Governor Thomas

little scandal was caused by this action that the next year
£5,000 was given to Governor Thomas "for the Use of the
King" without stipulating the purpose for which it was to be
used.[78] With this money four companies were raised and sent
to Albany.[79]

In this manner the heated controversy ended. It is undoubtedly true that Governor Thomas was neither wise nor tactful
in dealing with the situation. Had he proposed raising a
volunteer militia in which no Quaker would be compelled to
serve, the Assembly would have made sufficient financial
grants and all would have been well. But Thomas chose "to
run a tilt with the religious opinions of a people who meas-
ured their merit by the extent of suffering for conscience
sake."[80]

After nine years of fighting the war was ended by the peace
of Aix-la-Chapelle in 1748. The northern colonies had borne
the brunt of the struggle. Pennsylvania had contributed little
either in money or soldiers, and her citizens had remained at
home engaged in profitable industries. Many people in the
province opposed this attitude of the Assembly, among them
Benjamin Franklin. In November 1747, seeing the danger of
an attack by the French and Spanish, Franklin published a
pamphlet called "Plain Truth"[81] in which he pictured the utter helplessness of the province; criticized the Quakers for
their unwillingness to relinquish their power in the Assembly,
and made a powerful plea for a militia. He told the Quakers
that although they themselves might be "resigned and easy
under this naked, defenseless state of the country," it was "far

---

actually expended a part of it for this black grain, and was never accused of
mis-appropriating the fund." P. 249.

[78] The governor wanted more but the Assembly would grant no more unless
he assented to the issuance of Bills of Credit. This he refused to do, so the
£5,000 only was voted. *Votes*, IV, 40-41.

[79] *Votes*, IV, 38, 40, and 41. Gordon, *op. cit.*, p. 251.

[80] Gordon, *op. cit.*, p. 227.

[81] *Pennsylvania Gazette*, November 12 and 14, 1747. A first edition may have
appeared in 1746, but it is doubtful if it was printed before 1747. See *Life and
Writings of Franklin*, Sparks ed., III, 1-3.

otherwise with a very great part of the people," who had no confidence that God would protect those who failed to take reasonable measures for their own security. A plan of association was drawn up, chiefly by Franklin, and signed by over 1,200 persons. It was not long before 10,000 men in the province and the Lower Counties (Delaware) were under arms and formed into companies and regiments.[82]

It was well that this action was taken, for Pennsylvania was soon to see war fought on her own soil.

French and Indian War

As the westward movement led the intrepid traders and trappers beyond the Alleghenies into the land claimed by the King of France war appeared imminent. Both the English and the French strove to gain the Indians for allies, a policy involving grave danger for the Western settlements. On the eve of the French and Indian War—the name given by the Colonists to the general European conflict known as the Seven Years' War—the difficulties between the West and the East became ominous, for the whole situation was now to be changed. Fighting was to take place on Pennsylvania's soil, and the Scotch-Irish frontiersmen could not see their homes burned and their lands wasted while the Quaker merchants in Philadelphia lived in peace and plenty. Although war was not proclaimed until May 1756, it began, so far as Pennsylvania was concerned, when George Washington was compelled to surrender Fort Necessity on July 4, 1754. What was the response of the Assembly when the French carried the fighting into the province of William Penn?

The chief complaint of the frontiersmen was that the

---

[82] Shepherd, op. cit., 530; Gordon, op. cit., p. 245. The Proprietors condemned this action in no uncertain terms. Thomas Penn said that it "strongly resembles treason." Shepherd, op. cit., p. 530. His chief objection seems to have been that these "associators" elected certain of their officers and also a military council, the orders of which were binding until the King should command otherwise. Later, however, the Proprietors became more favorable towards the movement. P. L. B., III, T. P. to Hamilton, Aug. 27, 1750. This was James Hamilton, the deputy governor at the time.

Quakers, by denying them a just representation, prevented adequate military preparation.[83] The two years preceding the fall of Fort Necessity were filled with disputes between the Governor and the Assembly,[84] while the frontier remained defenseless. Petitions began to pour in once again. On November 5, 1755, William Moore and thirty-five inhabitants of Chester County begged the members of the Assembly to cease their "unnecessary Disputes with the Governor, nor, by Reason of their religious Scruples, longer neglect the Defence of the Province."[85] Five days later several of the principal inhabitants of the city of Philadelphia sent "A Representation to the General Assembly" severely criticizing it.[86] Another remonstrance along similar lines was presented on November 25, 1755, by the Mayor, Aldermen, and Common Council of Philadelphia.[87] This was too much, so a committee was appointed to consider and investigate these petitions. The report, received on December 3, said that the remonstrance of November 25 was signed by inhabitants, *a great part of them not Freeholders,"* and was denounced "as presuming, indecent, insolent and improper."[88] With these caustic remarks the matter was dismissed.

But the people did not let it end here. The depredations along the frontier continued with increasing severity until at last the peace-loving Germans were willing to unite with the Scotch-Irish in demanding something more than supplies and volunteer militia bills. "The inhabitants of the remote parts of Philadelphia county, chiefly Germans, to the number of four hundred, marched to the city, unarmed, in a peaceable and orderly manner, to implore the protection of their rulers,

---

[83] In this contention the frontiersmen were strongly supported by the Proprietors. *Vide Penn Letter Book,* IV, T. P. to Morris and Peters, March 22, 1756; to Chew, Dec. 12, 1757, V.

[84] These disputes culminated in an attempt to overthrow the Proprietors and make Pennsylvania a Royal Province. *Vide supra,* p. 10, note 23.

[85] *Votes,* IV, 495.

[86] *Ibid.,* pp. 502-03.

[87] *Ibid.,* p. 519. These were partisans of the Governor.

[88] *Ibid.,* p. 530.

and the postponement of their unseasonable debates."[89] If the
Quaker-controlled Assembly would do nothing, then an appeal must be taken to England. Accordingly, a petition was
prepared and sent to the Provincial Agent to be presented to
the Privy Council. Expressing alarm at "the present Melancholy Scituation of these Colonys, involved in all the complicated Miseries & Distress of a cruel War," it said that "Numbers of your Majtys. good Subjects, on the sev¹ Frontiers,"
have recently "been barbarously murdered, by bloodthirsty
Savages; & whole Townships broke up, & driven from their
Habitations; . . . "[90] There can be but little doubt that this
harrowing picture is a true one. George Stevenson wrote
from York on November 5, 1755, that the great question
there is "whether we shall stand or run? most are willing to
stand, but have no Arms nor Ammunition." Appeals have
been sent to the Assembly, letters to the Governor and others,
"but no Answer. People from Cumberland are going thro this
Town hourly in Droves and the Neighbouring Inhab.ts are
flocking into this Town Defenseless as it is, . . . "[91] In Carlisle
the situation was so serious that a proposal was made to send
the women and children out of town. Sixty men from Carlisle
under Colonel Hamilton were ordered to join Major James
Burd to defend Sherman's Valley.[92]

The address sent to England urged that the Privy Council
advise the King to withhold his sanction from a certain military bill recently passed by the Pennsylvania Assembly. It
further requested that Quakers should be forever disqualified
from sitting in that body—a change which, if granted, would

---

[89] Gordon, *op. cit.*, p. 316.

[90] Printed in the *Pa. Mag.*, X, 294. For a good, though partisan account, of
the events of the year see *A Brief State of the Province of Pennsylvania* (1755),
by W. Smith.

[91] Miscellaneous MSS, York County Papers (Historical Society of Penna.).
The letter was written to the Rev. Wm. Smith. Stevenson said that he himself
may flee, but if so "it will not be to Quakers, I will go to Maryland."

[92] MS letter to James Burd at Shippensburg, dated Nov. 2, 1755, and written
from Carlisle. In the private collection of Mr. Edward Shippen Thompson,
Thompsontown, Pa.

have been completely revolutionary.[93] A committee appointed by the Council to investigate these charges condemned the conduct of the Assembly and declared entirely erroneous its construction of the Charter, which did not exempt the Colony from military service nor place solely upon the Proprietors the duty of protection.[94] The legislature, the Committee declared, was bound by the original compact to support the government and protect its subjects. The measures enacted for that purpose were inadequate. No more effective measures could be taken in that body controlled by those whose fundamental principles were opposed to military service. The report was adopted by the Privy Council and naturally caused quite a commotion among the Friends in Pennsylvania.[95]

The Province was, of course, defenseless against the attacks of the French and Indians, but to assess the blame is difficult. The petition given above charges the Assembly with a refusal to defend the Province, yet it objects to the approval of the military bill which the Assembly had passed for that very purpose. The objection, however, was that this bill did not compel the inhabitants to arm.[96] The charges against the Quakers as stated in the petition are doubtless true, but there is another side to the question. There was little gold or silver in the Province, for the greater portion had been drained from the country to pay for imports from England. The Assembly was in the habit of meeting extraordinary emergencies by issuing paper money. The Proprietors objected to this, and there was a constant controversy between the Assembly and the Governors on this subject. One Pennsylvania historian said that to "the irreconcilable differences on this point, and not to religious scruples, are no doubt to be ascribed much of the embarrassment of the English government in Pennsylvania in raising men, money, and the supplies for the prosecution of the war."[97]

---

[93] For a previous suggestion of a similar nature, *vide supra*, p. 22.

[94] Bolles, *op. cit.*, pp. 335-36.

[95] *Ibid.*, pp. 336-37.

[96] Gordon, *op. cit.*, p. 319. Smith, in his *Brief State*, says that the military bill was a trick.

[97] Charles J. Stillé, *Pa. Mag.*, X, 284-86.

But there is another side to the question which involved the old struggle over the taxation of the Proprietary lands. It costs money to fight, and the Governor, as we have seen, refused to allow the Proprietary estates to be taxed. Franklin stated it very well: "When the Indians were scalping the western people, and notice of it arrived, the concurrence of the Governor in the means of self-defence could not be got, till it was agreed that his Estates should be exempted from taxation: so that the people were to fight for the security of his property, whilst he was to bear no share of the burden."[98]

Whether or not the Quakers were at fault, the situation was indeed critical. After the defeat of Braddock, July 9, 1755, Governor Dinwiddie of Virginia proposed that Pennsylvania and Maryland unite with his province to build, equip, and garrison a fort at the Meadows. Unfortunately this plan was not adopted; the frontier settlements were left unprotected and suffered all the horrors of guerilla warfare.[99]

The pressure on the Quakers was apparently becoming greater, and the climax came in the spring of 1756 when the Governor and Council declared war against the Delaware and Shawnees Indians. On June 4, 1756, six of the Quakers presented to the House a paper requesting leave to resign. They said they had no desire to involve the House in unnecessary trouble, but since the present situation called upon them for military services which, "from a Conviction of Judgment, after mature Deliberation," they were unable to comply with, they concluded that it was "most conducive to the Peace" of their own minds and religious professions to withdraw. Their resignations were accepted.[100]

When the Assembly met in October 1756, four more members of the Quaker sect took similar action. They stated that they had been returned to the Assembly without any solicitation on their part, but were willing to withdraw because the

---

[98] *Documents Illustrative of the Formation of the Union*, p. 148.

[99] Bolles, *op. cit.*, I, 331. The Proprietors were in favor of military measures being taken. *Vide* Penna. *Statutes at Large*, IV, 472, and *supra*, p. 6, note 11.

[100] *Votes*, IV, 564-65. These men were James Pemberton and Joshua Morris, Phila. Co.; Wm. Callender, Phila. City; Wm. Peters, Chester; Peter Worral, Lancaster; and Francis Parvin, Berks.

Ministry had requested them to permit their seats to be filled "by Members of other Denominations" who could, without any scruples, enact laws for the defense of the Province.[101]

The control of the House now passed temporarily to another class of men who did not believe in the principles of non-resistance. The withdrawal of the Quakers, however, changed the political tendencies of the Assembly only in regard to questions of defense. The same hostility to proprietary encroachments was still shown. It was still in popular language the "Quaker Assembly" and remained so until 1776, for the new members were elected by the same constituencies and were of the same political party as their predecessors.[102] Vigorous war measures were taken at once and a new militia bill prepared which went so far as to subject all men to military duty. However, service could be avoided by the payment of a fine. The Governor vetoed the bill because of the Assembly's unwillingness to grant him the power to appoint the officers. But so eager were many to enlist that the Governor and the Provincial Commissioners were able to raise troops with the offer of bounties.[103]

The capture of Fort Duquesne in 1758 and the pacification of the Indians meant the end of the War as far as Pennsylvania was concerned. But the damage had already been done; the resentment of the Westerner for the Eastern oligarchy had been kindled anew. Some effects of the war in the western part of the province may be seen in the petition presented to

---

[101] *Ibid.*, p. 626. They were Mahlon Kirkbride and William Hoge, Bucks, and Peter Dicks and Nathaniel Pennock, Chester.

[102] The Society of Friends was, however, not responsible for their acts, hence repudiate the years from 1756 to 1776. After the Indian wars some Quakers returned to the Assembly and in 1763 there were fourteen members who were in good standing in the Society. Much confusion has arisen from the fact that everyone who qualified by an affirmation, everyone who was in sympathy with the past policy of the legislative body, every descendant of a Quaker family, was called a Quaker. This is clearly seen in the statement of a Quaker who said that "though there are but fourteen allowed members of our Society in the House, yet as *divers others are termed such* our adversaries take occasion of clamoring and abusing us on this account. . . ." (Italics my own.) See Sharpless, *op. cit.*, pp. 267-270.

[103] Bolles, *op. cit.*, I, 342.

the Assembly on April 27, 1758, by people from Berks County and the city of Reading. Their section, they said, was in great distress, which arose "from certain late Ravages committed therein by the *Indians,* and other Enemies, in Consequence of which, many of the Settlers have abandoned their Plantations, and praying immediate Succor, left that Part of the Country be wholly deserted by its Inhabitants, from an Apprehension of further Depredations and deeper Incursions of the Enemy upon them."[104] In April 1759, the borough of Lancaster advised the Governor that "A Continuance of the Distressed Situation and Circumstances of the Inhabitants . . . calls on us, in the most earnest Manner, again to remonstrate to your Honour . . ."[105] The following year the grievances of the people were aired once again, their chief complaint being inadequate representation in the Assembly.

b. DEMANDS FOR THE REFORM OF REPRESENTATION

The long and tense struggle over defense greatly exacerbated the differences between the East and the West and culminated in a persistent demand for a complete reform in the system of representation in the Assembly. Because of the unequal representation the frontiersmen could not force the Assembly to take more vigorous action. It was quite as natural for the frontiersmen, therefore, to rebel against the merchant and property-owning class as it was for this class to revolt from the rule of Great Britain.

The *Charter of Privileges* of 1701 provided that the Assembly should consist of four persons from each county, but that whenever the separation of the lower part of the province took place, the counties in Pennsylvania proper should be entitled to double their representation. In 1703 the "three lower countries," known as Delaware, withdrew, so the above proviso was enacted by the Assembly in 1705.[106] Only three

---

[104] *Votes,* IV, 820.

[105] *Votes,* V, 44.

[106] *Statutes at Large,* II, 212. Section two of the *Charter of Privileges* empowered the Governor and the Assembly to increase the number of representatives.

counties now remained in Pennsylvania—Philadelphia, Chester, and Bucks—and as long as the population was small there
was little, if any, injustice in this act. Then, too, as long as
the interests of the city of Philadelphia remained identical
with those of the county, the provision could evoke little opposition. With the occupation of the western part of the province by the Germans and Scotch-Irish, and the growth of
Philadelphia City, the inequalities in representation became
apparent. There is no evidence to show that William Penn
intended to deny to other counties which might be formed
the same representation.[107] In fact, the *Frame of Government*
of 1683 specifically provided that the number of representatives be enlarged from time to time in proportion "with the
increase and multiplying of the people." But whatever may
have been Penn's intention, the Quakers gave the charter
only the narrowest interpretation. Firmly intrenched in
power, they determined that no other group should endanger
their control. And that control was precarious, for the Quakers were not a majority, but, as Governor Thomas wrote to the
Board of Trade in October 1740, "from their union they
have a much greater influence on all public affairs here than
the other societies."[108]

From Markham's *Frame of Government* in 1696 to the
Revolution, the electors were "free denizens" of the age of
twenty-one who either owned fifty acres of land, ten of which
were "seated and cleared," or were "otherwise worth *fifty*
pounds, lawful money of this government, clear estate."[109] At
that time the only widely diffused wealth of the colony was

---

[107] *Vide* Shepherd, *op. cit.*, p. 548.

[108] *Statutes at Large*, IV, 471. John Adams recorded in his "Diary" that by
"means of a most unequal representation, the Quakers had a majority in their
House of Assembly, and, by consequence, the whole power of the State in
their hands." *Works*, II, 399. *Vide* Wm. Smith, *A Brief State*, etc., p. 5.

[109] Poore, *op. cit.*, II, 1533; Thorpe, *op. cit.*, V, 3071. No person could vote
unless he had been born or naturalized in England or in the Province, and had
resided here two years before the election. After 1700, twelve acres had to be
"cleared and improved." See the *Act of 1700, made at New-Castle*, chapter 28.
In Pennsylvania all elections were by ballot. C. F. Bishop, *History of Elections
in the American Colonies*, p. 67.

in land, which was abundant and cheap, whereas fifty pounds was a considerable fortune. Thus these requirements, by no means equivalent, practically disfranchised the lower classes in the city of Philadelphia and the boroughs, but established a fairly democratic suffrage for the country.[110] The tax lists for the country districts indicate that, while nearly one-half of the adult male population owned the requisite fifty acres of land, very few in addition could boast of a personal estate of fifty pounds. For the inhabitants of the city and boroughs who had no land the franchise was all but unattainable. In Philadelphia in 1775, out of a total of 3,452 male taxables, only 335 were assessed for fifty pounds or more.[111] In the country districts one man in every two taxables had the right to vote. It has been estimated that the taxables formed one-fifth of the total population, hence in the farming districts one in ten, and in the city one in fifty was qualified for the suffrage.[112]

To maintain their power the dominant Quakers and their eastern allies resorted to two methods: first, to keep Philadelphia City from becoming a power in the colony and to prevent the western counties, as they increased in population,

---

[110] *Vide* C. H. Lincoln, "Representation in the Pennsylvania Assembly Prior to the Revolution," in *Pa. Mag.*, XXIII; W. R. Smith, "Sectionalism in Pennsylvania during the Revolution," *Pol. Sci. Quart.*, XXIV, 211; A. E. McKinley, *The Suffrage Franchise in the Thirteen English Colonies in America*, pp. 279-284. "From 1706 onward the interest in the suffrage in Pennsylvania centers not in the electors, but in the masses of non-voters, who, legally disqualified, used every possible means to influence the elections. One sees them frequently in the background of the election picture with sticks or stones or even 'billets of wood,' instead of the forbidden ballots, trying by physical means to express their opinions. From the point of view of the ruling class they are 'servants,' or 'great numbers of disorderly persons,' or an 'outrageous Multitude,' who, by 'their rude and disorderly behaviour' disturb the elections, or who 'presumed to vote when they did not have the right so to do.' " McKinley, *op. cit.*, p. 284.

[111] James Wilson once remarked that he "had seen the Western settlem ᵗ of Pᵃ and on a comparison of them with the City of Philadᵃ could discover little other difference, than that property was more unequally divided among individuals here than there." Speech in the Federal Constitutional Convention, *Documents Illustrative of the Formation of the Union*, p. 361.

[112] McKinley, *op. cit.*, pp. 290-92. Taxables were those who paid a tax on the net value of their real and personal estates, as well as a poll tax.

from electing a majority in the Assembly; secondly, to prevent a coalition between the City and the West. In the East the danger was from the number of people; in the west from the number of counties. Their problem was simple—to keep the city populace disfranchised; to create new counties slowly, if at all, and to restrict their representation in the Assembly.[113] The struggle thus begun terminated only with the Revolution.

The Creation of Counties

The first county created in the West was Lancaster, admitted in 1729, with four representatives in the Assembly.[114] Being many times larger than the present county, it was not long before petitions for a division were received from the people living many miles away from the county seat. In 1747 one was presented from a "Number of Inhabitants of *Lancaster* County, living on the West-side of *Sasquehanna,* [sic] praying . . . that a new County may be erected on that Side of the River."[115] The need was apparent, not only because of the large population already there, but also because the inhabitants were practically isolated during the winter months. They were separated from the county seat by the Susquehanna River, a very wide stream in its course through Lancaster County, and at the main crossing over a mile in width. The administration of justice and protection against lawlessness were virtually impossible. Yet in spite of this situation the Assembly was in no great hurry to grant the request. The petition was ordered to lie on the table and was not read again until November 14, 1748, when the petitioners were granted leave to appear before the House and state their case. This was done, and "having answered such Questions as were asked of them for the Satisfaction of the House, they Withdrew; and further Consideration of that Petition was ad-

---

[113] *Pa. Mag.,* XXIII, 27.

[114] *Laws of the Commonwealth,* Dallas, I, 242.

[115] *Votes,* IV, 55-56. This petition was signed by well over two hundred people, many of whom made their "mark." Miscellaneous MSS, York County Papers (Hist. Soc. of Pennsylvania).

journed until" the following day.[116] The Assembly finally
resolved that the petitioners be given the privilege, at the next
session, of bringing in a bill and also that "if any others of
Lancaster County are against the Division of that County,
they have leave to be then heard."[117] After much debate the act
creating York County was passed on June 15, 1749.[118]

The same dilatory tactics were used by the Assembly with
all the petitions for new counties, thereby increasing the
antagonism between the West and the East. Cumberland
County was created in November 1749, with two representatives,[119] and in 1752 Berks and Northampton were admitted,
although they were given but one member each.[120] The
Assembly now felt, apparently, that it had gone far enough
in this matter, for in spite of the numerous demands for
similar action no more counties were created until 1771. Thus
from 1752 to 1771 the Assembly was composed of thirty-six
members: twenty-six representing the counties of Philadelphia, Chester, and Bucks (including two from the city of
Philadelphia), and the other ten representing the more popu-
lous German and Scotch-Irish settlements of the "back"
counties.[121]

The first real insight into the relationship of population
and representation is afforded by the report of a committee
of the Assembly on August 20, 1752. The report is not wholly
complete, for the committee said that some of the tax books
had been lost.[122] Taking Philadelphia County as a standard

---

[116] *Votes*, IV, 98-99.

[117] *Ibid.*, p. 100.

[118] Their first representatives—John Wright and John Armstrong—appeared
in the new Assembly which met on October 14, 1749. *Ibid.*, p. 115.

[119] Dallas, *op. cit.*, I, 329.

[120] *Ibid.*, pp. 347, 352. The first representative of Northampton County was
James Burnside, a native of Ireland. His opponent was the ex-surveyor general
William Parson, the Proprietary candidate, whom he defeated by a majority
of about 300. *Pa. Mag.*, XXI, 117-18.

[121] In 1740 there were only three non-Quaker members of the Assembly, and
in 1755, before they themselves had taken any measures to give up their seats,
twenty-eight of the thirty-six members were Friends. *Vide Pa. Mag.*, X, 291;
Sharpless, *op. cit.*, p. 75.

[122] *Votes*, IV, 226.

we find that the western counties of Lancaster, York, and Cumberland together had three less representatives and the city of Philadelphia one less than their true quotas, while on the same basis Chester and Bucks had five more than they should have had.[123]

A better estimate can be had in 1760 after the two new counties of Berks and Northampton had been created. On the same basis, we find that the discrepancies in representation hàd increased greatly. The three original counties had a total of 13,587 taxables (not including the city of Philadelphia), with a representation of twenty-four, while the western counties had a total of 15,443 taxables but sent only ten representatives to the Assembly.[124]

Of course these facts were well known, but during the French and Indian wars the agitation abated somewhat. With the termination of hostilities, however, the fight was renewed with even greater acerbity. While the grievances of the new counties were glaring in 1752, they were more so in 1760, and were growing worse each year, for these counties were de-

---

[123] Using the list of taxables given in the report we may construct a table showing the discrepancies in the number of representatives apportioned among the various counties. In the following table we have taken Philadelphia County as a standard. It had eight members in the Assembly and its number of taxables totaled 5,100, thus giving the county one representative for every 637+ taxables. The table shows how many representatives each county should have had on this basis, and also how many they actually had. In the list compiled by the Assembly Phila. City and County were taken together. In the figures for 1760 the city had 2,634 taxables, while the county had 5,678—a gain of 1,212. The figures, therefore, which we have used give the city an increase of 634 and the county 578, which seems entirely justified by the available data on the question of population. These figures are for the year 1751, save for the counties of Chester and Lancaster which are for 1752.

Counties	Taxables	Members based on taxables	Actual Members
Philadelphia County	5100	8	8
Philadelphia City	2000	3	2
Chester	3951	6	8
Bucks	3012	5	8
Lancaster	3977	6	4
York	2043	3	2
Cumberland	1134	1+	2

[124] Votes, V, 120.

veloping more rapidly in population, wealth, and tax-paying ability than were the old eastern counties.[125] Equity demanded an increase of western members, whether taxation or population be considered the true basis of representation. The Westerners sought the help of Governor John Penn to oppose the continued Fabian policy of the Assembly.[126] Nothing was accomplished by this except the intensification of sectional feeling. By this time greater representation came to be looked upon as the panacea for all the ills of the western counties. On March 23, 1764, a petition enumerating many complaints was presented to the House "from Upwards of Twelve Hundred inhabitants" of Cumberland County. It stated that "what lies at the Bottom of all their Grievances, and must be complained of as the Source of all their Suffering, is their not being fairly represented in Assembly. . . ."[127]

While the quarrel with England over the Stamp Act and the Indian affairs overshadowed for a time the question of representation, these matters tended to intensify the sectional, religious, and racial antipathies in the province. In fact, the Westerners felt all the more strongly that if they had been adequately represented in the Assembly many of these difficulties never would have occurred. As a consequence, petitions for greater representation and new counties began to descend upon the Assembly.[128] That body probably foresaw

---

[125] This was clearly recognized in a "Remonstrance and Petition from the Commissioners, Assessors and Freemen of the City and County of Philadelphia for the more equitable assessment of taxes." They said that the western counties "have encreased greatly in their Number of Inhabitants, the Quantity of cultivated Land, and their Ability to raise Taxes, while the State of the three interior Counties remains nearly the same." *Votes*, VI, 431. But it was one thing to recognize this for purposes of taxation and quite another for purposes of representation. A further cause of dissatisfaction was the feeling that the founder never had intended such a system of inequality. See *Votes*, IV, 211; *supra*, p. 32. The many petitions also contained numerous references to the original charter. The earlier constitutions created no such inequalities. See *Penn Letter Books*, IV and V, letters to Morris and Peters in 1756-57; letter to Chew, December 12, 1757.

[126] *Votes*, V, 313-14.

[127] *Ibid.*, V, 332-33.

[128] *Ibid.*, VI, 21, 29, 126, 196.

that it would ultimately have to accede to the demands of the West, so it took a step in January 1770, to make membership more difficult for the Westerners. A law was passed which provided that hereafter all members "shall be chosen from among the inhabitants of the City or County from which they were elected,"[129] thus preventing the western counties from choosing a member from the East who could with much less inconvenience be present at all times during the sessions of the Assembly.

Let us now see what difference ten years has made in the number of taxables and representation. The necessary information is available for the year 1771. Upon the same basis used before, we find that the eastern counties were over-represented to a greater extent than ever, having seven more members than was their just lot, while the western counties had eleven less than they should have had, despite the addition of one to the Berks County delegation.[130]

The creation of Bedford County in 1771 encouraged the Westerners, and immediately many petitions for new counties were received.[131] In 1772 Northumberland was created,[132] and the next year Westmoreland came into being.[133] The Assembly now thought it was time to call a halt, and the West received no increase in membership, either by enlarged representation or by the creation of new counties, until the year 1776. Nevertheless, the influence of that section was already felt, for Edward Biddle, of Berks County, was elected speaker of the Assembly on October 14, 1774.[134] But the East was still in control, for the preceding events gave the West only five

---

[129] *Ibid.*, VI, 213-14. The bill was passed on Feb. 1, 1770, as part of the act giving additional representation to Berks County.

[130] The counties of Chester, Philadelphia, and Bucks had a total of 15,365 taxables and twenty-four members in the Assembly. The western counties of Lancaster, York, Berks, Cumberland, and Northampton had 20,550 taxables, but sent only eleven members to the legislature. Proud, *op. cit.*, II, 275-76.

[131] See *Votes*, VI, 347; 440 and 442-43.

[132] *Votes*, VI, 383 and 388.

[133] *Ibid.*, p. 443. Each of these new counties had but a single representative in the Assembly.

[134] *Ibid.*, p. 546.

additional representatives, bringing their total to fifteen, in comparison with twenty-six for the East. The narrow and short-sighted policy of those in control was thus largely responsible for the violence and suffering which ensued. They unjustly maintained themselves in power by their manipulation of the representation in the Assembly and on them was wreaked the vengeance of the Westerner and the disfranchised mechanics and artisans of Philadelphia when the opportunity was afforded by the war with England.

6. *Crystallization of Antagonisms*

a. MARCH OF THE "PAXTON BOYS"

The sectional rivalry, hatred, and antagonism manifested itself at the end of the French and Indian War when the frontiersmen attempted to control the Indian policy of the colony regardless of any sentimental ideas or religious scruples of the Easterners. This attempt resulted in the Conestoga massacre and the march of the "Paxton Boys" to Philadelphia —events clearly indicative of a religious, sectional, and partisan hostility which could no longer be restrained.

The Westerners were determined to be protected against the Indian ravages. But in the difficulties which had already arisen between them and the Indians, the Assembly had almost invariably sided with the latter. As a result, practically the whole burden of defending the frontier fell upon the Scotch-Irish and German settlers.[135] The people along the Delaware lived in peace and quiet, and told the frontiersmen that their own aggressions and their own quarrelsome dispositions were the real cause of the border troubles. The war had undoubtedly weakened the prestige of the Assembly in the estimation of the Westerner because of its lack of energy, and resulted in an open defiance of its authority. This event was the march of the "Paxton Boys" upon Philadelphia. It is of great interest because it reveals much of the spirit and conditions of the time.

---

[135] *Vide* Charles H. Lincoln, *The Revolutionary Movement in Pennsylvania,* pp. 100-01; *Votes,* V, 292, 296-97, 298.

On December 14, 1763, a group of men, principally from Paxton township, fell upon the Indians living on the Conestoga Manor, an Indian settlement in Lancaster County under the protection of the province. These Indians had been partially Christianized and were supposed to be the descendants of the men with whom Penn had made his first treaties. Six were killed on the spot. Eleven days later about fifty men in arms broke open the doors of the Lancaster Almshouse, where the remainder had been taken for safekeeping, and butchered all who were there—about fourteen men, women, and children.[136] When the news of this affair spread eastward alarmed officials sent to New York the Moravian Indians quartered in Philadelphia. Governor Colden refused to receive them, so they were returned and were lodged in the Philadelphia barracks. On learning this their enemies in Lancaster County were aroused and started for the capital. Upon the request of the Governor[137] the Assembly immediately voted credits to enable him to take sufficient measures to subdue the rioters and defend the lives of the Indians.[138]

The rioters, whose force "though known to be small in the beginning, continually increased"[139] as they marched toward Philadelphia, determined to exterminate the Indians then under the protection of the government.[140] The Assembly immediately passed a bill for suppressing riots, which was read the next day to a concourse of 3,000 people at the State House. An Association was also formed for "ye Defence of ye Indians & ye City, in which Many Hand's of ye Inhabitants chearfully E[n]gaged & made ye necessary preparations for Opposing ye rioters."[141]

The Quakers were thoroughly alarmed, for many of them bearing arms appeared on the streets as the rioters approached

---

[136] Vide "Journal kept by Samuel Foulke," Pa. Mag., V, 66; Proud, op. cit., II, 326.

[137] Votes, V, 292.

[138] Ibid., p. 293.

[139] Alexander Graydon, Memoirs of His Own Time, ed. by J. S. Littel, p. 47.

[140] Foulke, op. cit., p. 69.

[141] Ibid., p. 70.

Germantown. The Reverend Mr. Henry M. Muhlenberg makes some interesting comments on this point in his *Journal.* "It is almost incredible," he writes, "that sundry young and old Quakers formed companies, and took up arms, particularly so to the boys in the streets; for a whole crowd of boys followed a distinguished Quaker, and in astonishment cried out, look here! a Quaker with a musket on his shoulder. It was by many old people looked on as a wonderful sign, to see so many old and young Quakers marching about with sword and gun, or deadly weapons, so-called. What increased the wonder was, that the pious lambs in the long French, Spanish, and Indian wars had such tender consciences, and would sooner die than raise a hand in defence against these dangerous enemies, and now at once like Zedekiah, the son of Chenaanah, with iron horns rushing upon a handful of our poor distressed and ruined fellow citizens and inhabitants of the frontiers."[142]

"In this state of consternation and dismay," as Graydon remarks, "all business was laid aside for the more important occupation of arms."[143] Governor Penn, in a panic, fled to the house of Franklin and requested him to form an association for the defense of the city. "Governor Penn," wrote Franklin, "made my house for some time his headquarters, and did everything by my advice; so that for about forty-eight hours I was a very great man; . . ."[144] Several clergymen were sent out to meet the rioters as they approached Germantown. The Governor also sent several of his Council, accompanied by four members of the Assembly—Franklin, Galloway, Chew, and Willing—to advise the rioters to disperse immediately. Foulke says that the men gave some poor excuses "to Cover the disloyal principles of ye faction, which Appears to be a

---

[142] "Extracts from the Journals of the Rev. Henry Melchior Muhlenberg," *Collections of the Historical Society of Pa.,* I, 75. When Rev. Brycelius, a minister sent out to talk to the men, told them "that even the Quakers had taken up arms, they laughed heartily, and wondered at such a phenomenon," *Ibid.,* p. 77.

[143] *Memoirs,* p. 47.

[144] *Works,* Smyth ed., X, 215.

presbyterian one—that Society thro' out the province being tainted with ye same bloody principles with respect to ye Indians & of disaffection to ye Government."[145] But Foulke was a Quaker from Philadelphia and perhaps never comprehended the true situation of the frontiersmen. A better account of the movement is given by Pastor Brycelius, a friend of Rev. Mr. Muhlenberg.

Mr. Brycelius met the "Boys" on the outskirts of Germantown where he was stopped and ordered to remain with them. Engaging in conversation he told them he had been a resident of Dublin, Ireland, and that "the love of peace and their common welfare had compelled him to see them and speak with them." He must have won their confidence, for he asked them "in the simplicity of his heart what their object and the intention of their down march might be." They said their objects were: first, that the Bethlehem Indians be given up and expelled; second, that they be given the opportunity to lay their "many weighty complaints" before the government. "The people in and around Philadelphia," they continued, "lived at their ease and in plenty, and had no idea of the distress and trouble of the poor" frontiersmen. Therefore, they had "come down to settle their affairs in Philadelphia."[146] They confessed, Foulke said, that they had been "invited and encouraged by many considerable persons in Philadelphia" and were told that "they should meet with no opposition in the execution of their design." Thus it is evident that the disaffection for the government was by no means confined to the West.

When the rioters found that the Indians were protected by the King's troops they desisted from their plans and dispersed. The Assembly's attempt to punish the "murderers" failed because popular feeling upheld the act.[147] "Party spirit,"

---

[145] *Op. cit.*, p. 70.

[146] Taken from the *Journal* of Rev. Muhlenberg, *op. cit.*, pp. 76-77. Brycelius "thought there were very few Germans among them, and the mass were English and Irish dissenters."

[147] Lincoln, *op. cit.*, p. 113. The Assembly did pass a law stating that persons charged in Philadelphia, Bucks, or Chester Counties with murdering an Indian

Graydon wrote, "at this time, ran very high, and the Paxton men were not without a number of clamorous advocates, who entirely justified them on the score of their sufferings from the savages . . ."[148] The whole matter was discretely dropped, but it was an ominous sign. Although the attempt to overawe the eastern Quaker conservatism had failed, it served to teach the dissatisfied elemets that by united action they might be successful.

The rioters returned home; the causes of discontent remained. So serious were conditions that the Proprietors directed the Governor to make every effort to settle the disputes between the factions, and especially to discourage the printing of partisan pamphlets.[149] Governor Penn found little difficulty in obeying this order, for in their wrath against the Stamp Act the factions momentarily lost sight of their former grievances. "The People," he wrote, "seem to have forgot former differences and are all united against the Stamp Act."[150]

b. ATTITUDE OF THE COLONY TOWARD THE STAMP ACT

In 1748 the Board of Trade, the agency in England which had supervision over the colonies, entered upon a new period of its history. Up to this time control had been lax. Now the Mother Country realized that a more effective government had to be established. Under the presidency of Sir John Monson, from 1737 to 1748, the Board had become little more than a bureau of information.[151] Monson's successor, the Earl of Halifax, inaugurated a new policy.[152] With his support the Royal Governors began to resist the claims of the

---

in Lancaster County be tried, "but no conviction for that offence was ever had, the number and power of the guilty protecting them from punishment." Gordon, *op. cit.*, p. 410.

[148] *Memoirs*, pp. 49-50. Franklin wrote a pamphlet entitled *A Narrative of the Late Massacres in Lancaster County* (MDCCLXIV), intended, as he said, "to strengthen the hands of our weak government, by rendering the proceedings of the rioters unpopular and odious." *Works*, Smyth ed., X, 215. The pamphlet is printed in *ibid.*, IV, 289-314.

[149] Shepherd, *op. cit.*, p. 570.

[150] *Penn Letter Book*, VIII, Thomas Penn to John Penn, February 26, 1766.

[151] Oliver M. Dickerson, *American Colonial Government*, pp. 35-36.

[152] *Ibid.*, p. 40.

colonial assemblies. Before this new policy could function the French and Indian War intervened.

The Treaty of Paris, which concluded the war in 1763, gave Great Britain a far-flung empire and the British people an enormous debt. The policy of vigorous control, thus interrupted by the war, was renewed at its close with even greater fervor, and the rule of "salutary neglect" came to an end. The new program of George Grenville, the Prime Minister, placed before Parliament in 1764, represented a drastic departure from the earlier system of colonial government.

As a part of the New Colonial Policy, the Stamp Act was passed with but slight opposition in the House of Commons, with unanimity by the House of Lords, and received the royal assent on March 22, 1765. Franklin, then in England, labored with untiring energy to prevent the passage of the act, but with no success. Parliament paid little attention to the warnings of Franklin—and none to the admonitions of the Pennsylvania Assembly.[153] The Stamp Act laid a duty on newspapers, legal documents, etc., to be collected by having stamps attached thereto. When this was passed Franklin wrote from England to Charles Thomson: "The sun of liberty is set, you must light up the candles of industry and economy." Mr. Thomson replied that he was "apprehensive that other lights would be the consequences."[154]

---

[153] In the summer of 1764 a letter had come to the Speaker of the Pennsylvania Assembly from a Committee of the Representatives of Mass. Bay, protesting against the "late Act of Parliament relating to the Sugar Trade" and the Resolutions of the House of Commons regarding the Stamp Duties, and other "Taxes to be laid on the British Colonies." (*Votes*, V, 355.) The letter was laid before the Assembly on September 12, and six days later a committee was appointed "to draw up Instructions" to Richard Jackson, the agent for the province, "to use his utmost Endeavors, in Conjunction with the Agents of the other Colonies to obtain a Repeal of the late Sugar Act," and also to remonstrate against a Stamp Duty, with any other Taxes and Impositions. (*Votes*, V, 359. A few days later the committee's report was adopted by the Assembly, and long and elaborate instructions were sent. They said the measures now contemplated by Parliament "will have a Tendency to deprive the good People of this Province of their most essential Rights as British Subjects." (*Ibid.*, p. 363.)

[154] Gordon, *op. cit.*, p. 432. On the right of England to levy taxes on the

The Assembly of Pennsylvania was in session when the news of the passage of the act reached Philadelphia, yet it took no public notice of it. The proposal of the Assembly of Massachusetts, that a congress of committees from the provincial assemblies be held at New York on the first Tuesday of October to consult on the present state of the colonies, was communicated to Mr. Fox, the speaker of the Pennsylvania Assembly, on June 8.[155] As the House was not then in session, Fox immediately called together some of the members who resided in Philadelphia or the vicinity. They instructed him to send a letter to Massachusetts saying that the plan was unanimously "approved by the Gentlemen who met," and that the matter would be laid before "our House, at their Meeting, on the Ninth of September next; . . ."[156]

When the Assembly convened it resolved that it ought "to remonstrate to the Crown against the Stamp Act" and appointed Messrs. Fox, Dickinson, Bryan, and Morton to represent the province in the Congress.[157] At the same time a Committee was appointed to draw up "Instructions," which were adopted the next day—September 11.[158] They directed the delegates to meet with the other Committees to "consult together on the present Circumstances of the Colonies, and the difficulties they are and must be reduced to by acts of Parliament for levying Duties and Taxes upon them, and to join with the said Committees in loyal and dutiful Addresses to the king, and the two Houses of Parliament, humbly representing the Condition of these Colonies, and imploring Relief by a Repeal of the said Acts." The Committee, however, was strictly enjoined to take care that such "Addresses . . . are drawn up in the most decent and respectful Terms, so as to

---

colonies, with reference to the Stamp Act, see "Examination of Dr. Benjamin Franklin In the British House of Commons Relative to the Repeal of the American Stamp Act, in 1766," *Works*, Smyth ed., IV, 412 *passim*.

[155] *Votes*, V, 419.

[156] *Ibid.*, p. 419.

[157] *Ibid.*, p. 420.

[158] *Ibid.*, p. 420. This committee was composed of Bryan, Dickinson, Morton, Knight, Sanders, M'Connaughy, Allen, and Taylor.

avoid every Expression that can give the least Occasion of Offence to His Majesty, or to either House of Parliament."[159]

But the real feeling of the Pennsylvania Assembly upon the Stamp Act was more fully expressed in ten resolutions reported by a committee declaring, among other things:

That it is the inherent Birth-right, and indubitable Privilege, of every *British* Subject to be taxed only by his own Consent, or that of his legal Representatives, in conjunction with his Majesty, or his substitutes: That the Taxation of the People of this Province by any other Persons whatsoever than such their Representatives in Assembly, is unconstitutional, and subversive of their most valuable Rights: That the laying Taxes upon the Inhabitants of this Province in any other Manner, being manifestly subversive of public Liberty, must, of necessary Consequence, be utterly destructive of public Happiness: That the only legal Representatives of the Inhabitants of this Province are the Persons they annually elect to serve them as Members of Assembly.

The resolutions also said that the inhabitants of Pennsylvania were "entitled to all the Liberties, Rights and Privileges of his Majesty's Subjects in *Great*-Britain, or elsewhere, and that the Constitution of Government in this Province is founded on the natural Rights of Mankind, and the noble Principles of *English* Liberty, and therefore is, or ought to be, perfectly free."[160]

The British ministry tried to reconcile the people to the law by appointing the officers to execute it from among the most reputable of the inhabitants of the provinces, and for this purpose held a meeting of the colonial agents in London at the office of Mr. Grenville. The agents were requested to nominate fit persons for the performance of these duties.[161]

---

[159] *Votes*, V, 421.

[160] *Ibid.*, p. 426. It might be interesting to note here that the above resolutions were very similar to ones later drawn up by the colonial assemblies on the eve of the Revolution. The idea of Natural Rights of Mankind, which later played such an important part in the arguments of the colonists, is likewise mentioned.

[161] Gordon, *op. cit.*, p. 438.

The attempt to placate the people in this manner had no effect, for the stamp officers were hanged or burned in effigy in several of the provinces. On Saturday, October 5, the ship *Royal Charlotte,* bearing the stamped papers for Jersey, Maryland, and Pennsylvania, convoyed by a sloop of war, arrived in Philadelphia.

On the appearance of these ships around Gloucester point, all the vessels in the harbor hoisted their colors at half-mast, the bells were muffled, and every countenance assumed the semblance of mourning. At four o'clock of the afternoon, many thousand citizens assembled at the state house to consider of the means for preventing the distribution of the stamps.[162]

Their first step was to make sure that the agent, Mr. Hughes, either resign his commission or refuse to execute the duties of his office. He promised to do the latter. According to the law the stamp duties were to commence on the first of November. On the previous day the newspapers were put in mourning for their own approaching extinction, for the editors had resolved to suspend publication until some plan should be devised to protect them from the penalties for publishing their papers without stamps.[163] Their term of suspension was short, for on November 7 a semi-sheet was issued from the office of the *Pennsylvania Gazette,* without title or mark of designation, headed, "No stamped paper to be had."

A committee succeeded in persuading over four hundred merchants and traders of Philadelphia to adopt non-importation agreements. Public offices were closed on the first of

---

[162] *Ibid.,* p. 439.

[163] The obituary notice in the *Journal* on October 31 read as follows: "The last remains of the *Pennsylvania Journal,* which departed this life the 31st October, 1765, of a stamp in her vitals; aged twenty-three years."

The editor of the *Staatsbote* announced on October 28 that his paper would suspend publication under the same plan. On the lower right-hand corner of the first page he printed a skull and cross-bones with the caption, "Dis ist der Platz für den Todespein erregender Stämpel." For an account of the opposition in Philadelphia, see J. Thomas Scharf and Thompson Westcott, *A History of Philadelphia,* I, 271 *ff.*

November and were not opened until May, when the news of the intended repeal arrived.[164] Even the Quakers remonstrated against the Stamp Act.[165]

Its repeal was due in part to the attitude of the Colonists, the action of the Stamp Act Congress, and the activity of the British merchants who were rapidly losing trade and who viewed with alarm the rise of colonial manufactures. The whole proceedings of the Stamp Act Congress were heartily approved by the Assembly of Pennsylvania.[166] The next year there appeared in the *Pennsylvania Chronicle* of December 2 the first of a series of twelve letters written by John Dickinson, afterwards known as the "Farmer's Letters." They dealt with the political situation and advocated resistance to the ministerial plan of taxation on constitutional grounds.

Thus in a very short time the hostility of the people and the Assembly was turned from the Proprietors toward the Crown. Yet this cessation of party strife within the Province was of short duration, for as the revolutionary movement developed the discontented classes in Pennsylvania seized this opportunity to vent their rage against the Assembly. This opposition became ever more bitter and finally led to the overthrow of the old system and to the substitution of a revolutionary government.

---

[164] The act was repealed on March 18, 1766, by a vote of 275 to 167.

[165] There were, of course, exceptions to this. In 1766 Joseph Galloway, an "open Champion for the Stamps," was the speaker of the Assembly. Samuel Purviance wrote that "this the Qu- -rs themselves are ashamed of." Stiles, *op. cit.*, p. 555. Galloway wrote a paper signed *Americanus,* "in which he used all his art to persuade the people to submit to the enslaving Statute." Letter of Alison to Stiles, *ibid.*, p. 428. The non-importation agreement signed in 1765 contained the names of many who later went over to the Tory ranks. *Vide* Scharf and Westcott, *op. cit.*, I, 272.

[166] *Votes,* V, 442, January 8, 1766.

II

THE PROPRIETARY GOVERNMENT AND THE REVOLUTIONARY MOVEMENT

THE attempt to enforce the new British Colonial policy was the signal for the mighty upheaval which resulted in the independence of the thirteen English colonies scattered along the Atlantic seaboard. The Stamp Act was followed in rapid succession by other acts which continued to arouse the colonists. The culmination of this policy came in 1774 when the so-called "Intolerable Acts" were passed. With these the united and active opposition to British authority begins.

1. *Attitude of the Proprietary Government and the Early Opposition*

The "Intolerable Acts," which included the act closing the port of Boston, increased the tension between the colonies, particularly Massachusetts, and England. Samuel Adams had already formed committees of correspondence to bring the colonists together and to secure their coöperation. The leaders in this movement for united action needed the support of Pennsylvania.

In the preceding chapter we have seen that due to the faulty system of representation the Assembly was controlled by the three eastern counties. The body in session in 1774 had been elected in October 1773, and was dominated by the "Eastern Party"—a coalition of the Quaker, German, and commercial interests—led by Joseph Galloway, the arch-conservative; the very personification of opposition to violence. Although the limited franchise undoubtedly lessened the representative quality of the Assembly, the majority, in deprecating all violence or illegal action in the struggle with Great Britain, acted as the moderate element wished.[1]

[1] P. L. Ford, "The First Pennsylvania Constitution," *Political Science Quarterly*, X, 426.

On May 19, 1774, Paul Revere arrived in Philadelphia bearing a Public Letter from the people of Boston announcing the passage of the Boston Port Bill.[2] He also brought with him private letters to men in Pennsylvania which were even more alarming, declaring that unless Philadelphia joined the people of Boston the latter were powerless to make any effective opposition. Their conduct in this crisis, they declared, depended upon the attitude of Philadelphia.[3] The leaders of the "Popular" party at once realized that measures other than those of the Assembly were necessary to give the colony even the semblance of supporting Massachusetts. At the same time they were fully aware that the support given must be moderate, for any extreme action might fail of acceptance, even in the mass meeting by means of which they hoped to influence the sentiments of the people of Pennsylvania. Charles Thomson, Joseph Reed, and Thomas Mifflin, the leaders of this party, arranged a plan of action—a clever piece of political machination. The letter from the people of Boston was publicly read at the Coffee-House the same day it was received, and notice was given that it would be read the following evening at the City Tavern, where there was a large room accommodating several hundred people.

At this assemblage it was necessary to have the presence of John Dickinson, author of the famous "Farmer's Letters," a Quaker, and a man of great prominence, whose sentiments on the present controversy were not generally known. Thomson promised that he would not come to the meeting without Dickinson. It was agreed that Mifflin and Thomson should propose the most vigorous action, and then that Dickinson "should moderate that fire by proposing measures of a more

---

[2] *Pa. Gaz., Postscript,* May 18, 1774.

[3] Stillé, *Dickinson,* p. 105. "A Philadelphian," writing in the *Pa. Gaz.* had already sounded a note of warning: "Liberty, Property and Life are now but Names in America. . . . We dare not call even our Lives our own. . . . New York, Philadelphia and Charles Town cannot expect to escape the fate of Boston. . . . Our Brethren in Boston may perhaps stand in need of our Counsels." Issue of May 18.

gentle nature."[4] On Friday evening, May 20, between two and three hundred people gathered at the City Tavern.[5] Joseph Reed, who opened the meeting, urged the most spirited action. Thomson rose and supported him, but with the excitement, the heat of the room, and his own vigorous speech—pressing for an immediate declaration in favor of Boston and making common cause with her—he fainted away, and was carried into an adjoining room. Dickinson then arose and recommended an "Address to the Governour to call the Assembly," and the appointment of a committee of correspondence. As Reed said: "The contrast between the two measures advised and Mr. Dickinson's great weight precipitated the company into an adoption of the latter, which being so gentle in its appearance was a great relief against the violence of the first, & therefore although opposed was admitted." A Committee of Correspondence was created to serve "until an Alteration is made by a more general Meeting of the Inhabitants," and was instructed to inform the people of Boston of the sense of the meeting, which was that "we truly feel for their unhappy situation, that we consider them as suffering in the general Cause, that we recommend to them Firmness, Prudence and Moderation, and that we shall continue to evince our firm Adherence to the Cause of American Liberty."[6] As Mr. Reed wrote: "This even, such as it was, was a great point gained. It gave birth to a Public Body in appearance, & that once established by prudent management led to other open actions."[7]

The Committee of Correspondence the next day prepared

---

[4] Joseph Reed's "Narrative," *New York Historical Society Collections*, 1878, p. 271. Charles Thomson wrote that the meeting was planned by Dickinson and himself, and that Reed and Mifflin were asked to take part in it. This, however, is doubtful, and Thomson corroborates the rest of the account. *Cf. Ibid.*, Introduction, p. xii.

[5] *Pa. Gaz.*, June 8, 1774. The whole proceeding is given here.

[6] *Pa. Gaz.*, June 8, 1774.

[7] Reed's "Narrative," pp. 269-72; letter of Thomson to Wm. H. Drayton, *New York Historical Society Collections, 1878*, pp. 219-20; Stillé, *Dickinson*, pp. 341-44.

and sent back to the Committee of Boston an answer. It was much milder than the instructions noted above. It simply stated what had been done and said that "you are considered as now suffereing in the *General Cause.*" However, it made no commitments but promised that the Committee would "take the necessary Steps to obtain the general Sentiments of our fellow Inhabitants of this Province, as well as of our Sister Colonies. . . ."[8] To fulfill this promise the Committee forwarded the news to the Southern colonies, accompanying the information with letters intimating the necessity of a congress of delegates from all the colonies. The Committee also devised measures to call a general meeting of the inhabitants of the city at the State House. "This required great address," as Thomson said, for "The Quakers had an aversion to town meetings & always opposed them. However it was so managed that they gave their consent & assisted in preparing the business for this public meeting, agreed on the persons who should preside & those who should address the inhabitants."[9] The men who managed this affair were assuredly consummate politicians.

In the meantime the Assembly's Committee of Correspondence was urged by popular clamor in Philadelphia to send a message such as had been sent by the meeting of May 20. But Mr. Galloway, the Speaker, was not in the city, and as the committee was reluctant to act without him nothing was done.[10] Later this committee sent a letter, somewhat cool in tone, which said that they "hope and earnestly recommend that the great cause of American rights may be left to the management of the Representatives of the people in every colony, as they alone are vested with a constitutional power of enquiring into and redressing those grievances, under which the subject may at any time be oppressed."[11]

---

[8] "Copy of a Letter from the Committee of Philadelphia to the Committee of Boston," *The Franklin Papers, Miscellaneous,* I. (Library of Congress.)

[9] Stillé, *Dickinson,* p. 344.

[10] *Pa. Mag.,* XXVI, 303.

[11] *Pa. Gazette,* July 13, 1774.

Many people in Pennsylvania thought that this was no body to talk about redressing grievances. One writer wanted to know by "whose authority did they act? Were they a Committee of Correspondence?" He said that it appeared that Galloway and the rest had taken upon themselves to write the letter "without any due authority from the people of the Province, who will disown the whole of it, and authorize their true Committee to write a letter that will be to the purpose."[12]

The activity of the popular party continued, and on May 30 a meeting of the different societies was held. It was decided that all business be suspended on the first of June—the day the Boston Port Bill was to go into effect.[13] On that day there was a "Pause in the business of this city, and a solemn pause it indeed was. If we except the Friends, I believe nine-tenths of the citizens shut up their houses. The bells were rang muffled all the day, and the ships in the port had their colours half hoisted."[14] Christopher Marshall wrote in his *Diary* that the bells of Christ Church "were muffled, and rung a solemn peal at intervals, from morning till night. . . . Sorrow, mixed with indignation, seemed pictured in the countenances of the inhabitants, and indeed the whole city wore the aspect of deep distress, being a melancholy occasion."[15]

The Quakers were not the only sect opposed to this action. The Episcopalians protested against the account of the observance of June 1 in the *Pennsylvania Packet,* saying they "desired, by the Rector [of Christ Church] to acquaint the Public, that the Bells were not rung with his Knowledge or Approbation, and that, by his express Direction, there was no particular Observance of the Churches under his Care. . . ."[16]

---

[12] Force, *American Archives,* 4th ser., I, 486.

[13] *Ibid.,* p. 365; Marshall, *Diary,* pp. 5-6. A committee of the Society of Quakers informed the public that no person was authorized to represent them at the above meeting. Force, *op. cit.,* 4th ser., I, 365; *Pa. Gaz.,* June 1, 1774.

[14] Force, *ibid.,* p. 365.

[15] Entry for June 1, 1774.

[16] *Pa. Gaz.,* June 8, 1774. The protest declared, "It is well known, that the established Church is restrained from any religious Observance of Days, except those appointed by the Church, and the public Authority of Government." A

On June 8 a petition was presented to Governor John Penn "Signed by near nine hundred respectable Freeholders, in and near the City of Philadelphia," requesting him to call the Assembly to consider the proceedings of Parliament toward America.[17] Already rumors have got abroad that the Pennsylvania Assembly had supported the people of Boston, an impression which the Governor hastened to correct. In a letter to Lady Juliana Penn, dated Philadelphia, May 31, 1774, he wrote that he was "surprised that Ld Townshend should have said that the Assembly for this Province had returned thanks to the people of Boston for their spirited behaviour in defence of their rights," for the statement was untrue as the Assembly was not sitting at the time "& have not sat since." Penn said that he was much "concerned that any misrepresentations should be made of the conduct of this Province, especially such as tend to increase the prejudices already entertained against it. Every step will be taken that can to keep things in as moderate a state as possible, but at present a great number of people are very busy in all the Colonies in keeping up the flame & what will be the end of it, God knows." Referring to the petition to him to call the Assembly, Penn said: "I shall treat as it deserves. I have however been informed that the movers of this extraordinary measure have no expectation of succeeding in it but that their real design is to gain time by it in order to see what part the other Colonies will take in so critical a Juncture. . . ."[18]

The conclusion of Penn's letter shows that he was remarkably well informed, for Charles Thomson said: "Tho it was hardly expected the governor would comply, yet it was necessary to take this step in order to prevent farther division in the City & to convince the pacific that it was not the intention of the warm spirits to involve the province in the dispute with-

clear warning that these committees had no authority so far as they were concerned.

[17] Force, *op. cit.*, 4th ser., I, 391-92; Thomson to Ramsey, *New York Hist. Soc. Coll., 1878.*

[18] "Letters of Governor John Penn," *Pa. Mag.*, XXXI, pp. 233-35.

out the consent of the representatives of the people."[19] That they also desired to gain time in order to see "what part the other Colonies will take" is likewise true, for Marshall says in his *Diary* that the Committee "wrote to other Provinces to know their minds on the alarming occasion, which was sent by express, and wait till its return."[20]

Governor Penn replied to the request for calling the Assembly, "Gentlemen, upon occasions when the peace, order, and tranquillity of the Province require it, I shall be ready to convene the Assembly; but as that does not appear to be the case at present, I cannot think such a step would be expedient or consistent with my duty."[21] This refusal to act afforded the patriots a plausible pretext to call the meeting they had already planned. On the tenth and eleventh of June, gatherings were held by the leaders at the Philosophical Hall "to advise, consult and deliberate upon the propositions that were to be laid before the general meeting of the inhabitants. . . ."[22] They must have felt confident of success, for already a meeting of about 1,200 mechanics of Philadelphia and its environs had been held to consult upon the course to be pursued. They chose a committee of correspondence to communicate with the mechanics of New York, from whom they had received letters, and appointed two men to coöperate with the "Committee of merchants, and to strengthen their hands, and to form such resolutions, as will convince the world Americans were born and determined to live free, . . ."[23]

On June 18 the meeting was held in the State House Yard, about eight thousand inhabitants attending. Thomas Willing, a leading merchant of the city, and John Dickinson presided. The meeting, which was very orderly, resolved that the act of Parliament closing the port of Boston was unconstitutional and that it was expedient on the part of America to convene a

[19] Stillé, *Dickinson*, p. 344.
[20] May 21, 1774.
[21] *Ibid.*, June 8.
[22] *Ibid.*, p. 7.
[23] *Pa. Gaz.*, June 15, 1774.

Continental Congress. Several other resolutions were made and a committee of forty-three persons was selected to transact further business. Committees were established in every county of the province and constant communication was maintained between them and the committee of Philadelphia.[24]

The part the interior was to play in the opposition to England was clearly perceived, and the recognition by the leaders of Philadelphia of the potentialities of the Westerners was of the greatest importance in the ultimate success of the revolutionary movement. After the gathering at the State House, Dickinson, Mifflin, and Thomson made an excursion, under color of a pleasure tour, through two or three frontier counties in order to discover the sentiments of the inhabitants, particularly the Germans. "The travelers found the public sentiment favorable to their purpose."[25] A fête was held in the woods near Reading, to which many farmers were invited, and the party was assured that the Germans were almost unanimous in the cause. One said that his father had fled from great oppression in Germany, and on his deathbed charged his sons to defend the liberties they enjoyed in this country, even with their lives if necessary.

Since the frontier counties preferred a convention with more equal representation to the Assembly, it was agreed to hold a meeting of the delegates of these county committees at Philadelphia on July 15. A circular letter, requesting the appointment of delegates, was addressed to all the counties of the province, and is characteristic of the usual verbosity of the period: "We will not offer such an affront to the well-known public spirit of Pennsylvanians, as to question your zeal on the present occasion. Our very existence in the rank of freemen, and the security of all that ought to be dear to us, evidently depends on our conducting this great cause to its proper issue, by firmness, wisdom, and magnanimity."[26]

---

[24] Marshall, *Diary*, p. 7; Stillé, *Dickinson*, p. 110; *Willing Letters and Papers*, ed. by Thomas W. Balch, p. xii; *Pa. Gaz.*, June 22, 1774.

[25] Thomson to Drayton, *op. cit.*, p. 279; see the interesting letter of Mrs. Deborah Logan, who accompanied the party, given in Stillé, *Dickinson*, p. 314.

[26] *Pa. Gaz.*, July 6, 1774.

Everywhere throughout the colony gatherings were held under the direction of the county committees. They denounced the action of the British Parliament, urged the colonies to unite, supported the Philadelphia Committee, and agreed to send delegates to the Convention to be held in Philadelphia.[27] The West seemed thoroughly aroused. James Wilson wrote from Carlisle on July 12: "In the interior parts of the Province the public attention is much engrossed about the late conduct of the Parliament with regard to America, and the steps which the colonies ought jointly to take to maintain their liberties; against which, to say the least of the matter, a very dangerous blow seems to be aimed. . . ."[28]

The Provincial Committee, composed of deputies from the City and County of Philadelphia, and the counties of Bucks, Chester, Lancaster, York, Cumberland, Berks, Northampton, Northumberland, Westmoreland, and Bedford, met at Carpenters' Hall on July 15 and elected Thomas Willing chairman and Charles Thomson clerk.[29] These deputies considered themselves the true representatives of the people, although they were without the least semblance of legal authority. They told the Assembly which was to meet July 18 to choose delegates for the Continental Congress, and formulated instructions for them.[30] The meeting lasted from July 15 to 22 and adopted sixteen resolutions along with the "Instructions." One of these stated: "There is an absolute Necessity that a Congress of Deputies from the several Colonies be immedi-

---

[27] For an account of these various county meetings see the *Pa. Gaz.* from June 22 to July 20, and the *Pa. Arch.* 2d ser., XIII. It is interesting to note that the Carlisle meeting was held in the Presbyterian Church. *Vide Hamilton Library Historical Papers*, V, no. 10, Carlisle, 1902. Address by Edward W. Biddle.

[28] *The St. Clair Papers*, ed. by Wm. H. Smith, I, 324; To Arthur St. Clair at Ligonier, July 12.

[29] For the full proceedings of this body see *Pa. Arch.*, 2d ser., III, 545-622.

[30] For these "Instructions" see *ibid.*, pp. 551-64. The committee to draft these, composed of Dickinson, Wm. Smith, Reed, Kidd, Price, Atlee, James Smith, James Wilson, Broadhead, Okely, and Scull, had been appointed on July 16. *Ibid.*, p. 549. The "Instructions" were the work of John Dickinson. Gordon, *op. cit.*, p. 492.

ately assembled, to consult together and form a general Plan of Conduct to be observed by all the Colonies, . . ."[31] A committee was appointed to wait upon the Assembly with the above resolutions.

Unsuccessful in their attempts to get the Governor to call the Assembly, the Philadelphia committee, whose chairman was John Dickinson, requested the speaker of that body to summon its members to meet on the first of August to consult on the public affairs. This move was likewise endorsed by the meetings in the counties, and the speaker consented to do so. In the meantime Penn had been forced to call the House together because of the pressure which the "back settlers" had brought on account of trouble with the Indians.[32] It was perhaps a good thing for him that he was compelled to do so, for the extra-legal body meeting in Philadelphia was not moderate by any means. The Assembly would be moderate and probably would be able to stem the ever-swelling tide. Governor Penn was clearly aware of this, for in another letter to Lady Juliana, dated June 24 he said: "If the Assembly take notice of the Boston affair as most probably will be the case, they will be more moderate in their Resolves than the People in their Town Meetings, which it is impossible to prevent, . . ."[33]

Thomas Wharton saw clearly that the legislature might be swayed by popular clamor toward action displeasing to the authorities in England. In a letter to his brother written July 5 he said:

Thou may somewhat admire to see my name among the Committee lately appointed at a grand meeting of our citizens, as thou knows I have for some years declined taking an active part in public measures, but I shall freely say that the inducements to me on this extraordinary occasion were the solicitations of great numbers of my fellow citizens, and a sincere desire in myself to keep the transactions of our city within the limits of moderation and not indecent or offensive to our parent state. . . .

---

[31] *Pa. Arch.*, 2d ser, III, 547, ninth resolution; also *Votes*, VI, 517.
[32] *Pa. Mag.*, XXXI, 236.
[33] *Ibid.*, p. 236.

He remarked that the Governor would "not have called the house, and thereby given them an opportunity constitutionally to unite with the other Colonies," had he not been compelled to do so.[34]

The Assembly was not slow in taking advantage of the "opportunity constitutionally to unite with the other Colonies," for on July 21 it resolved itself into a grand committee to consider the "sundry letters from the committees of our sister colonies," and gave "leave for our Provincial Committee to attend and hear" our debates.[35] The next day, in the very words of the Provincial Committee, it resolved: "That there is an absolute Necessity that a Congress of Deputies from the several Colonies be held as soon as conveniently may be. . . ."[36]

On the same day the eight Pennsylvania delegates were chosen "to meet with the Delegates of the other Colonies."[37] Mr. Galloway, upon the earnest solicitation of the House, consented to serve, but only on condition that the instructions he had drawn governing their conduct should first be adopted by the Assembly. These were of a most pacific nature and will be given in full, for the question of instructions to the Pennsylvania delegates in Congress became of great importance as the Revolution developed.

The Trust reposed in you is of such a Nature, and the Modes of executing it may be so diversified in the Course of your Deliberations, that it is scarcely possible to give you particular instructions respecting it. We shall therefore only in general direct that you are to meet in Congress the Committees of the several *British* Colonies at such Time and Place as shall be generally agreed on, to consult together on the present critical and alarming Situation and State of the Colonies, and that you, with them, exert your utmost En-

---

[34] *Pa. Mag.*, XXXIII, 434-39. "Extracts from the Letter Book of Thomas Wharton." (He was one of the Quakers some years later exiled to Virginia.) The same idea is reiterated in another letter of August 2, 1774.

[35] Marshall's *Diary*, p. 8.

[36] *Votes*, VI, 519.

[37] *Ibid.*, p. 520. The delegates were Galloway, Samuel Rhoads, Thomas Mifflin, Charles Humphreys, John Morton, George Ross, and Edward Biddle.

deavours to form and adopt a Plan, which shall afford the best Prospect of obtaining a Redress of *American* Grievances, ascertaining *American* Rights, and establishing that Union and Harmony which is most essential to the Welfare and Happiness of both Countries. And in doing this, you are strictly charged to avoid every Thing indecent or disrespectful to the Mother State. You are also directed to make Report of your Proceedings to the next Assembly.[38]

> *Signed by Order of the House*
> Joseph Galloway, *Speaker.*

The plans of the Provincial Committee were thwarted in one respect, for the Assembly confined the choice of delegates to its own members, thus excluding two men whom the Committee had in view—John Dickinson and James Wilson. This action, severely criticized by the popular party, was really a rebuke to the meetings then being held.[39]

It was Galloway's plan to control completely these delegates. In a letter to William Franklin, dated September 3, 1774, he comments on their attitude and the efforts he has already taken to form a party among them committed to his measures.[40] His plans were not entirely successful, for in the October elections Dickinson was sent to the Assembly and on the fifteenth of that month was added to the Pennsylvania delegation to Congress. Here was a formidable opponent![41]

---

[38] *Ibid.,* pp. 520-21.

[39] For this whole question, *vide Pa. Mag.,* I, 101-02, and XXVI, 304-08; Galloway's *Examination,* p. 42; "Memoirs," *Historical Society of Penna.,* XIII, 346. For a brief description of the delegates, see Stillé, *Dickinson,* pp. 117-19.

[40] *New Jersey Archives,* 1st series, X, 475-77.

[41] It must be said that Galloway's position and intentions regarding the first Continental Congress are clearly manifested from both his public acts and his private correspondence. He was opposed to the policy of the British Ministry, but was extremely averse to the rash measures proposed by the people from Boston and Va. *Vide* Ernest H. Baldwin, "Joseph Galloway, the Loyalist Politician," *Pa. Mag.,* XXVI, 307. *Vide* the letter of Galloway to Samuel Verplanck, written on Jan. 14, 1775. (Printed in *Pa. Mag.,* XXI, 477-78.) In this letter Galloway says he did not approve of the "explicit approbation our Assembly have given to the Proceedings of the Congress." For the effect of this election on the Assembly see *infra,* pp. 65-66.

2. *Meeting of the First Continental Congress*

It is not necessary for our purpose to discuss the work of the Congress, but one thing which may be learned from its meetings is the attitude of the members towards Pennsylvania, their opinions of the conditions in the Quaker Colony, and their influence upon the revolutionary movement there. As early as August 9, 1774, delegates to the Congress began to arrive in Philadelphia,[42] but it was not until September 5 that the fifty-five members met in Carpenters' Hall and elected the Honorable Peyton Randolph chairman and Charles Thomson, of Pennsylvania, secretary.

From the very beginning it was apparent that Congress would add to the factional strife in Pennsylvania, for immediately a quarrel arose over the place of meeting. The city of Philadelphia offered Carpenters' Hall and Galloway, as speaker of the Assembly, offered the State House. Silas Deane wrote: "The last is evidently the best place, but as *he* offers, the other party oppose."[43] The people had won. In the same letter Deane also says that he hopes Philadelphia and Pennsylvania "will be firm and resolute, though there are not wanting enemies to the general Cause, and who, aided by party, are restless in their endeavors to defeat or retard our proceedings."

That this is true is unquestionable, for the New England delegates found many obstacles to their plans for opposing the policies of Great Britain. The story is no better told than by John Adams himself. In a letter to Timothy Pickering, August 6, 1822, he described the journey of the Massachusetts delegates to the meeting of Congress. He said that when they arrived at Frankford, in the suburbs of Philadelphia, they were met by Dr. Rush, Mr. Mifflin, Mr. Bayard, and several others of the most active "Sons of Liberty" in the city who had come out not so much to welcome them as to give them a timely warning as to their conduct. The men from Massachu-

---

[42] Marshall's *Diary*, p. 9.

[43] The letter is given in Edmund C. Burnett, *Letters of the Members of the Continental Congress*, I, 4-5.

setts were told that they were suspected of favoring independence. "Now," said the Philadelphia gentlemen, "you must not utter the word independence, nor give the least hint or insinuation of the idea, either in Congress or any private conversation: if you do, you are undone, for the idea of independence is as unpopular in Pennsylvania and in all the Middle and Southern States as the Stamp Act itself. No man dares to speak of it."[44]

While this statement was written in Adams' eighty-sixth year, we have no valid reasons to suppose it erroneous or exaggerated.[45] Wherever the Massachusetts delegates went they found little sympathy with their opinions. Not only did the Quakers seem cold, but many others who were conspicuous in public life manifested little enthusiasm. Adams had difficulties in convincing the Quakers about New England's sincerity regarding liberty when they knew that their own sect was not tolerated there.[46]

A good account of the spirit at the time of the meeting of the first Congress is given by Joseph Galloway. He says that two parties were immediately formed, "with different views, and determined to act upon different principles. One intended candidly and clearly to define American rights," and to petition for a redress of their just grievances, but "to avoid every measure which tended to sedition, or acts of violent opposition. The other consisted of persons, whose design, from the

---

[44] Adams, *Works*, II, 512; *Pa. Mag.*, XIII, 415-17.

[45] There might be some question as to whether the delegates from Massachusetts had any ideas about independence at this time. John H. Hazelton, in *The Declaration of Independence—Its History*, says: "Of the opinions of John Adams during this year respecting independence, we have found no contemporaneous record; . . ." p. 9. Adams, in his *Diary* for 1774, says nothing about the warning given or of the conversation on the way from Frankford to Philadelphia. See *Works*, II, 357-58. Benjamin Rush later wrote that he went to Frankford to meet the New England delegates and rode back to the city in the same carriage with John Adams and two of his colleagues. He says little more, except that Adams asked many questions. *"An Account of Sundry Incidents, . . .,"* p. 80 ff.

[46] Adams, *Works*, II, 398-400. On Sept. 10, 1774, Adams records that Mr. Reed said that "the sentiments of people here are growing more and more favorable each day."

beginning of their opposition to the Stamp Act, was to throw off all subordination and connexion with Great-Britain; who meant by every fiction, falsehood and fraud, to throw the subsisting Governments into anarchy, to incite the ignorant and vulgar to arms, and with those arms to establish American independence. The one were men of loyal principles, and possessed the greatest fortunes in America; the other were congregational and presbyterian republicans, or men of bankrupt fortunes, overwhelmed in debt to the British merchants. . . ."[47]

The great subject which principally occupied the attention of Congress—the rights of the colonists—was referred to a committee composed of two men from each colony. Galloway and Edward Biddle were the members from Pennsylvania. The committee was directed to state "the rights of the colonies in general; the instances in which those rights are violated, and the means most proper to be pursued for obtaining a restitution of them." The very able declaration reported by the committee was opposed by Mr. Galloway, but was supported by his colleague.[48]

On October 20, 1774, the Assembly of Pennsylvania gave a dinner to the whole Congress at the City Tavern.[49] John Adams recorded in his diary that the "whole House dined with us, making near one hundred guests in the whole; a most elegant entertainment. A sentiment was given: 'May the sword of the parent never be stained with the blood of her children.' Two or three broad-brims over against me at table; one of them said, this is not a toast, but a prayer; come let us join in it. And they took their glasses accordingly."[50]

The Congress adopted resolutions prohibiting the importa-

---

[47] Printed in Burnett, *op. cit.*, I, 54-5.

[48] *Pa. Mag.*, I, 102, "Edward Biddle," by Craig Biddle.

[49] *Pa. Gaz.*, Oct. 26, 1774. About the middle of September 1774, some men of Philadelphia entertained the Delegates to Congress, and over five hundred persons were present. Many toasts were drunk, including ones to the King, Queen, Prince of Wales, and "Perpetual Union to the Colonies." *Pa. Gaz.*, Sept. 21, 1774.

[50] *Works*, II, 400.

tion, purchase, or use of goods coming from Great Britain or
her dependencies after the first day of December, unless the
grievances of America should be redressed before that date.
On October 26 Congress adjourned and the proceedings were
published.[51] Joseph Hewes, a delegate from North Carolina,
in a letter to James Iredell on October 31, wrote: "I have the
pleasure to inform you that they [the resolves of Congress] are
generally approved of here by all ranks of people; the Germans
who compose a large part of the inhabitants of this province
are all on our side; the sweets of liberty little known in their
own country are here enjoyed by them in its utmost lati-
tude. . . ."[52]

The statement of Mr. Hewes is borne out by subsequent
events. Since the Pennsylvania Assembly was the first colonial
legislature to meet after the adjournment of Congress much
depended on its action. On December 10 it adopted and confirmed all the measures of that body, thus becoming the first
constitutional House of Representatives to ratify the acts of
the general Congress. Despite the optimism of some, this action was wholly unexpected by the Governor and was regarded
by Mr. Reed as very significant, as it was "expressive of the
approbation of a large number of Quakers in the House, a
body of people who have acted a passive part in all the disputes
between the mother-country and the Colonies."[53]

This action must be credited largely to Mr. Dickinson. After
a journey to New York, Mr. Galloway returned to his country
estate, Trevose, the first week in December. But three days
before he could return to Philadelphia and take his seat in the
Assemly, that body, under Dickinson's leadership, ratified the
acts of Congress.[54] Dickinson tried to get Galloway to change
his mind about the matter, fearing his opposition would have

[51] When Congress organized the doors were closed and the members pledged
to secrecy.

[52] Burnett, *op. cit.*, I, 83.

[53] Letter to Lord Dartmouth, *Pa. Mag.*, XIII, 420.

[54] *Ibid.*, XXVI, 425-26.

a bad effect on the public cause, but he steadfastly refused.[55]

The opposition to the Assembly's action was of no avail, for the work had been done. Some idea of this feeling is seen in a letter addressed to Samuel Wharton. After lauding the New York Assembly for their refusal to take "any of the proceedings of Congress into their consideration," and their intention to "act for themselves," it said that "had our contemptible house done the same, we might have expected some good, but Dickinson's politicks turned the scale, and caused the vote to pass as it did. . . ."[56]

On December 15, 1774, the Pennsylvania Assembly appointed its delegates to the Second Congress which was to meet on May 10, 1775. These were Edward Biddle, from Berks County, who had been elected Speaker of the House in October, John Dickinson, Thomas Mifflin, Charles Humphreys, John Morton, George Ross, and Joseph Galloway, who, despite his protests, was reappointed.[57] At the same time a committee was appointed to prepare instructions for them.[58]

That the meeting of Congress in Philadelphia had an important effect upon Pennsylvania politics is undeniable. Some of its members held quite radical views. During their sojourn in Philadelphia they made many friends, had many private conversations, and were often invited to dinner, thus exerting much influence in the cause of popular measures. John Adams, in a letter to his wife, written from the seat of Congress on October 7, 1774, said: "The spirit and principles of liberty here are greatly cherished by our presence and conversation. The elections of last week prove this. Mr. Dickinson was

---

[55] *Ibid.*, XXI, 477; *Cf.* Reed, William B., *Life and Correspondence of Joseph Reed*, I, 91; Galloway's *Candid Examination*. See the sarcastic letter in the *London Chronicle* of Jan. 5, 1775, in which the writer, "A Boston Saint," describes the quarrel between Galloway and Dickinson. Printed in *Pa. Mag.*, XXV, 418.

[56] *Pa. Mag.*, XXXIV, 43, "Extracts from the Letter Book of Thomas Wharton." The letter is addressed "Dear Brother Samuel Wharton," and is signed "J. W." It was dated Philadelphia, January 31, 1775.

[57] *Votes*, VI, 555.

[58] *Ibid.*, p. 556.

chosen, almost unanimously, a representative of the county. The Broad-brims began an opposition to your friend, Mr. Mifflin, because he was too warm in the cause. This instantly alarmed the friends of liberty, and ended in the election of Mr. Mifflin by eleven hundred votes out of thirteen, and in the election of our Secretary, Mr. Charles Thomson,[59] to be a burgess with him. This is considered here as a most complete and decisive victory in favor of the American cause. And, it is said, it will change the balance in the Legislature here against Mr. Galloway, who has been supposed to sit on the skirts of the American advocates, . . ."[60]

This same spirit is also seen in the selection of Edward Biddle, a man from the frontier county of Berks, as speaker of the Assembly—the first time a "Westerner" ever held that position. Likewise, the action of the Pennsylvania Assembly in ratifying the acts of Congress shows that even the conservative elements were being carried along in the movement of opposition. However, as we shall see later, there were limits beyond which the Assembly would not go.

3. The Revolutionary Committees

The most important factor in the overthrow of the old government of Pennsylvania and the establishment of a new and more democratic constitution, was the work of the various committees established throughout the province. Their origin dates back to the "Association" formed in opposition to the revenue laws of 1767, which lasted for about two years. Under it committees were established in the capitals of the Provinces, in the country towns, and subordinate districts. Thus an example was at hand for the Revolutionists. As Charles Thomson remarked: "In the commencement of the present opposition these Committees had been revised, extended and reduced to system; so that when any intelligence of importance which it was necessary the people at large

---

[59] Adams recorded in his *Diary* that "This Charles Thomson is the Sam Adams of Philadelphia, the life of the cause of liberty, they say."

[60] *Letters of John Adams addressed to his Wife*, ed. by Charles Francis Adams, I, 33.

should be informed of reached the Capital, it was immediately dispatched to the county Committees and by them forwarded to the Committees of the districts, who disseminated it to the whole body of the people. . . . The expenses of expresses when necessary was defrayed by private contributions—and as the persons employed in this service were animated in the Cause, their zeal was a spur to their industry and the news spread with incredible despatch."[61]

These committees, particularly that of Philadelphia,[62] were fully aware of the state of the political parties and the general disposition of the Province. They saw the quarrel with Great Britain being brought to a crisis, and the opening of a scene which required altogether different exertions from those made heretofore.[63] The Philadelphia Committee, for instance, wanted to appoint the delegates to Congress, not having sufficient confidence in the Assembly, "and more particularly in the Speaker [Galloway], whose influence was great —but whose attachment to the Cause of his Country was even then suspected, . . ."[64]

A new impetus was given to the movement when the First Congress recommended the formation of such committees throughout the colonies.[65] Carrying out this suggestion, notices were scattered throughout Berks County calling the inhabitants together. A respectable number met on December 5, 1774, at the Court House in Reading and proceeded by ballot to elect a County Committee of Observation.[66]

But perhaps the most potent reason for their rapid spread

[61] The following account is taken largely from the excellent history of this movement written by Charles Thomson. "Thomson Papers," *New York Hist. Soc. Coll.*, 1878, pp. 218-19.

[62] The Philadelphia Committee here referred to consisted of forty-three members and was created at the meeting in the State House Yard on June 18, 1774. *Vide supra*, p. 56. A Committee of Correspondence had already been formed on May 20, 1774, headed by John Dickinson. *Vide* Burton A. Konkle, *George Bryan and the Constitution of Pennsylvania*, p. 100.

[63] Thomson, *op. cit.*, p. 219.

[64] *Ibid.*, p. 225.

[65] See *Pa. Gaz.*, Nov. 16, 1774.

[66] M. L. Montgomery, *History of Berks County in the Revolution*, p. 28.

and importance in Pennsylvania was the fact that, due to the restricted suffrage and the inadequate representation, thousands of the inhabitants played no part in the government. This fact coupled with the love of liberty and authority—traits nurtured by the frontier—led these people to create agencies of government under their control and direction. The Quakers fully realized the possible danger from these committees and in their monthly meetings of December and January forbade their members serving on them.[67] These Quaker meetings were filled with serious and prolonged discussions, often lasting until late at night. "The debates ran high," Marshall said, "respecting their conduct in these troublesome times that are expected. In regard thereto, their members were enjoined not to concern themselves in the public disputes, nor to interrupt any of the king's officers in the discharge of their duty, but to pay all humble and dutiful obedience unto the king or his ministers' mandates . . . ; not to join, nor be in any of the city, county, provincial, or general committees, if so, whoever offends is to be dealt with as walking contrary to their discipline."[68]

Alarmed at all these public gatherings and committees, the Quakers felt that more drastic action was necessary. At a meeting for the Sufferings of Pennsylvania and New Jersey Quakers they issued a testimony against usurpation of author-

---

[67] Reference is often made to these Quaker meetings as their "illegal Cabals." They were so called in support of a petition of the inhabitants against the Quaker Assembly, discussed on pp. 27-28, *supra*. Smith, in his "Brief State," says that the Quakers maintained themselves in power by entering into "Cabals in their yearly Meeting, which is convened just before the Election, and being composed of Deputies from all the monthly Meetings in the Province, is the finest Scheme that could possibly be projected, for conducting political Intrigues, under the Mask of Religion." P. 26. Sharpless says that this accusation is untrue *(A Quaker Experiment in Government*, p. 75, note), but there is too much evidence to the contrary. For example, Governor Thomas wrote in 1740 that by "the positive directions of their yearly meeting, which was at first designed for the regulation of the religious concerns of that Society (but in this instance have taken upon them to direct the civil affairs of the government), there are but three returned out of thirty that are not of that profession." *Statutes at Large*, IV, 470.

[68] *Diary*, entries for December 30, 1774 and January 2, 1775.

ity, insurrections, conspiracies, and illegal assemblies—this last expression was obviously intended to include the Provincial Conventions and the Continental Congress itself.[69]

4. State of Affairs in the Early Days of 1775

By the early part of 1775 much progress had been made in the revolutionary movement. Committees were active throughout the province and a call had been issued by the "General Committee" for a Provincial Convention. A sharp division of sentiment regarding resistance to the Crown was already manifest. Loyalists who were not silenced or driven away by means of handbills or personal warnings were tarred and feathered.[70] In the counties anything savoring of opposition was favored by the revolutionists. A group of men in York, writing to Messrs. William and Thomas Bradford, printers of Philadelphia, said: "In order to assist in supporting so successful a Paper as yours—We, the Subscribers, do request you to send each of us a News Paper Weekly, . . . The Spirit of Liberty which appears in your Publication has gained you many Friends in this County. So that ere long we expect your Subscribers will increase much in this Part of the Province."[71]

The passage of the non-intercourse and non-importation agreements by the first Congress sharpened the division of sentiment. The Quaker and Proprietary elements in the Assembly and elsewhere were now called Tories, while those favoring the committees and the adherents of the Provincial Convention were called Whigs.[72] Galloway wrote that the men of property were beginning to think and speak their sentiments, and he hoped they would soon take the lead to which their consequence entitled them.[73] He was still optimistic and thought that the situation was improving at the beginning of 1775 and that the people of Pennsylvania were "altering

---

[69] Wilbur H. Siebert, *The Loyalists of Pennsylvania*, p. 22.

[70] Siebert, *op. cit.*, p. 23; Scharf and Westcott, *op. cit.*, I, 293-94; 296.

[71] *Pa. Mag.*, XIV, 445: Letter was dated April 6, 1775.

[72] Konkle, *op. cit.*, p. 105.

[73] *Pa. Mag.*, XXI, 478—Galloway to Verplanck, Jan. 14, 1775.

their sentiments and conduct." "We have been successful," he wrote, "in baffling all the attempts of the violent party to prevail on the people to prepare for a war against the mother country'. . . I hope all violence will soon cease and peace and order take place of licentiousness and sedition. The Tories (as they are called) make it a point to visit the Coffee House dayly and maintain their ground, while the violent independents are less bold and insolent, as their adherents are greatly diminished."[74]

While this might have been true on the surface, there was a deep, underlying hatred on the part of the West and of the lower classes in Philadelphia for the "men of property" in control of the Assembly and the government of Pennsylvania. An unjust system of representation, inadequate protection against the Indians, property qualifications for voting, all tended to maintain the friction between these classes.

a. PROVINCIAL CONVENTION

Such was the state of feeling when the Provincial Convention met in Philadelphia on January 23, 1775. The General Committee had issued the call, and the various county committees had met to take action on the question and to appoint delegates.[75] Three counties were unrepresented—Bedford, Westmoreland, and Bucks. The first two undoubtedly because of the season of the year and the great distance from Philadelphia;[76] the latter because of the action of the Loyalists. Bucks County, composed largely of Quakers, was predominately Tory. The situation is readily seen in the following letter of Joseph Galloway: "A Committee has been appointed for this County by a few warm People of neither Property or significance among us. But I think they have found it so contrary to the sense of the County that they will not attend the Provincial Congress. . . ."[77]

---

[74] *New Jersey Arch.*, 1st ser., X, 573.

[75] For the action of the various county committees and a record of their meetings see *Pa. Arch.*, 2d ser., XIII, 271-78.

[76] *History of Bedford, Somerset, and Fulton Counties*, p. 81.

[77] *Pa. Mag.*, XXI, 478—Galloway to Verplanck.

The Convention met from January 23 to 28 in the State House—showing how public opinion had changed—and drew up some very important resolutions.[78] It approved the conduct and proceedings of the Continental Congress and resolved to "faithfully endeavour to carry into execution, the measures of the association entered into, and recommended, by them, . . ." However, it said it earnestly wished to see harmony restored. It urged the setting up of woolen manufactures in as many different branches as possible, recommended the manufacturing of iron into nails and wire, the making of steel, paper, and glass, and also pledged itself—and called upon all the inhabitants of the Province—to use their own manufactures and those of the other colonies in preference to all others. The Convention finally resolved that "the committee of correspondence for the city and liberties of Philadelphia, be a standing committee of correspondence for the several counties here represented, and that if it should at any time hereafter appear to the committee of the city and liberties that the situation of public affairs render a provincial convention necessary, that the said committee . . . do give the earliest notice thereof to the committees of the several counties."[79]

The pretext for convening the Convention was to encourage domestic manufacturing; the real object was to familiarize the people with the necessity of subverting the old charter and establishing a new constitution on a more popular basis. The Convention was clearly an extra-legal body and was used to supervise the conduct of the lawful Assembly. Even some of the most ardent patriots opposed this scheme because it was designed to interfere with the regular functions of the House, which had been up to this time, as we have seen, in complete harmony with Congress and the other colonies. From the time of the meeting of the Provincial Convention until June 1776, there was a sort of dual authority in Pennsylvania; the Whigs favoring the General Committee and the Conferences,

---

[78] See the excellent speech of James Wilson. It was a powerful plea for Massachusetts. *Works*, III, 247-69.

[79] *Pa. Arch.*, 2d ser., III, 625-31. This contains the full proceedings of the Convention.

their opponents supporting the Assembly and the old charter.[80]

Thus it is evident that even before the convening of the Second Continental Congress these popular bodies, having no sanction at law, were already beginning to play an important part in the opposition to England. No attempts were made as yet to subvert the existing order, primarily because the Assembly was keeping pace with the general opinion throughout the province. On March 9, 1775, Governor Penn sent a message to the Assembly suggesting that in the present critical condition of affairs it would be more respectful to the authorities in England if each Colony should state its peculiar grievances in separate petitions rather than by making common complaint through a general Congress. To this suggestion the Assembly returned an emphatic refusal. It told the Governor in a very polite but firm manner that separate action was not to be considered; that the present dispute was not one which affected Pennsylvania or any other colony singly, but was one of common concern.[81] It likewise disdainfully rejected the proposition of the House of Lords that each colony should vote its own supplies under certain conditions.

This firm action was followed two months later by an even more emphatic stand in dealing with the British Government. The events of Lexington and Concord had occurred in the interim, and the Assembly was in no pacific state of mind. A letter had come from Franklin in London stating that troops were coming to America,[82] and the very next day—May 2—Governor Penn sent a message to the Assembly accompanying a resolution of the House of Commons[83] proposing a plan of reconciliation. He urged the members to consider it with calmness. "Let me most earnestly entreat you, Gentlemen," he said, "to weigh and consider this Plan of Reconciliation, held forth and offered by the Parent to her Children."[84] This

---

[80] *Pa. Mag.*, XIII, 421.

[81] *Votes*, VI, 577.

[82] Burton A. Konkle, *The Life and Times of Thomas Smith*, p. 61.

[83] Plan or Resolution of the British House of Commons, Feb. 20, 1775.

[84] *Col. Rec.*, X, 251; *Pa. Arch.*, 4th ser., III, 513-15.

was the first legislature to which the resolution was communicated. The answer of Pennsylvania, which came two days later, was important—even momentous. The plan was coldly rejected. The Assembly said: "We have taken into our serious consideration your message of the 2d instant, and 'the resolution of the British House of Commons therein referred to.' Having 'weighed and considered this plan with temper, calmness and deliberation that the importance of the subject and the present critical situation of affairs demand,' we are sincerely sorry, that we cannot 'think the terms pointed out' afford 'a just and reasonable ground for a final accomodation' between Great-Britain and the colonies." The House further stated that it would "esteem it a dishonourable desertion of sister colonies, connected by a union founded on just motives and natural faith, and conducted by general councils, for a single colony to adopt a measure, so extensive in consequence, without the advice and consent of those colonies engaged with us by solemn ties in the same common cause."[85]

On the same day some Philadelphians petitioned the Assembly to grant at least fifty thousand pounds "towards putting this Province into a State of Defence, in such Manner as to the House shall appear most proper and effectual."[86] Concerning this petition John Montgomery, in a letter to James Wilson, May 6, 1775, said: ". . . a Pretty Long and warm Debate insued, and finding the opposition pretty strong the Debate was postponed untill Tuesday next when we expect Mr. Ross to assist us and also time to bring over some of the members in opposition. I am Doubtfull of Success of getting the money in that way. . . ."[87]

The sum was not granted because the Assembly now occupied itself with completing Pennsylvania's delegation to the

---

[85] *Pa. Gaz.*, May 18. The editor said: "We are informed that the above Message passed without one dissenting voice." In another answer to the governor's message the Assembly reiterated its position advocating common action and refused any benefits unless shared by all. *Votes*, VI, 584-85; *Col. Rec.*, X, 252-54.

[86] *Votes*, VI, 585-86.

[87] MS., (Hist. Soc. of Penna.)

approaching meeting of the Second Continental Congress. Benjamin Franklin returned to Philadelphia on May 5 and the next day he, together with Thomas Willing, a merchant of Philadelphia, and James Wilson, a young lawyer from Carlisle, were added to the list of delegates.[88] After many requests to be released from serving in the Assembly, Joseph Galloway was finally excused.[89] On May 9 the Assembly drew up the instructions for its delegates. They were virtually the same as those drawn up on July 23, 1774, for the first Congress.[90]

5. Associators

Another important factor in the overthrow of the old régime and in the creation of a new democratic government was the formation of the Military Associations, or "Associators," as the members were called. They played a conspicuous part in subverting the established authority and were, for the most part, the disfranchised element—the people who had been petitioning for more counties and greater representation; the mechanics and artisans of Philadelphia who had been denied any share in the government by the ruling aristoc-

---

[88] *Votes*, VI, 586.

[89] *Ibid.*, p. 587. After his bitter experience in the Assembly in 1774 Galloway was more determined than ever to refuse the appointment as a delegate to the Second Congress. He wrote: "I am determined to oppose the appointment in our sitting in May, and exert every nerve to prevent it." The vote of the Assembly excusing him marked the close of his political career in the Province of Pennsylvania. From the summer of 1775 to December 1776 he remained at his country home, subjected to continually increasing insults and attempted violence. He was virtually a prisoner at Trevose. A mob once threatened to hang him, but he escaped and never slept at Trevose again. As Graydon said: ". . . taking the hint, probably, from a halter coiled up in a box, that was said to be sent him, he gave up the contest, . . ." (*op. cit.*, p. 117). When an order for his arrest had been issued he hastily loaded some valuables into a wagon and in company with several other prominent Loyalists fled, in December 1776, to the British Camp at New Brunswick, N.J. *Vide Pa. Mag.*, XXVI, 430-33.

Mr. Biddle had been appointed to attend the Second Congress, but on his way from Reading to Philadelphia he fell overboard into the Schuykill River, became ill and was left an invalid. See *Pa. Mag.*, I, 102.

[90] *Votes*, VI, 587. For the "Instructions" of July 23, 1774, see *supra*, p. 59-60.

racy; the frontiersmen who felt that the Assembly had not given them adequate protection against the Indians.

The Address of the Lords and Commons to his Majesty, declaring Massachusetts Bay in a state of rebellion, was published on April 13, 1775. British troops were ordered to Boston, and on April 24, at five o'clock in the evening, the express brought to Philadelphia the news of the battles of Concord and Lexington.[91] Heretofore Pennsylvania had stood almost alone among the colonies in refusing to prepare for war. But now the Quaker and German sectarian influence could no longer restrain the people, and active preparations were begun. This gave a great impetus to the military associations and companies began drilling regularly.[92]

A military spirit, confined largely to the Western part of the state, had existed in Pennsylvania ever since the French and Indian Wars. Therefore it did not take these frontier people long to organize military companies where no such organizations existed. Four weeks after the fighting at Lexington a meeting was held at Hannastown in Westmoreland County, one of the westernmost settlements in the State, and another one was held even farther west at Pittsburgh. Here were the backwoodsmen! The Hannastown meeting unanimously subscribed to a series of resolutions advocating liberty and independence. An "association" was formed, and with it as a nucleus a regiment was organized in Westmoreland County under the command of Colonel Proctor.[93]

The same story might be told for all the important cities and counties in the interior. In Reading, by the last of April,

---

[91] Marshall's *Diary*, pp. 17-18.

[92] *Ibid.*, April 29. "Went and drank coffee at James Cannon's. He was not there, being gone to [the] State House Yard to help consult and regulate the forming of the militia." May 1. "This day a number of the associators to the militia met in each of the wards of this city, to form themselves into suitable companies, and to choose their respective officers."

[93] *History of the County of Westmoreland*, George D. Albert, pp. 73-75. For the record of the Hannastown meeting see *Am. Arch.*, 4th ser., II, 615; *St. Clair Papers*, I, 363-65. Arthur St. Clair drew up the resolutions which were adopted.

1775, there had been raised "two companies of foot under proper officers; and such is the spirit of the people in this free county, that in three weeks time there is not a township in it' that will not have a company raised and disciplined, ready to assert at the risk of their lives the freedom of America."[94] In Lebanon there was "great alarm." The minister of the congregation of Moravian brethren at Hebron, a mile east of Lebanon, wrote on May 10, 1775: "All men from 15 to 50 years, are expected to register themselves. Two companies are ready." Four days later the *Hebron Diary* says: ". . . our whole neighborhood has presented a warlike appearance."[95]

At a meeting of the Committee of Observation for Lancaster County on May 1, presided over by George Ross, "The Association of the Freemen and Inhabitants of the County of Lancaster" was signed by 108 men.[96] A member of the Committee of Bucks—the stronghold of the Tories—writing to the Philadelphia Committee says that some townships have already begun drilling and forming associations, and "many others, animated with the same zeal for the welfare of their country, will, I trust, readily fall in with the plan, a knowledge of which, we have great reason to fear, we shall be soon called upon to give a proof of:—The unanimity, prudence, spirit and firmness, which appeared in the deliberations of yesterday, do honour to Bucks County, and will, I hope, in some measure, wipe off those aspersions we too deservedly lay under."[97]

Patriotism now became rampant and much of the "unanimity" referred to above was secured by devious means. The writer from Bucks said, "A disciple of those species of creatures called Tories, being formally introduced to a tar barrel, of which he was repeatedly pressed to smell, thought it prudent to take leave abruptly, lest a more intimate ac-

---

[94] Letter dated "Reading, April 26, 1775." Force, *Am. Arch.*, 4th ser., II, 400.

[95] J. H. Redsecker, "The Hebron Diary During the Revolutionary Period," *Historical Papers and Addresses of the Lebanon County Historical Society*, I (1898-1901), Lebanon, 1902.

[96] *MS*, (Historical Society of Pennsylvania).

[97] *Pa. Gaz.*, May 10, 1775.

quaintance with it should take place." Benjamin Rush wrote that there were four classes of Whigs, the first being the "Furious Whigs who consider the tarring and feathering a Tory a greater duty and exploit than the extermination of a British army."[98] James Allen, the scion of a well-known family, became an Associator. "My Inducement principally to join them," he said, "Is that a man is suspected who does not; & I chuse to have a Musket on my shoulders, to be on a par with them; & I believe discreet people mixing with them, may keep them in Order."[99]

Christopher Marshall recorded in his *Diary* on May 7: "It's admirable to see the alteration of the Tory class in this place, since the account of the engagement in New England: their language is quite softened, and many of them have so far renounced their former sentiments as that they have taken up arms, and are joined in the association; nay, even many of the stiff Quakers, and some of those who drew up the Testimony, are ashamed of their proceedings." But only a relatively small proportion of the Quakers were willing to take up arms, so writers demanded that those who refused to join the Associators should pay an additional tax. One suggested that "an Association be recommended to the Conscientious, suitable to their Principles."[100] This the General Committee did on May 24, 1775, when it gave to all those who did not "associate" the opportunity to contribute voluntarily.[101]

John Adams, in Philadelphia to attend the meeting of the Second Congress, felt quite encouraged with what he saw there. On May 29 he wrote that the city turns out two thousand men every day.[102] A few days before this Adams

---

[98] The remaining classes given by Rush were: 2—"Speculative Whigs," who infested the public councils as well as the army; 3—"Timid Whigs," whose hopes rose and fell after every victory or defeat; 4—"Staunch Whigs; these were moderate in their tempers, but firm—inflexible and perservering in their conduct." *An Account of Sundry Incidents,* etc., pp. 88-89.

[99] Extracts from his "Diary," printed in the *Pa. Mag.,* IX, 186.

[100] *Pa. Arch.,* 2d ser., I, 581.

[101] *Peters MSS,* VIII, 46, (Hist. Soc. of Penna.)

[102] *Letters to his Wife,* I, 40.

wrote to James Warren: "The Martial Spirit throughout this Province is astonishing, it arose all of a Sudden, Since the News of the Battle of Lexington. Quakers and all are carried away with it. Every day in the Week Sundays not excepted they exercise, in great Numbers."[103] On June 10 Adams wrote, "Two days ago we saw a very wonderful phenomenon in this city; a field day, on which three battalions of soldiers were reviewed, making full two thousand men, battalion men, light infantry, grenadiers, riflemen, light horse, artillery men with a fine train, all in uniforms, going through the manual exercise, and the manoeuvres with remarkable dexterity. All this has been accomplished in this city since the 19th of April; so sudden a formation of an army never took place any where. . . ."[104]

On June 23, 1775, the Committee of the City and Liberties of Philadelphia petitioned the House to raise a "Military Association within the City and Liberties" to equip, train, and drill ablebodied men. They also urged the appointment of a "Committee of Safety and Defence, with discretionary Powers."[105] Four days later the Assembly appointed a committee "to consider of, and report to the House, such Measures as may be expedient for putting" Philadelphia and the province "into a State of Defence."[106] On June 30 their resolutions were considered and adopted. The "Association" was approved and in case of an invasion by British troops the Assembly agreed to pay all the necessary expenses of the officers and men in the actual service of repelling such hostile attempts. Furthermore, a board of commissioners was created to provide implements of war; "Minute-Men" were to be selected in each county "to be in readiness upon the shortest Notice to march to any Quarter in Case of Emergency"; and a Committee of Safety of twenty-five members was appointed, thus supplanting the Committee of Correspondence, "for calling forth such and so many of the Associators into actual Service, when Necessity

[103] "Warren-Adams Letters," p. 51.
[104] Letters to His Wife, I, 42.
[105] Votes, VI, 589-90.
[106] Ibid., p. 591.

required, as the said Committee shall judge proper."[107]

The work of the Assembly can best be seen in the description written by Charles Thomson. He said: ". . . in the summer of 1775 though a majority of the Assembly were of the people called quakers they agreed to arm the inhabitants & ordered five thousand new muskets with bayonets & other accoutrements to be made. And as they had not money in the treasury, & could not have the concurrence of the Governor in raising money to pay for them, they, by a resolve of their own, to which there was only three dissenting voices, ordered 35,000 pounds to be struck in bills of credit & pledged the faith of the province for the redemption of it, thus virtually declaring themselves independent & assuming to themselves the whole power of government."[108] While the Assembly deserves great credit for this action, the approval of the military associations was little more than the recognition of a *fait accompli*. Yet possibly it did give the movement greater impetus by legalizing it and providing the necessary laws.

The counties were just as energetic as Philadelphia. By August York County had formed a battalion of five hundred Minute Men, and over 3,400 had already joined the Association and were "preparing as fast as possible."[109] The ministers began preaching to the Associators, and special services were held for them during the months of June and July in Philadelphia, Lancaster, and other towns. With this backing of the clergy and the support of various churches, the military organizations acquired a firmer and even more honorable position in their respective communities.[110]

---

[107] *Ibid.*, p. 593. Benjamin Franklin was chosen President on July 3, 1775. *Col. Rec.*, X, 282. For a list of the members of the Committee of Safety see *Pa. Arch.*, 2d ser., III, 681-82. For the resolution concerning the "Minute Men" see *Peters MSS*, VIII, no. 50 (Historical Society of Pennsylvania).

[108] Thomson's "Letter to Drayton," pp. 281-82. Thomson gives the year 1776, but this obviously is an error. This action was completely revolutionary in character, and, as Stillé points out, "Can be defended only on the plea of an overruling necessity." For these resolutions see *Votes*, VI, 593.

[109] *Pa. Gaz.*, Aug. 30, 1775.

[110] *Vide Pa. Gaz.*, June 21 and July 12, 1775; J. I. Mombert, *Authentic History of Lancaster County*, p. 234. One of these sermons was printed at the re-

The Quakers and the German sects opposed to bearing arms looked upon these proceedings with alarm. We have already seen that the Quakers were enjoined not to attend the public meetings nor belong to the various committees.[111] The German sects held practically the same views. From the Diaries in the Moravian Archives at Bethlehem we may ascertain their position. On June 1, 1775, it is recorded that several of the brethren went to see Jacob Arndt, a leading member of the County Committee of Observation and Inspection and a captain of Associators, to inform him of their views about military training and fighting. They said: ". . . although we are desirous of the good of the land in which we live, and that we would not *oppose* the current of events, still we cling to the liberty, which as a people of God we enjoyed in all countries, to be freed from actual military service; and that we were willing to bear our share of the burdens of the country."[112]

The status of the Quakers and these German sects opposed to warfare now depended to a great extent on the attitude of the Assembly. That body because it desired their support treated them most leniently. On June 30, 1775, the Assembly, taking into consideration the fact that "many of the good people of this Province are conscientiously scrupulous of bearing arms," agreed to "earnestly recommend to the Associators . . . that they bear a tender and brotherly regard towards this class of fellow-subjects and countrymen." But at the same time it recommended to these "conscientious people"

---

quest of the company of militia and bore the following title: "A Self-defensive War Lawful, proved in a Sermon, preached at Lancaster, before Captain Ross's Company of Militia, in the Presbyterian Church, on Sabbath Morning, June 4th, 1775, by the Rev. John Carmichael, A. M., now published at the request of said Company." Printed by Francis Bailey. See "A Sermon to the Soldiers," preached at Windham, July 31, 1775 (MS, Historical Society of the Lutheran Church, Theological Seminary Library, Gettysburg, Pa.), also *Life and Correspondence of the Rev. William Smith, D. D.*, by Horace Wemyss Smith. The MS Diary of Rev. John Cuthbertson records the following for August 1, 1775. "Exhorted Capt. Ross's Company." Archives Division, State Library, Harrisburg.

[111] *Vide supra*, pp. 68-69.

[112] Extracts from the Diaries in the Moravian Archives at Bethlehem, Pa. John W. Jordan, "Bethlehem during the Revolution," *Pa. Mag.*, XII, 386-87.

that they "cheerfully assist in proportion to their abilities, such persons as cannot spend both time and substance in the service of their country without great injury to themselves and families."[113]

This was simply a recommendation, nothing more. It imposed no obligations on the Quakers; it compelled them to do nothing; it simply appealed to them to do whatever they thought fit to aid those in distress. The Quakers responded at once and at their meeting in Philadelphia early in July agreed "to recommend it to their brethren, in their several meetings in this province and New-Jersey to promote subscriptions to raise money for the relief of the necessitous of all religious denominations, who are reduced to losses and distress in this time of public calamity." The money was to be distributed by a committee of Quakers appointed by the meeting.[114]

As the relations between the colonies and England became more acute, and as fighting had actually begun, the position of the Quakers became more difficult. Demands were made upon Pennsylvania for troops, and the Quakers were beginning to feel that attempts were being made to change the charter government. Because this would mean the end of their control, the Quakers firmly and unequivocally stated their position in their Yearly Meeting held in Philadelphia in 1775. They said that while they did not approve of the proceedings of the British Ministry and "thought them ill-advised," they did not believe in war or revolutions, and would not "be a party in overturning the beneficent charter of William Penn, nor . . . aid in throwing off our ultimate allegiance to the Kings of Great Britain." They further stated that they were utterly opposed to the measures being taken and disavowed all responsibility for them. They could neither recognize a revolutionary government, hold office under it, nor affirm allegiance to it.[115]

Difficulties began almost immediately and were intensified

---

[113] *Votes*, VI, 594; *Pa. Gaz.*, July 5, 1775.

[114] *Pa. Gaz.*, July 12, 1775.

[115] *Minutes of the Yearly Meeting of the Friends in Philadelphia, 1775.*

as the momentous events rolled on. On October 27, 1775, an
Address to the Assembly by a committee of Quakers on behalf
of their society emphasized their religious scruples against
bearing arms, and claimed that they were "intirely relieved
from divers Oppressions" by a contract entered into between
them and William Penn. The address ended by saying that
the Quakers were "not insensible of the Difficulties and Trials
which attend your station in this Time of public Calamity,
and are desirous that divine Wisdom may influence your
Minds, and guide your Councils, so that your Determination
may tend to the Honour of God, the Promotion of Peace,
and the Happiness of the People."[116]

This action of the Quakers taxed the patience of the
Patriots, and a petition and remonstrance was drawn up by
the Committee of the City of Philadelphia on Tuesday, October 31. The Committee, sixty-two in number, marched
two by two to the State House to present it to the Assembly
in person.[117] It denounced the *Address* of the Quakers by saying that "it bears an aspect unfriendly to the liberties of
America, and maintains principles destructive of all society
and government, . . . " Pointing out that the Quakers would
enjoy equally the benefits of the struggle without contribut-
ing a single penny, and with perfect safety to their persons,
it concluded: "Upon the whole, your petitioners rest assured
you will exert every power you are possessed of, for the security and happiness of the good people of this province, and
that you will do equal justice to all your constituents, and
therefore they again repeat their request, that you will not,
at a time when the united strength of *North America,* and the
aid of every individual, is wanted to preserve our common
rights, exempt many of the wealthiest among us from co-
operating with their countrymen in some way or other, for
their common safety."[118]

[116] *Pa. Gaz.,* Nov. 1, 1775. It was signed by John Pemberton, the clerk of
the meeting.

[117] Scharf and Westcott, *op. cit.,* I, 300.

[118] *Pa. Gaz.,* Nov. 8, 1775. *"Signed, by an unanimous order of the Committee, George Clymer, Chairman."* Similar ideas were expressed by the Asso-

Similar petitions were presented to the Assembly by the Committee of the Privates of the Association of the city of Philadelphia and its Districts and by the Officers of the Military Association of the City and Liberties of Philadelphia.[119] The latter protested against the "leniency shown towards persons 'professing to be conscientiously scrupulous against bearing Arms.' "[120]

The fears of the Quakers that attempts were being made to change the government of Pennsylvania were apparently not unfounded, for the committees and the Associators were becoming more and more active. So much so, in fact, that the Committee of Chester County felt itself called upon to make a denial of any such intentions. It asserted that persons evidently inimical to the liberty of America were disseminating propaganda to the effect that the military Associators intended overturning the constitution of Pennsylvania and declaring independence. Such a report "could not originate but among the *worst of men,* for the *worst* of purposes." The Committee declared its abhorrence of "an idea so pernicious in its nature, as they ardently wish for nothing more than a happy and speedy reconciliation, on constitutional principles, with that state from which they derive their origin."[121]

Because the Assembly was lax in making provisions for the militia in the fall of 1775, petitions were presented praying for more money, provisions, and arms.[122] Then, unable to resist the pressure of popular opinion, on November 8 it adopted after considerable discussion a set of resolutions for enlisting men and providing for them. Thus the Associators became a regular milita. The resolutions, however, compelled no one to enlist; they simply recommended that all "Male white Persons within this Province, between the Ages of Sixteen and Fifty years, who have not already associated, and are

---

ciators of Donegall Township, Lancaster County, in a petition to the Lancaster Committee. *Vide* Pennsylvania Miscellaneous MSS, V (Library of Congress).

[119] *Ibid.,* supplement, Nov. 15th.

[120] *Votes,* VI, 599.

[121] *Pa. Gaz.,* Sept. 27, 1775. Signed by Anthony Wayne, chairman.

[122] *Vide Votes,* VI, 600, 644.

not conscientiously scrupulous of bearing Arms," join the Association immediately. Those who did not associate, the House said, "ought to contribute an Equivalent to the Time spent by the Associators in acquiring the military Discipline." At the same time eighty thousand pounds were ordered struck in Bills of Credit.[123] While these resolutions went a little further than those of June 30 they were not mandatory and consequently accomplished very little.

These Associations had existed for some time without any rules or uniform regulations. Finally on August 19, 1775, the Committee of Safety drew up "Articles of Association in Pennsylvania."[124] Composed of thirty-two sections, the first quaintly stated that "if any officer make use of any profane oath or execration when on duty, he shall forfeit and pay for each and every such offence the sum of *Five Shillings*: And if a non-commissioned officer or soldier be thus guilty of cursing or swearing, he shall forfeit and pay for each and every offence the sum of *One Shilling*."

On November 25 the Assembly, following this example, adopted the "Rules *and* Regulations *for the better Government of the Military* Association *in* Pennsylvania." Consisting of thirty-eight articles, they made elaborate "rules for establishing rank or precedence amongst the Pennsylvania Associators," which was to be according to counties, in the order of their establishment. It was agreed that "All National Distinctions in Dress or Name" be avoided, "it being proper that we should now be united in this General Association for defending our Liberties and Properties, under the sole Denomination of *Americans*." All the Associators were urged to adopt, sign, and agree to these regulations in order that one general system might prevail in Pennsylvania.[125]

---

[123] *Ibid.*, p. 646.

[124] These are given in *Pa. Arch.*, 2d ser., XIII, 253-57; also in *Votes*, VI, 658-60. Some alterations were made on April 3, 1776 (*Votes*, VI, 705), and again on April 5 (*ibid.*, pp. 706-10). See also *Pa. Gaz.*, supplement, no. 2438 and same paper for Dec. 6, 1775.

[125] *Votes*, VI, 655-58. The *Pa. Gaz.* for February 14, 1776, said that the signing of the articles of Association "is become very general in the city and districts, and like to be universal among those who have heretofore associated."

But in spite of all these rules, regulations, and agreements the discipline of the Associators was none too good. Insubordination was rife; riots and desertions, as well shall see later, were all too numerous. One illustration of the usual insubordination is attributed to Judge Richard Peters, who commanded a company of Infantry Associators. When he called upon the paymaster to settle his first six months' accounts, the latter remarked to him that the accounts were very large and added: "Pray, captain, how many men do you command?" "Not one," replied the Judge. "How," exclaimed the paymaster, "such heavy accounts as these and not command one man!" "No," rejoined the Judge, "not one, but I am commanded by ninety."[126] James Allen was of the opinion that the Associators would be of little use in defending the City, "as they . . . have no subordination."[127]

As already mentioned, one of the grievances most frequently complained of by the Associators was that the Quakers were not only exempt from military service, but also were freed from any additional pecuniary payments beyond the ordinary taxes. Conscientious objectors had been told by the Assembly that they ought to contribute, but no compulsion was attached thereto. After much insistence on the part of the Associators, the Assembly, before it adjourned on November 29, 1775, passed an act taxing Non-Associators. The eighth article said that "Commissioners are required to charge every such person not associating, over and above the rates and assessments set upon him by virtue of the laws of this province, the sum of Two Pounds Ten Shillings."[128]

The enforcement of this tax seems to have been lax, for in the early months of 1776 the Assembly received many petitions from the Associators objecting to the mode of levying the said taxes.[129] One from the officers of the battalions from Berks County stated: "The great Advantage given to the Non-

---

[126] *Pa. Mag.*, XXV, 367-68. "A Collection of Puns and Witticisms of Judge Richard Peters." From the MS of Samuel Breck.

[127] *Diary of James Allen*, Oct. 14, 1775.

[128] *Pa. Gaz.*, no. 2450.

[129] *Votes*, VI, 668-69.

Associators, in Point of Interest, would entirely defeat the Association, if the People in general were not actuated by a patriotic Spirit."[130] The Privates of the Military Association of Philadelphia stated that they had signed the Articles of Association "notwithstanding the many Difficulties to which they are thereby subjected, and the strong Inducements to them to become Non-Associators by the easy Terms of Exemption, being firmly persuaded that, on a Re-consideration, this Honourable House will remove every reasonable Cause of Complaint, . . ."[131]

When the Assembly convened in February 1776, the privates of the military association of Philadelphia petitioned against the easy manner in which military duty could be evaded. At the same time they demanded the right to vote, declaring that all persons who expose their lives in defense of their country should be entitled to all the privileges and rights of citizens. The officers of the same association concurred in the petition. Concerning the first point the petition stated: "So apparent already are the Effects of this Regulation, that persons of" a lazy, timid, and disaffected nature "affect to ridicule those whose Patriotism would lead them to Activity and Action when necessary, by representing this Honourable House as rating their Lives at 50S. a Piece. . . ."[132] The Committee of Inspection of Bucks County recommended that "an additional Tax be laid upon the Estates of Non-Associators proportionate to the Expenses of the Associators necessarily incurred for the general Defense of Property."[133]

On March 14, 1776, Congress took steps to put an end to one of the grievances complained of by recommending to the "several Assemblies, Conventions and Councils, or Committees of Safety of the United Colonies, immediately to cause all Persons to be disarmed within their respective Colonies, who are notoriously disaffected to the Cause of *America,* or

---

[130] *Ibid.,* pp. 668-69.
[131] *Ibid.,* p. 671; for other petitions see *ibid.,* pp. 671-75.
[132] *Pa. Gaz.,* March 6, 1776.
[133] *Ibid.*

who have not associated, and refuse to associate to defend by Arms these United Colonies against the hostile Attempts of the *British* Fleets and Armies: . . ."[134]

On May 22, 1776, the Assembly of Pennsylvania, acting on the above recommendation, ordered the arms of the non-associators to be collected by the various committees of Observation and Inspection.[135] Some disaffected persons in Berks County refused to deliver up their arms, whereupon the local committee resolved that it would afford all the assistance in its power to the Collectors. In case the Collectors neglected or refused to do their duty necessary steps would be taken to enforce the order.[136] The opposition to this measure must have been widespread, since the Convention which framed the new Constitution passed an ordinance for its more effectual enforcement.[137]

In spite of the increased representation granted to the Western counties by the Assembly on March 14, 1776,[138] many grievances still remained and the disaffection continued among the Associators, particularly those on duty in Jersey. Addressing the Pennsylvania Associators at Amboy, General Roberdeau said: "I find myself under the unpleasant necessity of taking notice of a dissatisfied spirit, which some how or other has crept in among some of us."[139] On August 8 the commanding officers of the detachment of Associators left for the defense of Philadelphia stated that they had given notice for the last time "to the persons who have entered into the several companies, and do not attend their duty," that they "will be severely dealt with unless they immediately alter their conduct."[140]

One of the reasons for this unrest was that many of the As-

---

[134] *Votes*, VI, 694.

[135] *Pa. Gaz.*, May 22, 1776.

[136] *Ibid.*, June 26, 1776. One Henry Kettner was confined for not doing so, and he publicly acknowledged his misconduct.

[137] *Ibid.*, Aug. 7.

[138] *Votes*, VI, 693; *infra*, p. 99.

[139] *Pa. Gaz.*, Aug. 21.

[140] *Pa. Eve. Post*, Aug. 8.

sociators had marched away leaving their families in need.
They demanded that some provision be made for their dependents. The Assembly saw the justice of their contention,
and to provide for their families resolved:

That if any associator, called into actual service, shall leave a
family, not of ability to maintain themselves in his absence, the
Overseers of the Poor, with the concurrence of one Justice of the
Peace of the city or county where such associators did reside, shall
immediately make provision by way of out-pension for the maintenance of such family, and a true and proper account being kept
thereof, shall be returned to the Assembly in order that the same
may be made a provincial expense, and paid accordingly.[141]

Another source of grievance arose when Congress recommended that the Pennsylvania Assembly appoint two brigadier generals to command the Associators. This aroused a
storm of protests,[142] that of the committee of privates of the
military association of Philadelphia being most instructive
because of the light it throws on the antagonism between the
Associators and the organized government of the colony. It
vehemently opposed this action because "many of the Associators have been excluded, by this very House, from voting
for the Members now composing it," and because "the Counties, which have the greatest Number of Associators, have not
a proportional Representation" in the Assembly and consequently could not have an equal voice in the nomination. The
protest concluded by saying that the House was composed
of persons whose religious professions were averse to military
measures, and therefore could not be called the representatives of the Associators, and whose action, ever since the
first opposition to Great Britain, seemed more disposed to

---

[141] *Pa. Gaz.*, July 17, 1776. In July the Committee of Safety of Philadelphia
supervised the work and the various committees of Inspection and Observation
throughout the Province appointed committees to carry out this important
service. *Ibid.*, Aug. 28. Records remain of the relief extended to the families of
deserving Associators. *Vide Pa. Mag.*, XXV, 591-92; Pennsylvania Miscellaneous
MSS, VI (Library of Congress), "Payments on Acct of poor Families gone into
actual Service." The records are from August 13, 1776, to February 21, 1777.
Fifty-eight payments are recorded amounting to about £250.

[142] *Votes*, VI, 741-42.

break "the Union of the Colonies, and submit to the Tyranny of" that country. The Associators declared, of course, that they would not submit to the appointment of general officers for them.[143] So strong was the opposition that steps were taken to have the representatives of the Associators meet and elect the said brigadier generals. The meeting was held at Lancaster on July 4, 1776. Daniel Roberdeau was elected First Brigadier General and James Ewing the Second.[144] This whole affair clearly shows how much the Associators distrusted the Assembly. That body was drawing its last breath and could make no opposition.

6. *Closing Days of 1775*

From the summer of 1775 to the close of the year the political atmosphere was, as we have already seen, growing more heated. John Dickinson labored throughout the summer in the Continental Congress to promote reconciliation with England. John Adams states that the "proprietary gentlemen, Israel Pemberton and other principal Quakers now united with Mr. Dickinson, addressed themselves with great art and assiduity to all the members of Congress whom they could influence, even to some of the delegates of Massachusetts; but most of all to the delegates from South Carolina . . . I became the dread and terror and abhorrence of the party."[145]

Benjamin Franklin wrote from London on several occasions that nothing would be accomplished by sending petitions. In a letter to Charles Thomson on February 5, 1775, he said that "from the constant Refusal, Neglect or Discouragement of American Petitions these many years past, our Country will at last be convinc'd that Petitions are odious here and that petitioning is far from being a probable Means of obtaining Redress."[146]

---

[143] *Ibid.*, pp. 742-43.

[144] *Pa. Arch.*, 5th ser., V, 16 *passim*.

[145] "Diary," *Works*, II, 408-09.

[146] Charles Thomson Papers, I (Library of Congress). See also another letter of Franklin to Thomson on March 13, 1775, in *American Historical Review*, IX, 524.

But Dickinson was far from being so convinced and was finally successful in getting Congress to adopt in July 1775, the Second Petition to the King, which he drafted.[147] He wanted to send it by Richard Penn, who was going to England, but Adams opposed this and had a long harangue with Dickinson. It was soon after this that Adams referred to him as "A certain great Fortune and piddling Genius, . . ."[148] On September 16, 1775, Dickinson met Adams on the street and completely ignored him, whereupon Adams bowed and doffed his hat.[149] Charles Lee wrote that "the writer of the Farmer's Letters wou'd [sic] have passed for the first of citizens, capable of leading the world—but now . . . I am afraid the most honorable inscription on his monument must be *un passable homme du plume*—My God, why does not your whole Province arouse themselves, kick the Assembly from the seat of representation which they so horribly disgrace and set 'em to work German Town stockings for the Army—an employment manly enough for 'em. . . ."[150]

But Lee's proposal for kicking the "Assembly from the seat of representation" would have been too precipitate, and the criticism of Dickinson was perhaps a little too harsh, for outsiders did not understand the peculiar situation in Pennsylvania as did Charles Thomson. He wrote that this experiment was necessary, for otherwise "it would have been impossible ever to have persuaded the bulk of Penna. but that an humble petition drawn up without those clauses against which the ministers & parliament of Great Britain took exceptions in the former petition, would have met with a favorable reception and produced the desired effect. But this petition which was drawn up in the most submissive & unexceptionable terms, meeting with the same fate as others obviated objections that would have been raised & had a powerful effect in suppressing

---

[147] Nevins, *op. cit.*, pp. 101-02.
[148] Letter to James Warren, July 24, 1775. *Warren-Adams Letters*, I, 88.
[149] Adams, "Diary," *Works*, II, 423.
[150] Letter to Benjamin Rush, "Lee Papers," *New York Historical Society Collections*, 1871, I, 227.

opposition, preserving unanimity & bringing the province in a united body into the contest[151]

While opposition to the measures the Colonists were taking against England might have been suppressed, factional strife within Pennsylvania was constantly increasing. In October the last Assembly under the charter of 1701 was elected. Some important changes in membership resulted, and among the new members were Benjamin Franklin and Thomas Mifflin. The latter was reëlected from Philadelphia but retired in November. Joseph Reed, a leader of the so-called "radicals," was chosen in his place on January 26, 1776. "As the Governor had withdrawn himself in a great degree from the affairs of Government," according to Charles Thomson, the Assembly reappointed the Committee of Safety, adding several new members, and invested "them with the executive powers of government reserving to themselves the legislative authority. . . ."[152]

On November 4 the Assembly chose as its delegates to Congress for the ensuing year John Morton, John Dickinson, Robert Morris, Benjamin Franklin, Charles Humphreys, Edward Biddle, Thomas Willing, Andrew Allen, and James Wilson.[153] The last three were not members of the Assembly;

---

[151] Thomson's "Letter to Drayton," pp. 284-85. For Dickinson's work in drawing up the Second Petition to the King, see Stillé, *Dickinson*, pp. 157 *ff*. Franklin was on the Committee but how far he actually approved of it is uncertain. Writing to a friend he said: "It has been with difficulty, that we have carried another humble petition to the crown, to give Great Britain one more chance, one opportunity more, of recovering the friendship of the colonies; which, however, I think she has not sense enough to embrace, and so I conclude she has lost them for ever." Franklin's *Works*, Sparks ed., I, 396.

[152] Thomson's "Letter to Drayton," p. 285. Thomson's account at this point is not very accurate. No trace of the latter part concerning the delegation of powers is given in the minutes. However, this might have been tacitly understood. He said that at the first meeting the Assembly appointed a Council or Committee of Safety. This action was not taken until five days after the first meeting, and it was not the *appointment* but the *reappointment*. *Votes*, VI, 626. Franklin asked to be permitted to retire on Feb. 26, 1776. The House agreed and David Rittenhouse was elected in his place at a special election. *Votes*, VI, 684.

[153] *Votes*, VI, 644.

Willing was a judge of the Supreme Court of the Province, and Allen, a brother-in-law of the Governor, was the Attorney General. These two represented the moneyed and intellectual aristocracy of the Province. That the larger group—men approved by the first Provincial Convention—came from the liberals showed how greatly opinion had changed.

On November 9 the new Instructions for the delegates, principally the work of John Dickinson, were adopted by the Assembly. The first part was practically the same as those previously adopted, but the last part, which was to become of the greatest importance, was significant. Independence was still looked upon with horror, so the Assembly said:

Though the oppressive Measures of the *British* Parliament and Administration have compelled us to resist their Violence by Force of Arms, yet we strictly enjoin you, that you, in Behalf of this Colony, dissent from, and utterly reject, any Propositions, should such be made, that may cause, or lead to, a Separation from our Mother Country, or a Change of the Form of this Government.[154]

While these instructions were adopted without one dissenting voice,[155] it is undoubtedly true that they ran counter to the wishes of a large and constantly increasing party called the Whigs. Thomas Paine described the whole procedure as follows:

A set of instructions for their delegates were put together, which in point of sense and business would have dishonored a schoolboy, and after being approved of by a *few*, a *very few*, without doors, were carried into the house, and there passed *in behalf* of the whole *colony*; whereas, did the whole colony know with what ill will that house had entered on some necessary public *measures*, they would not hesitate a moment to think them unworthy of such a trust.[156]

---

[154] *Ibid.*, p. 647.

[155] *Pa. Mag.*, XV, 15.

[156] Thomas Paine, *Writings*, ed. by D. E. Wheeler, II, 73—"Of the Present Ability of America with some Miscellaneous Reflections."

The Whigs favored a policy directly opposed to that laid down in these instructions, for they were already insisting upon a speedy declaration of independence and the subversion of the charter government of the Province. But such measures were opposed to the wishes and policies of those in control of affairs. As was mentioned before, there was a limit to the opposition to England beyond which the old Assembly would not go. That limit had now been reached. The resultant situation is very clearly stated by John Adams. "The gentlemen in Pennsylvania," he said, "who had been attached to the proprietary interest, and owed their wealth and honors to it, and the great body of Quakers, had hitherto acquiesced in the measures of the Colonies, or at least had made no professed opposition to them; many of both descriptions had declared themselves with us, and had been as explicit and as ardent as we were. But now these people began to see that independence was approaching, they started back. . . ."[157]

It is now evident that the war with England was affording the elements long disfranchised by the old régime an opportunity to assert their claims to a participation in the government. Through their various committees and military associations they were gradually usurping power which legitimately belonged to the constituted authorities. The Assembly, however, was not completely reactionary, for it slowly kept pace with the developing spirit of opposition to English rule.

But when the question of independence was broached the Assembly "started back," as John Adams said. To many people in Pennsylvania a separation from England was unthinkable. Separation would undoubtedly mean the end of the Charter and the end of the rule of that class which had held sway from the very beginning of the colony. It was natural, then, that they should vigorously oppose independence and that over this question a relentless struggle should ensue.

---

[157] "Diary," *Works*, II, 407.

III

POLITICAL CONDITIONS IN 1776 AND THE MOVEMENT FOR A CONSTITUTIONAL CONVENTION

1. *Political Conditions Early in 1776*

IN THE beginning of 1776 Pennsylvania was in a feverish
political state. So complex were the problems to be met;
so different were the opinions held as to modes of redress to
be taken—even among the accredited friends of liberty—that
a description of parties and party feeling is exceedingly difficult. It is certain, however, that it was not a season of universal patriotic enthusiasm. Even among the lower ranks of the
people such a feeling was far from prevalent.[1] Many were
apathetic to the events which occurred; some were listless in
the opposition to the policies of England; while others were
even hostile to the rebellious activities of the colonists.

There were, however, two definite parties violently opposed
to each other—the Whigs and the Tories. The latter included
the greater portion of the Society of Friends,[2] the "proprietaries and proprietary officers, their dependents and con-
nexions, embracing a large proportion of the wealthy and distinguished of the province,"[3] who saw in the change of government the loss of official emolument and influence. Furthermore, a change would mean the end of their power, so they
shrank with horror from the idea of a permanent separation

---

[1] Graydon's *Memoirs*, p. 134. He was in a good position to judge, for he
went on a recruiting expedition into the country and had a very difficult
time getting recruits. Albert J. Beveridge, in his *Life of John Marshall*, I, 80-84,
shows that 1776 was a dark year in the revolution.

[2] Thomas McKean later wrote that they "foresaw the consequences of an
equal representation, as it would affect themselves, and this was a principal
cause of their aversion to a change in the form of our government as a body."
Letter to John Adams, 1823, Adams, *Works*, X, 75.

[3] Gordon, *op. cit.*, p. 525.

from England. This party, the very bulwark of conservatism, represented the wealth and aristocracy of the province. In Philadelphia the New England delegates to Congress found themselves in continual warfare with the advocates of Proprietary interests who stood firmly in the way of the measures they proposed.[4]

The Whigs were the revolutionary or active-movement party, but they were divided into what might be denominated the Right and the Left wings.[5] The Right, or conservative wing, led by Dickinson, Morris, Thomson, and Wilson, wanted the old charter preserved. They were in favor of independence, but insisted that it should not be proclaimed until every means of conciliation had been exhausted and a more perfect union formed. In the early stages, as Graydon remarked, "many sincere whigs" considered "a separation from the mother country as the greatest evil that could befal [sic] us. The merchants were on the whig side, with few exceptions; and the lawyers, who, from the bent of their studies, as well as their habit of speaking in public, were best qualified to take a lead in the various assemblies that became necessary, were little less unanimous in the same cause."[6] The Left Wing, or extremists, stood for vigorous action. They insisted that the authority of Great Britain no longer be recognized and that the charter government of Pennsylvania be overthrown.[7] This was the party of democracy, composed of the Irish and Scotch-Irish settlers in the outlying districts and the disfranchised elements in Philadelphia and elsewhere in the East.[8] It was led at first by Dr. Franklin, McKean, and

---

[4] *Vide* James T. Austin, *The Life of Elbridge Gerry*, I, 194; Adams, *Letters to his wife*, I, 45.

[5] Dr. Rush divided the Whigs into five classes, viz: "1—Such as contend for *power;* 2—Such as contend for *liberty;* 3—Such as contend from *resentm^t;* 4—Such as contend for *mili^y glory;* 5—Such as aim only at *interest."* "Historical Notes of Dr. Benjamin Rush, 1777." *Pa. Mag.,* XXVII, 147.

[6] Graydon, *Memoirs*, p. 117.

[7] *Vide Pa. Mag.,* XIII, 424.

[8] Jonathan D. Sergeant, according to John Adams, said that "the Irish interest in this city [Philadelphia] has been the support of liberty. . . . The Irish and the Presbyterian interest coalesce." Adams, *Works,* II, 426.

George Clymer. Later such frontier chieftains as Robert Whitehill, and military officers like Colonel Daniel Roberdeau,[9] of the Philadelphia battalions, became prominent in its management. They demanded the overthrow of the Charter because of its undemocratic nature; because it gave the Western population an inadequate representation in the Assembly, and because it denied the ballot to the working classes and the unpropertied freemen in the city of Philadelphia.

The types of people who were drawn into these groups is clearly set forth in a statement by Alexander Graydon. He said that the young lawyers, with few exceptions, were Whigs.

In the country the same spirit was prevalent at the bar, the members of which, some of whom were of the first eminence, distinguished themselves by their zeal in opposition to the ministerial claims; and as these very forcibly appealed to the pocket, the great body of German farmers, extremely tenacious of property, were readily gained. . . .[10] As to the genuine sons of Hibernia, it was enough for them to know that England was the antagonist. . . . The spirit of liberty and resistance . . . drew into its vortex the mechanical interest, as well as that numerous portion of the community in republics, styled *The People*. . . . But notwithstanding this almost unanimous agreement in favour of liberty, neither were all disposed to go the same lengths for it, nor were they perfectly in unison in the idea annexed to it.[11]

The moderate Whigs and the Tories, heretofore opposed to each other, were now uniting in an effort to control the Assembly. This tendency was dangerous for the radical leaders since it might unify the opposition to England but prevent the overthrow of the Charter government. As Charles Thomson wrote,

Had the Whigs in Assembly been left to pursue their own measures there is every reason to believe they would have effected their

---

[9] Roberdeau was later elected a brigadier general. See *supra*, p. 89, note 144.

[10] The German sectarians, of course, were not found in these ranks because of their opposition to war. Many did enlist, however. See the *Hebron Diaries*.

[11] Graydon, *op. cit.*, pp. 121-22.

purpose, prevented the disunion which had unhappily taken place & brought the whole province as one man with all its force & weight of government into the common cause.[12]

But the Whigs in the Assembly were not allowed to "pursue their own measures," for the Radical party, aided by Congress, gained control and established a government of their own. When the Assembly met in February 1776, those who favored the continuance of the charter form of government still had the whip hand. Despite this fact, as we have seen, they acted vigorously in raising troops,[13] voting money, taxing non-associators, drawing up rules and regulations for the Associators, and in general putting the province in a state of defense.[14]

It really mattered little, however, what the Assembly did along these lines, for it had instructed its delegates in Congress to oppose independence. The radicals, determined to secure independence, had come to the conclusion that the only way to accomplish this was to abolish the Charter and create a new and more democratic government which would be under their control. Such action they knew would meet with bitter opposition,[15] for many people who supported the cause of the colonies would not go so far as to favor a com-

---

[12] Thomson's "Letter to Drayton," p. 281.

[13] "The Hon. General Assembly have voted 1500 Men for the immediate Defence of this Province, viz. two Battalions of Riflemen, and one Battalion of Musket-men." *Pa. Gaz.*, Mar. 13, 1776.

[14] Some of these measures had been passed in the latter part of 1775, but it was the same Assembly which met again in February, 1776. As Charles Thomson wrote: "And at the very moment when the Assembly were giving the most solid proofs of their attachment to the Cause and gradually entrenching on the powers of the governor in order to arm and put the province into a state of defence, the Com^tt were adopting measures to dissolve them and substitute a convention in their stead." "Thomson to Drayton," p. 283.

[15] "The question of Independence became so warm at Northumberland that it was decided to have a discussion on the subject. A scaffold was erected and the discussion took place. Colonels Cooke and Hunter took the stand on the side of liberty and independence, and Dr. Plunkett and Charles Cooke took the side of loyalty. Considerable warmth was manifested on both sides." *History of Northumberland County*, p. 127.

plete separation from England.[16] The sons of Chief Justice
William Allen, for example, warmly supported the opposition to England, but declared that should independence become the avowed object of the war, their hostility to the Royal
Government would not be continued.[17] On March 6, 1776,
James Allen wrote in his *Diary:* " . . . peace is scarcely thought
of—Independancy predominant. . . . I love the Cause of liberty; but cannot heartily join in the prosecution of measures
totally foreign to the original plan of resistance."[18] Be it remembered, too, that the Allens, or at least James Allen, were
not friendly to England. On July 26, 1775, this same James
Allen had written:

The Eyes of Europe are upon us; if we fall, liberty no longer
continues an inhabitant of this Globe: for England is running fast
to slavery. The King is as despotic as any prince in Europe; the
only difference is the mode; & a venal parliament are as bad as a
standing army.[19]

Many people must have felt the same way, for Joseph Reed,
in a letter to General Washington, dated Philadelphia, March
3, 1776, said:

Notwithstanding the act of Parliament for seizing our property,
and a thousand other proofs of a bitter and irreconcilable spirit,
there is a strong reluctance in the minds of many to cut the knot
which ties us to Great Britain, particularly in this colony and to
the southward.[20]

By the end of February plans for a provincial convention
and the ultimate establishment of a new frame of government
seem to have matured.[21] According to Christopher Marshall, a
member of the Philadelphia Committee, it was decided on
February 28 and 29 to call a convention for the second day of
April.[22] This daring move immediately aroused a furious po-

---

[16] *Vide supra,* p. 93.
[17] *Pa. Mag.,* IX, 176-77.
[18] MS Diary of James Allen, (Hist. Soc. of Penna.); *Pa. Mag.,* IX, 186.
[19] *Ibid.*
[20] Reed, *op. cit.,* I, 163.
[21] *Ibid.,* p. 162.
[22] *Diary,* Feb. 28 and 29.

litical storm. Judge Yeates, on the one hand, wrote that the "measure . . . is . . . condemned by the thinking people . . . ,"[23] while Thomas Paine expressed the contrary opinion that "a more judicious proposal could not be thought of: . . ."[24]

In the meantime a conference was held between some members of the Philadelphia Committee and a few Assemblymen. As the attitude of the latter seemed favorable, the Committee met on March 4 and agreed to a temporary suspension of the call for a Convention.[25] The great question involved was the increase of representation in the Assembly, for it was at this time that the flood of petitions descended upon the House. The Philadelphia Committee then wrote a long and vigorous letter to the county committees explaining its action, and bitterly denounced the unequal representation in the Assembly. It attributed much of the present opposition to that body to this fact, and stated that its proceedings might more properly be called the proceedings of the three original counties. Referring to the conference with members of the Assembly mentioned above, the letter said that it was "found, with great satisfaction, that those Gentlemen indulge themselves in the hopes that a full and equal representation would be obtained in consequence of the petitions now before the Honorable House. . . ."[26]

The Committee had the political situation fathomed very accurately, for the Assembly resolved on March 8 to admit seventeen new members.[27] No decided change in the Assem-

---

[23] *Letters and Papers Relating Chiefly to the Provincial History of Pennsylvania*, ed. by Thomas Balch, p. 248.

[24] Writing as "The Forester," *Pennsylvania Journal*, May 8, 1776. Paine said that "to every man of reflection, it had a cordial and restorative quality."

[25] Marshall's *Diary*, March 4.

[26] The letter is given in the *Penna. Packet* for March 11, 1776. The action which the committee took seems to have been of a temporary nature only—merely a suspension of the call—in order to see what the Assembly would do about the question of increased representation. After admitting seventeen new members on the 8th, the Committee of Inspection and Observation met on the 13th and "recalled their resolve to call a convention." *Pennsylvania Gazette*, March 20, 1776.

[27] *Votes*, VI, 688. Four additional representatives were given to the City of Philadelphia, two each to the counties of York, Lancaster, Cumberland, Berks,

bly took place, however, for the Quakers and the eastern oligarchy still controlled thirty votes, whereas the Scotch-Irish and German counties had only twenty-eight. The inclusion of the six votes of Philadelphia City with those of the first group seems justified because the suffrage requirements disfranchised the large middle and lower classes, thus vesting control in the hands of a small group of property owners. The Assembly realized its precarious situation and was willing to do most anything to preserve its existence. But this questionable magnanimity came too late, for already the real control of affairs-had begun to pass into the hands of the extra-legal committees and conventions. It was apparent that this concession had been extorted from the Assembly and consequently meant little.[28] Although this increase in membership stayed for a time the calling of a convention, it ultimately availed the old order but little, for as Thomas Paine said, "such an augmentation would increase the necessity for a convention; because, the more any power is augmented, which derives its authority from our enemies, the more unsafe and dangerous it becomes to us."[29]

The popular party, encouraged by this action of the Assembly, now sought to have the odious instructions to their delegates removed. On March 20 the Committee of Philadelphia met to draw up a remonstrance requesting the House to rescind these.[30] After a considerable debate and delay that body finally decided on April 6, "by a great Majority," that it would not alter the instructions given at its "last sitting, to the Delegates for this Province in Congress."[31]

---

and Northampton, and one each to Bedford, Northumberland, and Westmoreland. *Ibid.*, p. 693.

[28] See the interesting letter of John Adams to James Warren concerning this action. "Warren-Adams Letters," *Massachusetts Historical Society Collections,* LXXII 213-14.

[29] "The Forester," *Pennsylvania Journal,* May 8, 1776.

[30] Marshall's *Diary,* March 20, 1776. John Adams wrote that this "Virtuous, brave and patriotic Body of Men 100 in Number, voted with only one dissentient Voice to petition their Assembly now sitting, to repeal their deadly Instructions to their Delegates in Congress." "Warren-Adams Letters," p. 213.

[31] *Votes,* VI, 726. The "moderate" men were likewise trying to get these instructions rescinded in the hope of restraining the more radical party. On

a. THE ELECTIONS OF MAY 1

The elections for the additional representatives just granted were to be held on May 1, 1776. It was a crucial time and each party put forth the most strenuous efforts to elect its candidates. Meetings were held night after night and all means known to the politicians of the time were employed. There were two tickets, the Whig, the party of the patriots or revolutionists, and the Tory and Moderate men. In Philadelphia the Whigs met on April 19 at Wm. Thomas's schoolhouse in Videll's Alley, with Christopher Marshall in the chair and James Cannon secretary. They agreed to support George Clymer, Col. Roberdeau, Owen Biddle, and Fred. Kuhl.[32] The Tories and Moderate men chose Samuel Howell, Andrew Allen, Wilcocks, and Willing. The candidates having been selected, the parties now issued their appeals to the people. These took the form of newspaper articles, pamphlets, handbills, and meetings. The printed articles were usually sharp and spiteful, many of a most vindictive nature. One read as follows:

To the Tories. Mind How ye Fight Your Lies Tomorrow, Gentlemen. As we know ye can't go on without some, We'll give you leave to use a few; . . . I recommend to you for a handbill. To the Electors. We, the King's Judges, King's Attornies, And King's Custom-House Officers, Having had a long run in this city, Grown rich from nothing at all, and Engrossed every thing to ourselves, Would now most willingly keep Everything to Ourselves.[33]

The Associators played an important part in the elections. As early as March 29 we find the officers of the several battalions in Lancaster County meeting to take action on the

---

March 3, 1776, Joseph Reed wrote: "We shall endeavour to get the Assembly to amend the association, take off the instructions from the delegates, and increase the representation. I hope we shall succeed in all, but some violent spirits have obstructed our measures by calling a convention, or attempting to do so, before we know what the Assembly will do. Great contests have ensued upon it, and the event is yet doubtful." Reed, *op. cit.*, I, 153.

[32] Scharf and Westcott, *op. cit.*, I, 311; Marshall, *Diary*, April 18-27.

[33] Charles Evans, *American Bibliography*, V, 231; Hildeburn, *Issues of the Philadelphia Press*, II, 269.

matter. They resolved that "the members of Assembly intended to be chosen in May next . . . ought to be Associators, such as have shown themselves to be spirited in the glorious Cause of American Liberty."[34]

The Whigs hoped, of course, to gain control of the Assembly at this election,[35] but they met with bitter disappointment. Everywhere their wish for national independence was understood and this lost them many of their former supporters. On a very full poll the whole Whig ticket with the exception of George Clymer was defeated in the exciting Philadelphia election. "This has been one of the sharpest contests," said Christopher Marshall, "that has been for a number of years. . . . I think it may be said with propriety that the Quakers, Papists, Church, Allen family, with all the Proprietary party, were never seemingly so happily united as at this election, . . ."[36]

The Whigs also suffered some defeats in the counties but, on the whole, were fairly successful there. The Moderate party, however, carried Northampton County by an overwhelming majority. The successful candidate, James Allen, was chosen without any opposition, polling 853 votes with only 14 against him.[37] There was indeed somewhat of an incongruity

---

[34] MS, Yeates Papers, (Hist. Soc. of Pa.). *Vide Pa. Mag.*, VII, 26.

[35] They had some reasons for being hopeful for in the election held in January to fill the office of Burgess made vacant by Thomas Mifflin, who resigned to go to camp, the candidate of the Popular Party, Joseph Reed, was elected. Marshall, *Diary*, Jan. 26-27; *supra*, p. 91.

[36] *Ibid.*, May 1. The poll was as follows, four to be elected: Samuel Howell, 941; Andrew Allen, 923; George Clymer, 923; Alexander Wilcocks, 921; Thomas Willing, 911; Frederick Kuhl, 904; Owen Biddle, 903; Daniel Roberdeau, 890. It must be said, however, that many advocates of independence had gone to the war. As Tom Paine remarked: "On our side, we had to sustain the loss of those good citizens who are now before the walls of Quebec, and other parts of the Continent; while the Tories, by never stirring out, remain at home to take advantage of elections; . . ." He further said that his party was under the disadvantage of "having many of our votes rejected, others disqualified for non-allegiance, with the great loss sustained by absentees, the maneuver of shutting up the doors between seven and eight o'clock and circulating the report of adjourning, and finishing the next morning, by which several were deceived. . . ." *Pa. Journal*, May 8.

[37] *Pa. Mag.*, IX, 186.

in the results of the election, as Tom Paine points out. Writing under the pseudonym of *The Forester,* he said that the elections were to choose

... four burgesses to assist those already elected, in conducting the military proceedings of this province, against the power of *that crown* by whose authority they pretend to sit; and those gentlemen when elected, are according to the rules of that house ... to take an oath of allegiance to serve the same King against whom this province, with themselves at the head thereof, are at war: and a necessary qualification required of many voters, was that they likewise should swear allegiance to the same King against whose power the same house of assembly had just before obliged them, either, to fine or take up arms. Did ever national hypocrisy arise to such a pitch as this![38]

The real question involved in the election was independence. Dr. James Clitherall of Charleston, who was in Philadelphia at the time, records in his *Diary* under date of May 13, 1776:

I soon perceived in this city that parties ran high—the body of the people were for Independency. The Proprietary, John Penn, and most of the gentlemen of the city attached to his interest, were against it lest the form of government should be changed, and they would no more acknowledge the old officers of the government. . . .[39]

A week later Elbridge Gerry, of Massachusetts, writing from Philadelphia, said:

In this colony the spirit of the people is great, if a judgment is to be formed by appearances. They are well convinced of the injury their assembly has done to the continent by their instructions to their delegates. It was these instructions which induced the middle colonies and some of the southern to backward every measure which had the appearance of independency: to them is owing the delay of Congress in agitating questions of the greatest importance, which long ere now must have terminated in a separation from Great Britain: . . .[40]

---

[38] *Pa. Journal,* May 8.
[39] *Pa. Mag.,* XXII, 469.
[40] Austin's *Gerry,* I, 179.

As Joseph Reed stated, "a terrible wordy war" was "waging on the subject of independence" in the press.[41] The papers were filled with articles by "Cato," "Cassandra," "Civis," "The Forester," "An Elector," "Plain Truth," etc., defending or denouncing the Assembly, supporting or condemning independence, favoring or objecting to a new form of government.[42] In the *Pennsylvania Packet* for March 25, 1776, out of 'a total of sixteen columns (not counting the Postscript), "Cato" used five and a quarter, "Cassandra" four, a conversation between "Cato" and "Plain Truth" two and three-quarters, making a total of twelve columns. The Editor of the *Pennsylvania Evening Post* on June 4, 1776, stated that there was so much news for the paper that advertisements had to be omitted, and the following notice was inserted: "Advertisements omitted will have a good place in next paper."

b. GROWTH OF THE IDEA OF INDEPENDENCE

When the contest with England began, the idea of a complete separation from the Mother Country was totally foreign to the minds of the colonists.[43] Men were willing to fight against England for a redress of grievances, but not for independence. Especially was this true in Pennsylvania with its large body of Quakers, German sectarians, and men of wealth attached to the Proprietary interest. These men "had hitherto acquiesced in the measures of the Colonists, or at least had made no professed opposition to them," as John Adams

---

[41] Reed, *op. cit.*, I, 182.

[42] See Adams, *Letters to His Wife*, I, 105, in which he says: "The writer of 'Cassandra' is said to be Mr. James Cannon, a tutor in the Philadelphia college. 'Cato' is reported here to be Doctor Smith." The latter was the Reverend Dr. William Smith, Provost of the College of Philadelphia. It is impossible to discover the names of all of these writers. Undoubtedly many did like Benjamin Rush, who later said that he "wrote under a variety of signatures, by which means an impression of *numbers* in favor of liberty was made upon the minds of its friends and enemies." *An Account of Sundry Incidents*, p. 80.

[43] As far as written records go this is true, but the idea must have been held. See the letter of Francis Alison, quoted in Stiles, *Itineraries and Correspondence*, pp. 425-26. The leaders would not commit themselves in writing.

said, but when "these people began to see that independence was approaching, they started back. . . ."[44] Many people in Pennsylvania and elsewhere felt the same way. Joseph Galloway stated that it was his belief that at the beginning of the Revolution not more than one-fifth or one-tenth "of the people had independence in view."[45] It was one thing to defend their traditional rights as Englishmen; quite another to break away from England itself.

But England deliberately turned her back on the colonists and flatly rejected every petition for a redress of grievances As Dr. John Witherspoon, President of Princeton, said: "All reconciliation, but upon the footing of unconditional submission, had been positively refused by Great Britain."[46]

Even yet it is doubtful whether independence could have been achieved had it not been for the foolhardy policy of the English Ministry. The first of a series of witless acts was the hiring of German troops to fight the colonists—a step which made the healing of the wounds virtually impossible. Joseph Shippen wrote that "whatever Objections we & thousands of others may have to . . . Independence, it appears to me, beyond a Doubt, that a public Declaration of it will be made as soon as it is fully ascertained that a large Army of Foreigners has been taken into British pay to be employed against the Colonies."[47]

The second was the inexcusable severity of the British themselves which came as a shock to all who considered themselves Englishmen. In October 1775, Falmouth [Portland], Maine, was burned, and on January 1, 1776, the city of Norfolk, Virginia, was bombarded. The slaves in Virginia had been armed

---

[44] *Vide supra*, p. 93.

[45] *The Examination of Joseph Galloway, Esq., Before the House of Commons*, (London, 1779), p. 2. Galloway first said one-fifth, but later changed this estimate to one-tenth. *Ibid.*, p. 4.

[46] John Witherspoon, *The Dominion of Providence over the Passions of Men* (Philadelphia, 1776), p. 68. To which is added, *An Address to the Natives of Scotland residing in America.* (Preached at Princeton on May 17, 1776).

[47] Edward Shippen Papers, 1727-1783 (Library of Congress). Letter of Joseph Shippen to Edward Shippen, May 11, 1776.

by Governor Dunmore, and all these events stirred up the wrath of the Colonists. On January 2, 1776, Congress protested against "the execrable barbarity with which this unhappy war has been conducted on the part of our enemies, such as burning our defenceless towns and villages . . . exciting domestic insurrections and murders, bribing savages to desolate our frontier. . . ."[48]

In addition to British policy other factors led to a change of feeling. The colonists realized that aid from France, or any foreign alliance, could not be secured unless independence was declared. At the same time by declaring independence the colonists would be in a better position to claim the rights of belligerents. Finally, mention must be made of Thomas Paine's *Common Sense,* a pamphlet which stated the case of the colonists in simple, plain, and direct language easily read and understood by all. "The period of debate is closed," Paine said. "Arms, as the last recourse, must decide the contest. The appeal was the choice of the King, and the continent hath accepted the challenge."

Even yet many people opposed independence, hence the leaders in Congress who wanted to declare the Colonies free were forced to delay. The events noted above, however, secured the support of a sufficient number of people to render it possible. But many could never take the fatal step and, as Alexander Graydon remarked: "Its adoption . . . rendered numbers malcontent; and thence, by a very natural transition, consigned them to the Tory ranks."[49] The final adoption of the Declaration of Independence will be discussed later.

The battle in the press, as we have mentioned, had become bitter and a few excerpts from some of the articles will be given so that the thought and opinion of the time may be

---

[48] "Observations on the American Revolution," Published by a Resolution of Congress, 1779. Printed in *Pa. Arch.,* 3d ser., VII, 563. See *infra,* pp. 143-44, for the attitude of the Provincial Conference concerning this matter.

[49] *Memoirs,* p. 284. Lt. Col. Wm. Allen, Jr., resigned his command in the army when Independence was declared. *Ibid.,* p. 161. He later swore that "he would shed his blood in opposition to Independency." Marshall's *Diary,* Sept. 4, 1776.

made clear. "Cato's" letter "To the People of Pennsylvania" in the *Pennsylvania Gazette* for March 13, 1776, defended the Assembly against the Committee of Inspection. The latter was charged with aspiring to

. . . the powers vested in an Assembly, fairly and constitutionally elected, to represent two or three hundred thousand people? For, whatever may be pretended about the necessity of a Convention, it is certain, that if such a body were to meet, and could succeed in assuming the powers of government, they must all at length be vested, for the sake of execution, in the hands of a *few men*, who consider themselves as leaders in the city of Philadelphia; and the province in general have but little to say in the matter.

This is a point which cannot be too strongly emphasized, for the change of government in Pennsylvania was essentially the work of a few men in Philadelphia, led no doubt by that master politician Benjamin Franklin.

"In carrying on our great controversy with England," Cato continued, "Pennsylvania has no need either to make the least sacrifice of its constitution, nor yet to yield in zeal to the foremost of the colonies." He extols the constitution and remarks: "Would any wise people, enjoying such a constitution, ever think of destroying it with their own hands; . . ."[50] In the *Packet* for March 18 there appeared some "Queries to the writer who signs himself Cato." This article upholds the Committee of Inspection and asks: "May not *constitutional power* (as it is called) sometimes become dangerous to a state?" The "Query" ends by bringing up the perennial question of representation:

Do not mechanicks and farmers constitute ninety-nine out of a hundred of the people of America? If these by their occupations, are to be excluded from having any share in the choice of their rulers, or forms of government, would it not be best to acknowledge the jurisdiction of the British Parliament, which is composed entirely of GENTLEMEN?[51]

---

[50] See also *Penna. Packet*, March 18, 1776.

[51] The answer of *The Forester* to *Cato* can be found in the *Penna. Journal and the Weekly Advertiser* for April 3, 10 and 24. "Cato" likewise said:

"Cassandra," in the *Pennsylvania Gazette* for March 20, states that the Committee of Inspection of Philadelphia, chosen by ballot, "got possession of their office by a more respectable number of voters than any Burgess which sat in the House of Assembly since the first day in which a comparison could be made."[52] Differing from "Cato" in regard to the efficacy of the constitution, "Cassandra" said: "I should gladly view the paragraph which gives our Assembly the power of legislating without the Governor; and Cato is too well acquainted with the King's Representative, to believe he would ever give his sanction to our opposition." Thus the battle continued in the press, reinforced by pamphleteers and by keen discussions in the taverns and coffeehouses.

2. *The Resolution of Congress of May 15*

The Assembly was to meet on May 20, but it was evident that its sessions would be short.[53] The Popular Party was deeply chagrined over the May elections and as soon as the results of the polling were known the contest was transferred to Congress.[54] There the advocates of independence had effective

---

" . . . the true interest of America lies in *reconciliation with Great Britain on constitutional principles.*"

[52] This was in reply to the remark of "Cato" which appeared in the *Packet* on March 18. "But suppose our Assembly really chargeable with any culpable neglect of duty, with what face could those of our present Committee, who are so loud in their clamours against them, pretend to step into their seats? Were they chosen for that purpose? No. They were considered as chosen for the purpose already mentioned; and although they consisted of *a hundred members,* they had not two hundred votes. Few people gave themselves any concern about the election, being well satisfied that any number of respectable citizens who would take the trouble of a Committee of *Inspection,* should be thankfully indulged with the office." He then asks if this would have been the case had "it been imagined that any among them would ever aspire at the power vested in an Assembly, fairly and constitutionally elected, . . ."

[53] James Allen, who had been elected to membership on May 1, wrote on the 15th that on the "20th of this Month the Assembly meets, but I believe we shall soon be dissolved. . . ." *Pa. Mag.,* IX, 186.

[54] The Tories and Moderates had, in reality, gone too far, for the patriots were now more determined than ever to overthrow the Charter and the Proprietary government. They immediately launched an attack on the old gov-

allies, for the New England delegates were earnestly advocating decisive measures which the Proprietary government had generally opposed. This is clearly seen in a letter written by Elbridge Gerry from Philadelphia on June 25, 1776, saying that since the first arrival of the New England delegates in Philadelphia they had been

... in a continual war with the advocates of Proprietary interests in Congress and this Colony. These are they who are most in the way of the measures we have proposed, but I think the contest is pretty nearly at end, and am persuaded that the people of this and the middle Colonies have a clearer view of their interest, and will use their endeavours to eradicate the Ministerial influence of Governours, Proprietors, and Jacobites, and that they now more confide in the politics of the New England Colonies than they ever did in those of their hitherto unequal Governments.[55]

In the midst of the gloom which the defeat in the elections cast over them, the patriot party was greatly encouraged by the successes of Washington around Boston during March and April, and the flight of an enemy hitherto deemed invincible. Washington himself apparently strengthened the patriots, for in a letter to Joseph Reed, written from Cambridge on April 1, 1776, he said:

I think a change in the American representation necessary: frequent appeals to the people can be attended with no bad, but may have very salutary effects. My countrymen I know from their form of government, and steady attachment heretofore to royalty, will come reluctantly into the idea of independency, but time and persecution bring many wonderful things to pass; . . .[56]

John Adams and the New England delegates had despaired of carrying out their policies so long as the old Assembly held sway in Pennsylvania. Aligned with the radicals of that prov-

---

ernment. The Committee of Inspection and Observation began by recommending that "the Justices of his Majesty King George the Third's Court of Quarter Sessions and Common Pleas" exercise no more authority until a new government is framed. Scharf and Westcott, op. cit., I, 311.

[55] Austin's Gerry, I, 194.
[56] Reed, op. cit., I, 180-81.

ince they now determined to make the final assault upon the charter of William Penn. As pointed out before, independence had long been talked of, but the old royal governments, and particularly the proprietary government of Pennsylvania, were opposed to such a measure. One way this opposition could be overcome was to set up new and more democratic constitutions. This movement had begun fairly early, for on June 9, 1775, acting upon the suggestion of James Wilson, Congress advised Massachusetts to set up a new government on her original charter.[57] This action aroused a considerable demand for new governments everywhere. In November, 1775, it was recommended by Congress "to N. Hampshire to form a Government to their own liking, during this Contest; and S. Carolina is allowed to do the same if they judge it necessary. I believe the Time is near," says Samuel Adams, "when the most timid will see the absolute Necessity of every one of the Colonies setting up a Government within itself."[58]

Early in January, 1776, according to the diary of Richard Smith,

Wilson moved and was strongly supported that the Congress may expressly declare to their Constituents and the World their present Intentions respecting an Independency, observing that the King's Speech directly charged Us with that Design. Several Members said that if a Foreign Force shall be sent here, they are willing to declare the Colonies in a State of Independent Sovereignity [sic].[59]

The opposition was too strong, however, so nothing was done. Yet the agitation persisted. John Adams tells us that he returned to his "daily routine of service" [he took his seat in Congress on Feb. 9, 1776], and to his "almost daily exhortations to the institution of Governments in the States, and a declaration of independence."[60] Again on March 14, Adams

---

[57] Konkle, *Bryan*, p. 106; Dealey, James Q., *The Growth of American State Constitutions*, p. 25; *Journals of Congress*.

[58] Samuel Adams to James Warren, Nov. 4, 1775, quoted in Burnett, *op. cit.*, I, 247-48: see *Journals of Congress*, Nov. 3 & 4.

[59] Burnett, I, 304; see the discussion on the Growth of the Idea of Independence, *supra*, pp. 104 ff., especially p. 105.

[60] Adams, *Works*, III, 25.

records in his *Diary* that the "state of the country so obviously called for independent governments, and a total extinction
of the royal authority," that we earnestly urged "this measure
from day to day, . . ."[61] It was, of course, a big step and no one
better realized this than John Adams. On April 16 he wrote:

The Time is now approaching when the Colonies will find themselves under the Necessity, of engaging in Earnest in this great
and indispensable Work. I have ever Thought it the most difficult
and dangerous Part of the Business Americans have to do in this
mighty Contest, to contrive some Method for the Colonies to glide
insensibly, from under the old Government, into a peaceable and
contented submission to new ones. It is a long time since the
Opinion was conceived, and it has never been out of my mind. . . .
At present, the sense of this Necessity seems to be general, and
Measures are taking which must terminate in a compleat Revolution. There is Danger of Convulsions, but I hope, not great ones.[62]

Carter Braxton, a member of Congress, wrote on April 14:
"Independency and total separation from Great Britain are
the interesting Subjects of all ranks of men and often agitate
our Body. . . ."[63] Most of the agitation concerned Pennsylvania whose support was badly needed. The Assembly, controlled as it was by the Quakers and the landed aristocracy of
the East, realized that the question was not simply independence, but also the overthrow of the old system and the creation of a new state government. It is only natural, then, that
it refused to rescind the instructions to its delegates in Congress forbidding them from voting for independence.[64]

But the sentiment in Congress had gone so far by the
spring of 1776 that the support of Pennsylvania for independence appeared to be all that was needed. Richard Henry
Lee, writing from Philadelphia to Charles Lee on April 22,
said:

---

[61] *Ibid.*, II, 33-34. See the resolution Congress passed which Adams considered "an important step."

[62] "Warren-Adams Letters," pp. 221-22.

[63] Burnett, *op. cit.*, I, 420.

[64] *Vide Pa. Mag.*, XIII, 425, article by Charles J. Stillé.

You ask me why we hesitate in Congress. I'll tell you my friend, because we are heavily clogged with instructions from these shamefully interested Proprietary people, and this will continue until Virg^n sets the example of taking up Government, and sending peremptory Orders to their delegates to pursue the most effectual measures for the Security of America. It is most certain that the people in these Proprietary Colonies will then force the same measure, after which Adieu to Proprietary influence and timid senseless politics.[65]

In May Lee again stated:

The Proprietary Colonies do certainly obstruct and perplex the American Machine. Those who wish delay, and want nothing done, say, let the people in the Colonies begin, we must not go before them, Tho' they well know the language in the Country to be, Let the Congress advise.[66]

As early as March Andrew Allen seemed to have divined that Congress would probably interfere in the affairs of Pennsylvania, for in a letter to Philip Schuyler he said that although the rumor then on foot that John Penn had invited the Six Nations to a conference at Philadelphia was "reported void of Foundation," he had the "greatest Reason to think it a deep laid Plot of your Eastern Neighbours directed to favor the Designs of the Colony of Connecticut in their Dispute with Mr. Penn, and also to blow up the Constitution and Government of this Province which has hitherto been a Barrier against their dark Designs. . . ."[67]

Thus by the spring of 1776 the party in Pennsylvania whose immediate desire was the abolition of the old Charter (having been decisively defeated in the May elections) and the party in Congress whose only object was to secure the general consent of the Colonies to a declaration of independence, had a common basis of action and a *rapprochement* was easily reached.[68] And the time, too, was propitious, for on May 8

---

[65] Quoted in Burnett, *op. cit.*, I, 428-29.
[66] *Ibid.*, p. 442.
[67] *Ibid.*, p. 398. March 17, 1776.
[68] *Pa. Mag.*, XIII, 426. See Adams, *Works*, I, 219.

"the City [was] alarmed with hearing a great number of heavy cannons firing down the river."[69] Congress was at this time vehemently discussing the question as to what should be done with the old colonial governments.[70] While the question was pending on May 9 the discharge of heavy cannon was heard again. This distant cannonade was the first indication that actual war had reached this part of the colonies, and the next day the resolution introduced by John Adams was adopted.[71] It recommended "to the respective Assemblies and Conventions of the United Colonies, where no government sufficient to the exigencies of their affairs hath been hitherto established, to adopt such government as shall, in the opinion of the representatives of the people, best conduce to the happiness and safety of their constituents in particular, and America in general." It was further resolved that "a committee of three be appointed to prepare a preamble to the foregoing resolution."[72]

That the members of Congress knew the consequences of their action is undeniable. James Duane, writing to John Jay on May 11, said: "A Resolution has passed a Committee of the whole Congress, recommending it to the Colonies to assume all the powers of government. It waits only for a preface and will then be ushered into the world. This in Confidence as

---

[69] Marshall's *Diary*, May 8. As early as March the Colony was in a state of alarm, for on the 19th the Committee of Safety sent a letter to the Committee of Inspection and Observation of Lancaster County, telling them of Howe's threatened invasion, and saying "although our intelligence will not warrant our drawing out the Troops immediately, yet we conceive it necessary that every Man be prepared, and in readiness to March at an hours warning." Yeates Papers (Hist. Soc. of Penna.)

[70] John Adams says in his "Autobiography": "In the beginning of May, I procured the appointment of a committee, to prepare a resolution recommending to the people of the States to institute governments. The Committee, of whom I was one, requested me to draught a resolve, which I did, and by their direction reported it." *Works*, II, 510.

[71] John Adams said: "It was a measure which I had invariably pursued for a whole year, and contended for, through a scene and a series of anxiety, labor, study, argument, and obloquy. . . ." *Ibid.*, III, 45. *Vide Journals of Congress*, May 10.

[72] Adams, *Works*, II. 489.

res infecta."[73] The resolution had a decided effect upon conditions in Pennsylvania. As Josiah Bartlett wrote: "The order of Congress concerning taking up Government under the people . . . has made a great noise in this province."[74] Franklin wrote that it "has occasion'd some Dissension in Philadelphia, but I hope it will soon be composed."[75]

The Loyalists and some patriot friends of the Charter, such as Mr. Dickinson and his followers, earnestly contended that all Congress desired could be effected by the existing institutions. They said there was "a government sufficient to the exigencies of Affairs" in Pennsylvania, therefore, there was no need for a Convention. It was not easy to resist this interpretation and it might have embarrassed the patriot party outside of the Assembly but for another move made in Congress. When the resolution was adopted a committee of three, consisting of John Adams, Edward Biddle, and Richard Henry Lee, was appointed to prepare a preamble which they presented to Congress on May 13. After an earnest debate it was adopted on the fifteenth. It went far beyond the resolution, for it struck at the root from which all authority under the charter grew. It denied the necessity or reasonableness of oaths of allegiance to any Government under the crown and declared that the exercise of all such authority be totally suppressed and that all functions of government be exercised under the authority of the people alone. "This Day," John Adams wrote, "the Congress has passed the most important Resolution that ever was taken in America."[76]

---

[73] Burnett, *op. cit.*, I, 443. Adams says that Duane called the Resolution a machine to fabricate independence. *Works*, II, 510.

[74] Letter to John Langdon, Philadelphia, May 19, 1776, given in Burnett, I, 458.

[75] *Writings*, Smyth ed., VI, 448.

[76] Letter to James Warren, Burnett, *op. cit.*, I, 445. For the *Preamble* see *Journals of Congress*, May 15. *Cf.* Reed, *op. cit.*, I, 185-86. Charles F. Adams, in his "Life of John Adams," said: "In Pennsylvania, where resistance had been the most dogged, and at which the stroke of the 15th of May had been especially aimed, it was not enough simply to take the strength out of the assembly. A new power was to be created in its place, a power based upon the popular will." *Works*, I, 219.

An extract from the *Diary* of James Allen, a supporter of the established order, written on May 15, will show the feeling of his group:

The Congress have resolved to recommend it to the different Colonies to establish new forms of Governments, to get rid of oaths of allegiance &c. I think the Assembly of this province, will not consent to change their constitution; and then heigh for a convention! A Convention chosen by the people will consist of the most fiery Independents; they will have the whole Executive & legislative authority in their hands. Yesterday the Resolve of Congress was read by Bradford at the Coffee-house. One man only huzzaad; in general it was ill received. We stared at each other. My feelings of indignation were strong, but it was necessary to be mute. This step of Congress, just at the time commissioners are expected to arrive, was purpously contrived to prevent overtures of peace . . . Moderate men look blank, & yet the Majority of the City & province are of that stamp; as is evident from the Election of new members. Peace is at a great distance, & this will probably be a terrible Summer. . . . I am obnoxious to the independents; having openly declared my aversion to their principles & had one or two disputes at the coffee-house with them. I am determined to oppose them vehemently in Assembly, for if they prevail there, all may bid adieu to our old happy constitution & peace.[77]

The Preamble, as is evident, caused most of the trouble, for it was a veritable declaration of independence. John Adams, in his "Autobiography," said: "It was indeed, on all hands, considered by men of understanding as equivalent to" such a declaration.[78] Carter Braxton wrote on May 17: "The assumption of Governt. was necessary and to that resolution little objection was made, but when the Preamble was reported much heat and debate did ensue for two or three

---

[77] *Pa. Mag.*, IX, 187.

[78] *Works*, II, 510. The same idea is reiterated by John Adams in a letter to his wife, written on May 17. He said: "Great Britain has at last driven America to the last step, a complete separation from her; a total absolute independence, not only of her Parliament, but of her crown, for such is the amount of the resolve of the 15th." *Letters to His Wife*, I, 109-10.

days."[79] In this debate James Wilson, of Pennsylvania, took a leading part. He had not been present when the resolution was passed, but when the Preamble was presented he objected to it most vigorously on the ground that the Pennsylvania delegates had not been authorized to vote for it. He asked for a short delay until the Assembly could meet, for he said that in Pennsylvania "if that preamble passes, there will be an immediate dissolution of every kind of authority: the people will be instantly in a state of nature. Why then precipitate this measure? Before we are prepared to build the new house, why should we pull down the old one, and expose ourselves to all the inclemencies of the season?"[80] Of course the Assembly of Pennsylvania would oppose the preamble. That was plain even to an outsider, for James Duane, writing to John Jay, said: "You know the Maryland instructions and those of Pennsylvania. I am greatly in doubt whether either of their Assemblies . . . will listen to a recommendation the preamble of which so openly avows independence & separation."[81]

All this was exactly what the "patriots" of Pennsylvania wanted. Their plans for abolishing the government under the Proprietors now had the sanction of Congress. In the minds of many this sanction increased their prestige, so they now turned to the work of destroying the existing government and of creating one in which they themselves would be supreme. James Wilson had the political situation fathomed quite accurately.

3. The Movement for a Convention

The advice of Congress, that governments sufficient to the exigencies of affairs should be established in such colonies where they did not already exist, was seized upon by the zealous Whigs of Pennsylvania as an excuse for the abrogation of the old government. The same day the Preamble was adopted

---

[79] Given in Burnett, op. cit., I, 453-54. In this letter Mr. Braxton says he thinks the Preamble was carried by a vote of 6 to 4. Allen says that it was carried by 7 colonies to 4.

[80] Given in Adams, Works, II, 490-91, "Debates in Congress."

[81] Jay Papers, I, 61.

—May 15—a large number of persons met at the Philosophical Hall, with Colonel McKean in the chair, to debate "the resolve of Congress of the fifteenth instant, respecting the taking up and forming new governments in the different colonies." They adjourned a little past ten until three the following day.[82]

The next day the meeting decided "to call a convention with speed; to protest against the present Assembly's doing any business in their House until the sense of the Province was taken in that Convention, . . ."[83] On May 18, upon the request of "a large company," the Committee of the City and Liberties of Philadelphia decided, with only five dissenting votes, that a general call be made of the inhabitants of the City and Liberties, to meet next Monday at nine o'clock forenoon at the State House, in order to take the sense of the people respecting the resolve of Congress of the Fifteenth instant, . . ."[84]

On May 20 this meeting was held. Between four and five thousand people assembled, in spite of the rain, in the State House Yard. The Resolve of Congress of the 15th was read and the "people, in testimony of their warmest approbation, gave three cheers."[85] Of the many resolutions proposed all but one were carried unanimously and were ordered to be sent to the various counties. They were as follows: That the instructions to the delegates "have a dangerous tendency to withdraw this province from that *happy union* with the other colonies, which *we consider* both as our *glory* and protection." "That the present House of Assembly was not elected for the purpose of forming a new government," and that it cannot do so without "assuming arbitrary power";[86] that a "protest be immediately entered, by the People of this City and Liberties, against

---

[82] Marshall's *Diary*, pp. 70-1.

[83] *Ibid.*, entry for May 16.

[84] *Ibid.*, p. 72.

[85] *Pa. Gaz.*, May 22, 1776. "The meeting was conducted with the utmost decorum and harmony."

[86] This was the one resolve not unanimously carried; Isaac Gray dissented. Marshall's *Diary*, May 20.

the power of the said House to carry the said Resolve of Congress into execution"; that the present government is not
"competent to the exigencies of our affairs"; that "a Provincial
Convention ought to be chosen by the people, for the express
purpose of carrying the said Resolve of Congress into execution." It was also unanimously resolved that they would support the measures "now adopted at all hazards, be the consequences what they may."[87] A *Protest* against any further action of the Assembly was then read and unanimously approved. Interestingly enough it set forth the words of the
Preamble rather than those of the *Resolution of Congress.*

This *Protest* was presented to the Assembly on the first day
of its organization, May 22, 1776. It declared that the power
of the Assembly was "derived from our mortal Enemy, the
King of *Great*-Britain," the Members of which were elected
by persons in "real or supposed Allegiance to the said King, to
the Exclusion of many worthy Inhabitants whom the aforesaid Resolve of Congress hath now rendered Electors." Continuing, it said that since the House was "in immediate Inter-
course with a Governor bearing the said King's Commission,"
it was "disqualified to take into Consideration the late Resolve of Congress," not being " 'an Assembly under the Authority of the People.' "[88]

Since it was anticipated that "some difficulties may arise
respecting the mode of electing Members for the said Convention," the Protest and resolutions together suggested that "the
Committee of the City and Liberties of Philadelphia, be directed to send the aforementioned Resolve of Congress to the
several Committees throughout the province." These committees were instructed to arrange for a Provincial Conference
which was to provide for the election of a "Provincial Convention, consisting of at least One Hundred Members, for the
Purpose of carrying the said Resolve of Congress into Execution: As we are fully convinced, that our Safety and Happi-

---

[87] For a full account of the proceedings see *Pa. Gaz.,* May 22, 1776.

[88] *Votes,* VI, 726-27. In the *Pennsylvania Journal* for May 22 there was a
query—"Who ought to form a new constitution of government?" The answer
was "The people."

ness, next to the immediate Providence of God, depend on our complying with, and supporting firmly, the said Resolve . . . that thereby the Union of the Colonies may be preserved inviolate."[89] Late that night the Committee of Philadelphia confirmed the resolutions which had been drawn up at this meeting of the people in the State House Yard and appointed men to take them to the various counties.[90]

From these declarations of the radical Whigs the importance of the resolves of Congress in overthrowing the old government of Pennsylvania is evident. Without them it is indeed a question whether those who favored a new constitution would have been able to achieve their ends. Some interesting comments on the above meeting and the methods used by the "patriots" may be gleaned from the *Diary* of Dr. Clitherall. He said:

. . . the rage of the people burst out in a protest against their present Assembly, who had instructed their Delegates not to vote for Independency. A meeting of the people was called. I attended it. The paper calling the meeting was produced recommending a number of resolves; the Committee of Inspection proposed the appointment of a chairman; . . . The different questions were then put; the people behaved in such a tyrannical manner that the least opposition was dangerous. They came seemingly with a determined resolution to comply strictly with the recommendations of the paper, and Colonel Cadwalader, one of their favorites, was grossly insulted for proposing a different form, preserving at the same time the sense of the resolves. The questions were put, at the first of which, a man because he would not vote as they did was insulted and abused, I therefore thought it prudent to vote with the multitude. . . .[91]

Opinion, as usual, was divided even among the Whigs themselves. Caesar Rodney, writing from Philadelphia on May 22, said: "The people of this City I think have acted rather Un-

---

[89] All of the resolutions and the Protest were signed by Daniel Roberdeau, as chairman of the meeting.

[90] Marshall, *Diary*, p. 73.

[91] *Pa. Mag.*, XXII 469-70. Dr. Clitherall concluded the above account by saying: "In the mean time the publick papers were filled with protests and remonstrances."

wisely—They have called a town-Meeting—by which they have determined to apply to the Committees of Inspection of the Several Counties" to call a convention. "This mode for Establishing a Government appears to be, and really is verry [sic] fair—Yet I think they are unwise—Because we are Certain that a verry powerfull force is expected from England against us, some are Come, the most will undoubtedly Arrive before Midsummer. We shall be obliged to Exert every Nerve, at every point, and we well know how necessary Regular Government is to this End—and by their mode it will be impossible for them to have any Government for three months to Come,—and during that time much Confusion—If the present Assembly should take order in the Matter, the work would be done in one Quarter of the time—However many of the Citizens seem to have little or no Confidence in the Assembly. . . ."[92] General Persifor Frazer, with the army at Long Island, opposed calling a convention, terming such a scheme "very impolitic and unnecessary at this time, . . ."[93]

In an unsigned draft of a letter written by James Wilson we get another glimpse of the confusion. He said that the affairs in Pennsylvania "have been in such a fluctuating and disordered Situation, that it has been almost impossible to form any Accurate Judgment concerning the Transactions as they were passing, and still more nearly impossible to make any probable Conjectures concerning the Turn that Things would take." Mentioning the Resolve of Congress of the 15th, he wrote that "many different Opinions were entertained" concerning it. "Some thought the Government of Pennsylvania sufficient for the Exigencies of its Affairs: Others were of contrary Sentiments upon this Point: Those others divided in their Opinion concerning the *Mode* of adopting a new Government. Some said that the Assembly were adequate to the Purpose of adopting a new Govern-

---

[92] MS, Revolutionary Collection, (Historical Society of Penna.)

[93] *Pa. Mag.*, XXXI, 140—"Extracts from the Papers of General Persifor Frazer." The above letter was written on June 7, 1776, to his wife who kept him informed of the events at home.

ment, others, that they were adequate to the Determination of the Question, whether a new Government was necessary or not, but could not constitutionally adopt one without new Powers from the People; others, that they were adequate to neither. . . ."[94]

Some Philadelphians thought that the people in the interior should be warned against the propaganda which might be spread by the men appointed to take the proceedings of the meeting of May 20 throughout the counties. On May 23 Edward Shippen, of Philadelphia, wrote to his friend Jasper Yeates, at Lancaster, that he was advised by some friends to notify him "that a certain bawling New England man called Doctor Young, of noisy fame together with Joseph Barge" was going up to Lancaster to endeavor "to persuade the people there to join in the late attempt to dissolve our Assembly and put everything into the hands of a Convention, . . . In what way your people may stand I know not, but surely they would not be willing to give up all our Charter privileges at one stroke; many of the people here who even wish for our Independence are averse to the measure now proposed, as tending to deprive us of some valuable Rights, without an Assurance of a Substitute; and the Assembly can as well carry the Resolve of Congress into Execution as a Convention."[95]

It is apparent that the political situation in Pennsylvania was in a hopelessly chaotic condition. As one person said, "the Convention Scheme has turned Every thinge up side down."[96] The only people who knew exactly what they wanted were the staunch Tories, who would preserve the old order at all costs, and the ardent revolutionists who sought its complete overthrow. The latter were so sure of themselves and of the success of their efforts that the Committee of Inspection

---

[94] Written to General Horatio Gates, probably in June, 1776. Preserved in the Dreer Collection, MS. Division, (Hist. Soc. of Penna.) Printed in *Pa. Mag.*, XXXVI, 473-75.

[95] Quoted in *The Life and Times of Thomas Smith*, Konkle, p. 66.

[96] Mary Worral Frazer, in a letter to her husband on June 23. *Pa. Mag.*, XXXI, 141.

and Observation of Philadelphia petitioned the justices of the courts of his "Majesty George the Third" to postpone the business of their courts "until a new government shall be formed, which they apprehend will be effected so speedily that the delay will be of small if any injury to the present suitors, . . ."[97]

The Moderates were soon actively combating the Popular party and protested to the Assembly about the proceedings of the meeting held on May 20. They took exception to the declaration that the petition was from "the Inhabitants of the City and Liberties of *Philadelphia,* in Behalf of themselves and others," and stated:

We the Subscribers, Inhabitants of the City and Liberties of *Philadelphia,* sensible of the many Advantages derived to us from our excellent Constitution and anxiously solicitous that they may be continued to us and our Posterity, deem it our indispensable Duty to declare, that we are not represented in the said Protest, neither have we empowered any Person or Persons whatever, on our Behalf, to sign the same.[98]

Another resolution of greater length and scope was drawn up on May 21 at a meeting of a respectable number of the inhabitants of Philadelphia. It was passed around to be signed and when presented to the Assembly on May 29 contained the names of about six thousand people from the city and adjacent counties.[99] Known as the "Address and Remonstrance," it denounced the "Protest," saying that it was based upon "sundry Allegations which we cannot conceive to be well founded; . . ." The signers said they thought "it an indispensable Duty to ourselves and our Posterity, to claim and support our Birthright, in the Charter and wise Laws of *Pennsylvania,*" and closed with a remonstrance against the said "Protest" because it held up "the Resolve of Congress . . .

---

[97] *Pa. Eve. Post,* June 4, 1776.

[98] *Votes,* VI, 732.

[99] *Pa. Gaz.,* June 12; Marshall, *Diary,* May 24. It was alleged that this remonstrance was "signed chiefly by men who hold offices under the crown, or by people connected with them, . . ." *Pa. Gaz.,* May 29.

as an absolute Injunction. . . . Whereas the said Resolve
is only a conditional Recommendation," and because it set
on foot "a Measure which tends to Disunion, and must damp
the zeal of Multitudes of the good People of *Pennsylvania,*
in the common Cause, who . . . never conceived, when they
engaged . . . for the support of the Charter-Rights of another
Colony, that they would be called upon to make a Sacrifice
of their own Charter . . ."[100]

On May 23, 1776, the address of the Committee of Inspection and Observation for the County of Philadelphia was
presented to the House. It likewise denounced the action
taken by the ultra-Whigs and viewed with the deepest concern the fact that the ground on which the opposition to the
British Ministry was first made had been so totally changed.
It asserted that a "System has been adopted by some Persons,
in the City and Liberties of *Philadelphia,* which tends immediately to the Subversion of our Constitution. . . ." It requested the Assembly to "most religiously adhere to the Instructions given to our Delegates in Congress," and to do
the utmost in their power to oppose "the changing or altering,
in any the least Part, of our invaluable Constitution, under
which we have experienced every Happiness, . . ."[101] A *Broad-
side* of the time stated:

> No Provincial Convention
> Let us act for ourselves, and choose
> Our Old Five Delegates.
> The Friends of the above Measure
> are desired to meet at the usual
> Places of Election, at eight o'Clock,
> in Order to
> Vote Against the Eleven Deputies[102]

Protests now began to be heard from counties other than
Philadelphia. One from Chester County repudiated the action

---

[100] *Votes,* VI, 731; *Pa. Gaz.,* May 22. This was bitterly attacked by "A Pro-
testor" in the *Pa. Journal,* June 12, 1776.

[101] *Votes,* VI, 728; *Pa. Gaz.,* May 29. It was signed by W. Hamilton, by order of the Committee.

[102] Pennsylvania Broadsides, 144 (Library of Congress).

of the meeting held on May 20 by saying that it looked "upon such a Change in Government to be of hurtful and dangerous Consequences, and which they cannot consent to, but do earnestly desire, that the Charter and good Constitution of this Province may be preserved inviolate."[103] On the other hand, the York County Committee wrote to two of their Representatives in the Assembly that "in case of a motion for the continuance of that body" they were immediately to "leave the same."[104]

The Committee of Philadelphia, alarmed by the growing opposition to their proposals, carried the matter to Congress in an address framed at a meeting held on May 24 in Philosophical Hall.[105] The *Address* or *Memorial,* presented to Congress on May 25, stated that the Committee "have beheld with great affliction the Assembly of the province of Pennsylvania WITHDRAWN from its union with Congress (in consequence of their instructions to their Delegates) upon the Resolve of Congress of the 15th instant, . . ." Denouncing the Assembly because it did not possess the confidence of the people and because it did "not contain a full and equal representation," the *Memorial* said: "The situation of our province . . . requires vigour and harmony in the direction of both civil and military affairs, but these can never be obtained when a people no longer confide in their rulers." The *Memorial* continued by saying: "The Committee have too much confidence in the wisdom of your body, to believe (when informed of the true situation of the province) that you meant to include the Assembly thereof in your recommendations to 'Assemblies' to form new governments."[106]

---

[103] *Votes,* VI, 738.

[104] *Pa. Gaz.,* June 12, 1776. Signed by R. M'Pherson, Chairman of the Committee, May 30, 1776.

[105] *Vide* Marshall, *Diary,* May 24, 1776.

[106] This *Address* or *Memorial* was presented to Congress and read on Saturday, May 25. (*Journals of Congress*). It was ordered to lie on the table, and also ordered: "That a copy of said memorial be delivered to Mr. R[obert] Morris, who desires the same in behalf of the Assembly of Pennsylvania." This *Memorial* also protested against a resolution of the Assembly which was to be presented to Congress. It is doubtful if it was presented, for no

The acerbity of the struggle now in progress is clearly manifested in the affair of James Rankin, an Assemblyman from
York County. Mr. Rankin sent "a bundle of remonstrances
to seven inhabitants" of York County "for the express purpose of getting" them signed by the people of York and then
returned to Philadelphia. It was charged that the remonstrances could "be calculated for no other purpose than to
draw this province off from the present union with the other
colonies, or to divide the people, so as to fall an easy prey
to our inveterate enemies." The York County Committee, at a
meeting held on May 30, declared that Mr. Rankin by so acting "has violated the trust reposed in him by the good people
of this County," and resolved that "should any person or persons be so lost to all sense of duty to the public, as to attempt
to procure signers to said poisonous and destructive remonstrance in this county, that the said person or persons be
considered as violators of the Resolves of Congress, and inimical to the liberties of America."[107]

Mr. Rankin answered this attack in a long letter "To the
Worthy Inhabitants of York County" by saying that his
intention was to supply his constituents with all the necessary
information upon the subject. He maintained that it was the
opinion of their delegates in Congress that by the Resolutions of May 10 and 15 that body did not mean to exclude
the Pennsylvania legislature, which the "Protest" of the Philadelphia Committee denied. Mr. Rankin said: " . . . finding
that the public service has been, and might still be, carried
on as vigorously by the Assembly of this province as by any
other public body on the continent, and observing a *Remonstrance* to that effect, signing by multitudes of the most
respectable names in the city of Philadelphia, and the neighbouring counties, . . . I thought it my duty to send you copies

trace of it is found in the *Journals of Congress.* However, one cannot rely
absolutely on the *Journal. Vide infra,* p. 130.

[107] *Pa. Gaz.,* June 12. The resolution was signed by Robert M'Pherson,
Chairman. In this issue also is found the letter of Mr. Rankin from which
the remarks given below were taken. Rankin was later accused of treason,
and his property subjected to confiscation by an act of the Assembly, passed
March 6, 1778. *1 Smith Laws,* 449 *ff.*

of those papers, that I might know the sentiments of the county I represent, in a matter of such consequence . . ." Considering his private rights as a freeman and his "public rights as a Representative in Assembly" grossly violated in this interruption of his correspondence, he concluded: "I know the weight of the Committee of the town of York, who first opened my letters, and I hope that I neither fear their threats, nor regard their censures, while in the honest discharge of my duty."

Despite his protestations that he did not "fear their threats, nor regard their censures," and the essential rightfulness of his position, he was forced to give way completely. On July 12 the Committee of Inspection and Observation for York County resolved: "That in case Mr. James Rankin makes suitable concessions (as he proposes) and gives sufficient surety for his good behavior in [the] future, he shall be restored to his liberty, and the confidence of his countrymen."[108] The next day Mr. Rankin wrote the following letter: "As I have in several instances, injured the Committee of York county by sundry public misrepresentations, as well as by personal insults, thereby obstructing the public measures now so necessary for the safety of our country, but being convinced of the bad tendency of my past conduct, and desirous of being restored to a good understanding and friendship with my countrymen, I do thus publicly ask forgiveness of them, and do promise, on the faith and honour of an honest man, that I will in future pay due regard to the rules and regulations of the Honourable Continental Congress, and behave, in all respects, as becomes a good citizen of the United States of America."[109] Such was the power of the committees!

4. *Attitude of the Associators*

The resolve of Congress and the movement for a new Pennsylvania government were enthusiastically supported by the Associators. Almost unanimously they declared that the

---

[108] *Pa. Gaz.*, July 31, 1776.
[109] *Ibid.*

present government was not "competent to the exigencies of affairs" and was not capable of making the necessary alterations. They supported most heartily the Committee of Philadelphia and the resolutions drawn up by the meeting held on May 20 in the State House Yard.

About nine hundred Associators of the Second Battalion and other inhabitants of Whitehall township, Northampton County, at a meeting on May 27 declared unanimously that "the present government was not competent to the exigencies of our affairs," and that a "Provincial Convention ought to be chosen by the people, for the express purpose of carrying the said Resolve of Congress into execution." It was likewise unanimously resolved: "That we will support the measures now adopted at all hazards, be the consequences what they may."[110] At a similar meeting in the same county on May 29 the Fourth Battalion declared their opposition to the Instructions to the Pennsylvania delegates in Congress, and resolved that "the present House of Assembly, not having the authority of the people for that purpose, cannot proceed" to alter the form of government or draw up a new constitution."[111]

The Committee of Privates of the City and Liberties of Philadelphia sent a copy of the "Protest" with the proceedings of the meeting held on May 20 to the Pennsylvania troops then in active service. The action taken at that meeting was heartily supported by the soldiers. The Committee of Privates of Colonel Bartraim Galbraith's Battalion meeting at Elizabethtown, N.J., on May 27, resolved unanimously: "That we join with you, Gentlemen, in your Protest, and the late Resolve of Congress for totally suppressing all power and authority derived from the Crown of Great Britain."[112]

The Associators of the First Battalion of Chester County met on June 10 and resolved to "carry into execution, to the utmost of" their power "the resolve of the Hon. the Continental Congress." They further declared that the petition

---

[110] *Pa. Eve. Post,* June 1, 1776; *Pa. Gaz.,* June 5.
[111] *Pa. Eve. Post,* June 6, 1776; *Pa. Journal,* June 5.
[112] *Pa. Gaz.,* June 5.

to the Assembly, signed by W. Hamilton, was "calculated to inflame the minds of the good people of this province, to sow dissensions, and to strike at the liberties of the people."[113] At a meeting of the Elk Battalion militia of the same county, under the command of Colonel William Montgomery, resolutions of a similar nature were adopted and signed by 660 men.[114] Likewise, the Associators of Colonel James Crawford's battalion met at their place of parade on June 10 in Leacock township, Lancaster County, and supported the Resolve of Congress of May 15 and the Protest of May 20.[115] The Philadelphia Battalions did the same, and Christopher Marshall said that the soldiers of Colonels McKean and Matlack supported the above "to a man."[116]

One might imagine the tactics used by the Associators to obtain support for these resolutions and the movement for a convention. Dr. Clitherall remarks "that before the meeting of the conference every method was taken to force men into Independency by this body [Committee of Privates]. They put the question to the City Battalion under arms, and any man who dared oppose their opinion was insulted and hushed by their interruptions, cheers and hissings. I do not mean by this," the Doctor continues, "that there was not a majority in their way of thinking, but to shew how unfair and partial their proceedings were."[117] What tactics were employed at the meeting of Colonel Hunter's battalion at Northumberland on June 10 have never come to light, so far as is known, but the question which was put to the men at that meeting, regarding the ability of the Assembly to meet the exigencies of affairs, was very fairly stated.[118]

---

[113] *Ibid.*, June 12. This refers to the "Address and Remonstrance" discussed on page 124, *supra*.

[114] *Ibid.*, June 19.

[115] *Ibid.*

[116] *Diary*, June 10.

[117] "Diary," *Pa. Mag.*, XXII, 471.

[118] See "Questions proposed on the 10th of June 1776 to Col.ᴸ Hunter's Battalion at Northumberland," Revolutionary Papers, Archives Division, (Penna. State Library), III, #68.

While the Associators were holding the meetings referred to above, the various county committees were similarly engaged. All the committees agreed to meet with the deputies of the other counties in a Provincial Conference to be held at Philadelphia on June 18.[119] For example, the Lancaster Committee decided by an overwhelming vote of 28 boroughs to 2 to send deputies to the Philadelphia meeting.[120] On June 14 the Committee of Philadelphia selected by ballot the twenty-five members who were to attend the Conference as deputies from that "City and Liberties."[121]

Thus it is evident that the Resolve of Congress of May 15 was the turning point in the movement for the overthrow of the charter government of the Quaker colony. Without the aid of Congress the efforts of the "radicals" in Pennsylvania to do so would have been hopeless. Before discussing the work of the Provincial Conference and the Convention it is necessary to see what the Assembly was doing in these critical times.

5. Meeting of the Assembly

The Assembly met on May 20 without a quorum.[122] The newly elected members from the various counties took their seats to serve during the remainder of the year,[123] but without taking the oaths of allegiance. It is evident that the Assembly was at a great disadvantage regarding the Resolves of Congress, for it was not in session at the time they were passed. Meanwhile the popular meetings and gatherings of committees and Associators which adopted the resolutions and petitions already described were being held. The Assembly thus faced petitions and counter-petitions, protests and remonstrances, scarcely knowing which way to turn. It did nothing regarding the Resolves of Congress other than to

---

[119] For the record of these meetings see the Philadelphia newspapers for the month of June, 1776.

[120] *Yeates Papers.* (Historical Society of Pennsylvania.)

[121] Marshall's *Diary*, June 14.

[122] *Votes*, VI, 726.

[123] *Ibid.*

appoint a committee on May 22 to take into "consideration the said Resolve of Congress, and the Preamble thereto; and to draw up a Memorial from this House, setting forth the different Meanings that have been assigned to the said Resolve, and requesting an Explanation in such Terms as will not admit of any Doubt, whether the Assemblies and Conventions, now subsisting in the several Colonies, are or are not the Bodies, to whom the Consideration of continuing the old, or adopting new Governments, is referred."[124]

Apparently the committee never made a report,[125] but this action was severely criticized. The *Address* or *Memorial* which the Philadelphia committee presented to Congress denounced it in no uncertain terms,[126] and a writer in the *Pennsylvania Gazette* said that it contained "an insult both upon the people and the Congress; because it solicits a qualification from the Congress, which the Congress, in the preamble to their resolves, say ought to come from the people: Neither does the resolve of Congress say anything about continuing the old government, but of *totally suppressing it*."[127]

While the exceedingly difficult position of the Assembly—placed between Scylla and Charybdis—merits our sympathy, yet their tactics in May are open to question. A letter "to the People" stated that the House had announced that it "had resolved to do business without the Governor: Consequently" it no longer acknowledges him in that character, yet its votes are "titled as before, John Penn, Esq, Governor." It was also stated that the Assembly had got rid of oaths of allegiance, but nothing appears upon its printed votes.[128] The letter con-

---

[124] *Ibid.*, VI, 727.

[125] *Penna.-Constitutional Conventions, Proceedings;* Harrisburg, 1825. Introduction, p. iv. No trace of a *Memorial* is found in the *Journals of Congress.* Perhaps the opposition was too strong.

[126] See *supra*, p. 124.

[127] "To the People," June 26, 1776.

[128] *Pa. Gaz.*, June 26, 1776. Concerning the title of the votes as mentioned above, it should be said that in the printed volume the name of the governor no longer appears on the right hand page after May 20, 1776. This had been done since the beginning. As to the question of taking the oaths, nothing appears in the printed minutes.

tinues: "No *Ayes* or *Nays* are to be found this sitting; for when any objecting members found that they could not carry their point, they withdrew their objections to avoid being known to the public."[129] Again, it criticized the House for its inactivity, especially regarding the request of Congress on June 1 for six thousand men. This lay on the table for a fortnight without being attended to, and when the members finally gave up hope of ever obtaining a quorum they admitted their inability to "proceed on the said Resolution."[130]

The Assembly was urged to make some concessions to the demands of the people,[131] but it went blindly on paying no heed to these requests. It simply refused to recognize the change of sentiment which undoubtedly had occurred throughout the province. Its fatal blunder was to refuse to accept the advice of such counselors of moderation as Wilson, Morris, and others, thereby losing their support and leaving the Whigs with nothing to propose as an alternative to a convention.[132]

Insistent demands were made for a change in the instructions to the Pennsylvania delegates in Congress, but again the Assembly delayed. On May 28, 1776, a "Petition of a Number of the Freemen and Inhabitants of the County of *Cumberland*" was presented to the House, requesting that "the last Instructions, which it gave to the Delegates . . . in Congress, wherein they are enjoined not to consent to any Step, which may cause or lead to a Separation from *Great-Britain*, may be withdrawn."[133] The petition was ordered to lie on the table, but was read a second time on June 5

---

[129] There were only three times in the year 1776 when a roll-call was taken. Two really were one vote on the question of increasing the representation. The other came on September 24, 1776, a few days before the final session, when a roll-call was had on the question of granting "One Thousand Pounds" to the Governor. *Votes*, VI, 743.

[130] This letter appeared in the *Pa. Gaz.*, June 26, 1776. *Vide infra*, p. 134; also pp. 142-43.

[131] See the petition from the people of Cumberland County, May 28, *infra*, note 133.

[132] *Vide* Lincoln, *op. cit.*, pp. 272-73.

[133] *Votes*, VI, 730.

and "after a Debate of a considerable Length," it was agreed that a committee consisting of Morris, Dickinson, Reed, Clymer, Wilcocks, Pearson, and Smith draw up new instructions to the Pennsylvania delegates.[134]

The new instructions were approved of and ordered to be transcribed on June 8, by a vote of 31 yeas to 12 nays.[135] They were printed in the *Pennsylvania Evening Post* on the same day, but were not transcribed on the records of the Assembly until June 14. In order that a comparison may be made with the earlier instructions, these new ones, so markedly different, will be given almost in their entirety. The introductory paragraph stated that the earlier injunction "to dissent from and utterly reject any Proposition, should such be made, that might cause or lead to a Separation from *Great-Britain,* or a Change of the Form of this Government," did not arise from "any Diffidence" of the abilities of the delegates, "but from an earnest Desire to serve the good People of *Pennsylvania* with Fidelity, in Times so full of alarming Dangers and perplexing Difficulties. The Situation of public Affairs is since so greatly altered, that we now think ourselves justifiable in removing the Restrictions laid upon you by those Instructions." A list of the objectionable acts of Great Britain followed, and the delegates were then authorized "to concur with the other Delegates in Congress, in forming such further Compacts between the United Colonies, concluding such Treaties with foreign Kingdoms and States, and in adopting such other measures as, upon a View of all Circumstances, shall be judged necessary for promoting the Liberty, Safety and Interests of America; reserving to the People of this Colony the sole and exclusive Right of regulating the internal

---

[134] *Ibid.,* p. 736.

[135] Marshall's *Diary,* p. 76. James Allen says there were thirteen negative votes. "The names of those 13 members, (of whom I was one) that voted ag^t changing the instructions were put on the Coffee house books." *Pa. Mag.,* IX, 188. The names of those who voted against the above instructions are not given in the minutes.

Government and Police of the same." A florid peroration then followed, stating that

The Happiness of these Colonies has, during the whole Course of this fatal Controversy, been our first Wish. Their Reconciliation with *Great-Britain* our next. Ardently have we prayed for the Accomplishment of both. But, if we must renounce the one or the other, we humbly trust in the Mercies of the Supreme Governor of the Universe, that we shall not stand condemned before his Throne, if our Choice is determined by that over-ruling Law of Self-preservation, which his divine Wisdom has thought fit to implant in the Hearts of his Creatures.[136]

Thus the radical demand proved irresistible. James Allen, on June 6, made the following comment in his *Diary:* "I have met the Assembly & sat from 20th May to this time & have been very active in opposing Independence & change of Government; but the tide is too strong, we could not prevent a change of instructions to our Delegates."[137] But how complete was the change which these new instructions wrought? They did not forbid the delegates from joining in a vote for a declaration of independence, as did those of November 9, 1775, yet they did not specifically empower them so to vote.[138]

Criticism was aroused at once. A letter to the *Pennsylvania Gazette* said that the reason which the Assembly gave was "vague, general and unsatisfactory." The writer continued by saying that many people considered the reasons given

as an artful and selfish compromise for the safety of the persons who were the promoters of them, and there is very little doubt to be made, but that the honour of first drawing them up, passing them or acting under them, would have been strongly contended for, and pleaded as an evidence of the loyalty both of the House of

---

[136] *Votes,* VI, 740.

[137] *Op. cit.*

[138] As we shall see later, Thomas Willing, one of the Pennsylvania delegates who voted against the Declaration of Independence, said that "the Delegates of Pennsylvania were not then authorized by their instructions from the Assembly . . . to join in such a vote." *Infra,* p. 157.

Assembly and their Delegates, in case the enemy had been able
to have penetrated this province. The new instructions left the
Delegates at large, yet we have no reason to believe that their
conduct in Congress is altered thereby.[139]

From the first of June the ultra-Whig members of the Assembly ceased to attend its sessions save long enough to secure the removal of the instructions to their representatives in
Congress. From June first to the fifth the Speaker was unable
to' muster a quorum. On the latter date a quorum was secured when the Whigs returned to hear the presentation to
the Assembly of the proceedings of the Virginia Convention
instructing their delegates in Congress, without reservation,
to declare the Colonies free and independent.[140] The committee of the Pennsylvania Assembly to draft the new instructions was appointed on that date. When their report was
adopted the Whigs, now indifferent to the Assembly and its
proceedings, by a secret understanding ceased to attend its
sessions forever.[141] From June tenth to the thirteenth the
House met both morning and afternoon, but failed to obtain a quorum.[142] The next day those present resolved: "That
they are earnestly desirous of carrying into Execution the
Resolution of Congress of the First Instant;[143] but that, as
they despair, after repeated Disappointments, of procuring
a Quorum of the House, they find themselves unable, at this
time, to proceed on the said Resolutions."[144] A good deal of

---

[139] *Pa. Gaz.*, June 26, 1776—"To the People."

[140] Reed, *op. cit.*, I, 187; *Votes*, VI, 735. The resolutions had been passed in
the Convention of Virginia on May 15, 1776, and were presented to Congress
on June 7 by Richard Henry Lee.

[141] Stillé gives two reasons for this action: 1st—That the Assembly really
had no actual authority since the resolves of Congress of May 10 and 15; and
2d—to paralyze the action of the Assembly, leaving the progress of the revolution to do the rest. *Pa. Mag.*, XIII, 386.

[142] *Votes*, VI, 739.

[143] *Vide supra*, p. 131.

[144] *Votes*, VI, 741—thirty-six members present. During this session the Assembly did attempt several constructive measures. On May 24 a committee was
appointed "to prepare and draw up Resolutions for rendering Naturalization
and the Oaths or Affirmations of Allegiance unnecessary in all Cases where

business was transacted on the fourteenth without a quorum and the House finally adjourned to Monday, August 26.[145] But before it was to meet again a new constitution, which put an end to its authority, had been written.

---

they are required or have been usually taken within this Colony." *Votes*, VI, 729. On May 30 a committee was appointed "to examine the Works already made for the Defence of this Colony, and report what other Fortifications are necessary, and the Places proper for erecting the same: And that they request the Favour of the Commander in Chief of the Forces of the United Colonies, and the other General officers and Engineers now in this City, to afford them their Advice and Assistance in this necessary and important Matter." *Ibid.*, p. 734.

[145] *Ibid*, p. 741. Marshall says that the Assembly adjourned, "sundry county members being gone out of town." *Diary*, June 15.

IV

THE PROVINCIAL CONFERENCE AND THE CONSTITUTIONAL CONVENTION

1. The Provincial Conference

BY THE summer of 1776 the Revolution was sweeping along with the mighty force of a March wind. The call had already gone forth for a Provincial Conference, and the County Committees had chosen their representatives who assembled in Philadelphia on June 18. The record of the first meeting of this body—the formal organization of the revolutionary government—is as follows:

This day a number of gentlemen met at Carpenters' Hall, in Philadelphia, being deputed by the committees of several of the counties of the province, to join in a Provincial Conference in consequence of a circular letter from the committee of the City and Liberties of Philadelphia, inclosing the resolution of the continental congress of the 15th of May last.[1]

The meeting had no legal foundation nor any basis at law, yet it was successful in all it undertook, and planned the convention which drew up a new constitution for Pennsylvania. Its whole action was thus purely revolutionary and was saved from the contumely usually bestowed on such bodies by the high character of some of its members. Benjamin Franklin, Thomas McKean, Dr. Benjamin Rush, and William Atlee were among its members. Franklin, however, was not present when the conference opened and if he attended at all, which is doubtful, his participation in the proceedings was negligible.[2]

---

[1] The Proceedings relative to Calling the Convention of 1776 and 1790, p. 35; Pa. Arch., 2d ser., III, 635 ff. (Ed. of 1875). The Pa. Evening Post for June 18 had the following: "This day the Provincial Conference met at Carpenters'-Hall in this city, which was numerous and respectable."

[2] Life and Writings of Franklin, Sparks ed., I, 406. In a letter to George Washington, dated June 21, 1776, Franklin says nothing about the Conference.

The strongest support for the movement to establish a new constitution came from the Associators. It is interesting to note that of the 108 members of the Conference, fifty-eight held military titles[3] and perhaps many others were members of the military associations.

The Conference immediately proceeded to the choice of officers, electing Colonel Thomas McKean, president; Colonel Joseph Hart, vice-president; Jonathan B. Smith and Samuel C. Morris, secretaries. All these officers, with the exception of Hart, who was from Bucks County, were from the city of Philadelphia.

The task which these men were called upon to perform was deemed by them an imperative one. The fate of the country was at stake and little time could be lost. Their meetings were held every day of the week, including Sunday. The resolutions passed by the Conference express not only the dissatisfaction with the old Provincial Assembly, prevalent among certain classes of the people, but are indicative also of the sources upon which the new movement relied for support. First of all, equal representation was accorded to each county and to the city of Philadelphia. On June 19 it was ordered, "That in taking the sense of this conference on any question which may come before them, the city and counties respectively have one vote."[4]

The Conference, as was to be expected, heartily approved of the Resolve of Congress of May 15, which was read on June 19—the first full day devoted to business. After "mature consideration," it was *"Resolved,* unanimously, That the said resolution of congress . . . is fully approved by this conference."[5] The same day it was also declared that "the present government of this province is not competent to

---

"I am just recovering from a severe Fit of the Gout," he wrote, "which has kept me from Congress & Company almost ever since you left us, . . ." *Life and Writings,* Smyth ed., VI, 449-50.

[3] *Proceedings,* pp. 35-6.

[4] *Pa. Arch.,* 2d ser., III, 635-37.

[5] *Ibid.,* p. 639.

the exigencies of our affairs," and that it was absolutely necessary that "a provincial convention be called by this conference for the express purpose of forming a new government
in this province on the authority of the people only."[6]

The next question concerned the electors. Who was to have
the right to vote? Obviously the old property qualifications
which would disfranchise the majority of the Associators
could not be maintained. Such a situation was intolerable.
The discussion was precipitated by the presentation of a
petition from the German Associators of the city and liberties
of Philadelphia praying that all taxable Associators be entitled to vote.[7] By granting this request the Conference saw
an opportunity to secure for the new movement the support
of a large element in the colony who had long been denied the
franchise, and who earnestly desired it. Naturally it took the
members but a short time to decide the matter. In the very
same session it was resolved: "That every associator in the
province shall be admitted to a vote for members of the
convention in the city or county in which he resided; *provided,* such associator be of the age of twenty-one years, and
shall have lived one year in this province immediately preceding the election; and shall have contributed at any time
before the passing of this resolve to the payment of either
provincial or county taxes, or shall have been rated or assessed towards the same."[8] Thus the previous £50 property
qualification was abolished and the franchise put on a democratic basis.

Having increased the ranks of their own party, the new
rulers proceeded to impose tests, oaths, and other requirements which served to decrease the number of their opponents. It was resolved that all persons qualified to vote for
representatives to the Assembly should be entitled to vote
for members of the convention. However, if any of the elec-

---

[6] *Ibid.,* p. 639.
[7] *Ibid.,* p. 639.
[8] *Ibid.,* p. 640.

tion judges or inspectors required it, the following oath or affirmation had to be taken:

I . . . do declare that I do not hold myself bound to bear allegiance to George the third, king of Great Britain, &c., and that I will not, by any means, directly or indirectly, oppose the establishment of a free government in this province by the convention now to be chosen, nor the measures adopted by the congress against the tyranny attempted to be established in these colonies by the court of Great Britain.[9]

But this was not all. An additional oath was required of those elected to the convention before they could take their seats. They had to swear to do their best to "establish and support a government in this province on the authority of the people only, . . ."[10] These measures, intended to exclude the Tories and the moderate Whigs from the new movement, prevented anyone opposed to the idea of separation from Great Britain and of establishing a new government from taking any part therein. As a further disqualification of the above-mentioned classes, it was resolved that "no person who has been published by any committee of inspection, or the committee of safety, in this province, as an enemy to the liberties of America, and has not been restored to the favor of his country, shall be permitted to vote at the election of members for said convention."[11]

One more qualification was added which caused some violent opposition. On June 21 it was resolved that no person elected to serve as a member of the convention could take his seat until he made a declaration of faith "in God, the father, and in Jesus Christ, his eternal son, the true God, and in the Holy Spirit, one God blessed for evermore"; and also an acknowledgment of his belief that the "holy scriptures

---

[9] *Ibid.*, p. 640. June 19. This was twelve days after Lee's famous motion had been made in Congress.

[10] *Ibid.*, pp. 641-42.

[11] *Proceedings*, p. 39.

of the old and new testament" were given by "divine inspiration."[12]

The addition of this last qualification aroused considerable opposition and Marshall recorded in his *Diary* that it was

... highly censured, and as it's represented, and not unjustly, that I strenuously supported it, I am blamed, and buffeted and extremely maltreated by sundry of my friends, as I thought, and who, I believed, were really religious persons and loved our Lord Jesus Christ, but now declare that no such Belief or Confession is necessary, in forming the new government. But their behavior don't affect me, so as to alter my judgment in looking upon such a Confession to be essentially necessary and convenient.[13]

There seems to be no valid reason for exacting such an oath; no need for such an invasion of the ecclesiastical sphere by the civil authorities. It was an open usurpation of unwarranted power and a portent of a more bitter religious struggle soon to come. It is possible that the members of the Conference firmly believed no man fit to take part in these momentous affairs who could not make such a profession of faith. On the other hand, it may have been a desperate bid for clerical support or an attempt to secure divine sanction for what might otherwise appear as sedition.

With the groundwork now completed the Conference turned its attention to the details of calling the Convention. The committee appointed to ascertain the number and proportion of members reported on Friday, the twenty-first. The report stated that full information as to the number of taxables in each county was not then obtainable, but it was believed that the number would not differ so much as to make it "of any probable disadvantage to allow an equal representation from each county, especially as the convention will

---

[12] *Ibid.*, p. 39. In view of the opposition aroused, it should be noted that this oath was less drastic than the one required of members of the old Assembly, and is a return to the original idea of liberty of conscience held by William Penn. *Vide infra*, pp. 179-80.

[13] Entry for June 28.

probably vote by city and counties . . . upon the questions which shall come before them."[14] It was therefore agreed that eight representatives be chosen from each county and eight for the city of Philadelphia.

The committee which had been appointed to consider the time of holding the election for these representatives reported on June 23, and their recommendation to hold the election on Monday, July 8, was approved, while the time for the meeting of the convention was fixed for the following Monday. A committee consisting of Dr. Rush and Colonels Hill and Smith was directed to prepare a draft of an address to the inhabitants of the province. Their report addressed "To THE PEOPLE OF PENNSYLVANIA," made on the same day—Sunday, June 23—stated in part:

Divine Providence is about to grant you a favor, which few people have ever enjoyed before, the privilege of choosing deputies to form a government under which you are to live. We need not inform you of the importance of the trust you are about to commit to them; your liberty, safety, happiness and every thing that posterity will hold dear to them to the end of time, will depend upon their deliberations.

The people were exhorted to choose such persons only as were "distinguished for wisdom, integrity and firm attachment to the liberties of this province, as well as to the liberties of the United Colonies in general." The address then talked about the unanimity in their councils and begged the people to try "to remove the prejudices of the weak and ignorant, respecting the proposed change of government, and assure them that it is absolutely necessary, to secure property, liberty and the sacred rights of conscience, to every individual in the province."[15]

---

[14] *Proceedings,* p. 40.

[15] *Ibid.,* pp. 41-2. The address also told the people not to be surprised at the early date for the election of deputies to the Convention, saying that the "season of the year, and the exigencies of our colony, require despatch in the formation of a regular government."

2. *Usurpation of Governmental Functions by the Conference*

It is generally the case that a body such as the one we are describing, called for a specific purpose, seldom confines its activities to those functions for which it is assembled. The Provincial Conference was no exception, for it not only issued a call for a constitutional convention, but actually assumed powers of government. As a revolutionary body the members justified their action by the alleged failure of the Assembly to meet the exigencies of affairs and by the fact that Congress had advocated the creation of new governments.[16] Since the Assembly was not then in session the Conference usurped its functions. Congress had called upon Pennsylvania on June 1 for six thousand militiamen as part of the "flying camp." The Conference, in considering this matter, read the resolve of the Assembly declaring its impotence to act[17] and said that unless it,

. . . being the only representative body of this colony that can at this time with propriety interpose in this business, undertake to accomplish the desires of the congress and of the assembly . . . the aforesaid flying camp cannot be raised in due time; and the liberties and safety of this province as well as of the other colonies may be thereby endangered:

AND WHEREAS, The militia of this province at first associated by the advice and under the authority of the committees of inspection and observation of the city and the several counties; Therefore,

---

[16] As this was merely a recommendation and nothing more, its action was not binding on Pennsylvania. See "Life of John Adams" by C. F. Adams, in *Works,* edited by the latter, I, 217. The author says that through "all the proceedings there is reason to presume that the chief agents were acting in constant consultation with the leading advocates of independence in Congress." *Ibid.,* p. 220.

[17] See *supra,* p. 134. While I have kept the date June 1 because it was the one used by the Assembly, it seems almost certain that reference to the resolution of Congress of June 3 is the one intended. Congress simply resolved on June 1 that "six thousand militia be employed to reinforce the army in Canada," making no mention of Pennsylvania. On June 3 Congress resolved that a "flying camp" of 10,000 men be established and called upon Pennsylvania for 6,000 of that number.

Resolved, unanimously, That this conference do recommend to the committees and associators of this province to embody 4,500 of the militia, which with the 1,500 men now in the pay of this province, will be the quota of this colony required by congress.[18]

Furthermore, complete and elaborate plans were adopted for the mustering, the organizing, and the commanding of these troops.[19]

The Conference took a decided stand for independence and appointed a committee to state its attitude. The report was read and considered on June 24, and "it was with the greatest unanimity of all the members agreed to and adopted, . . ." John Adams, in a letter written on the same day, says that the vote was "not only unanimous," but he was told by one of the members that "this was their opinion, and the opinion of the several counties and towns they represented, and many of them produced instructions from their constitutents to vote for that measure."[20]

The report denounced the actions of George the Third by saying that he had excluded the inhabitants of America from his protection "by an accumulation of oppressions, unparrelleled [*sic*] in history," and had paid no regard to the "numerous and dutiful *petitions* for a redress of our complicated grievances, but hath lately purchased foreign troops to assist in enslaving us, and hath excited the savages of this country to carry on a war against us, as also the negroes to embrue their hands in the blood of their masters, in a manner unpractised by civilized nations," and hath lately declared that he will show the colonists "no mercy until he hath reduced" them. Continuing in the same strain, it declared that the obligations of allegiance were dissolved by the despotism of the King, and said in conclusion: "We, the *deputies* of the people of Pennsylvania, assembled in full *provincial con-*

---

[18] *Pa. Arch.,* 2d ser., III, 655.

[19] *Ibid.,* p. 661.

[20] Letter to Samuel Chase, Philadelphia, June 24, 1776, *Works,* IX, 413. These men had no *constituents* in the true sense of the word. One is liable to be fooled by their cleverness.

ference, . . . for suppressing all authority in this province, derived from the crown of Great Britain, and for establishing a government upon the authority of the people only, now in this public manner in behalf of ourselves, and with the approbation, consent and authority of our constituents, unanimously declare our willingness to concur in a vote of the congress declaring the united colonies free and independent states, . . ."[21] Furthermore, the Conference recommended "to the said convention to choose and appoint delegates or deputies to represent this province in the congress of the united colonies."[22]

Recommendations were made to the Committee of Safety of the province[23] along with one to the various county committees. The wide power already assumed by these committees is shown by the latter which said:

Resolved, That it be recommended to every county and district committee in this province, to pay the strictest attention to the examination of all strangers or persons travelling through the city or counties, and permit no person [so doing] to remain therein, unless they produce a pass or certificate from the city, county or district committee from whence they last came; and it is further recommended to all Committees to furnish proper passes to all friends to American Liberty upon their application therefor.[24]

The Conference recommended that the Convention create a *"Council* of *Safety,* to exercise the whole of the executive powers of government, so far as relates to the military defence and safety of the province."[25]

On June 25 the Conference concluded its work by voting thanks to the Committee of the City and Liberties of Philadelphia for its part in calling the convention, and then drew up an "Address" to the "Associators of Pennsylvania." The latter was an attempt to justify the position of the Confer-

---

[21] *Pa. Arch.,* 2d ser., III, 657-58. Congress acknowledged receipt of this on the following day. See *Journals of Congress,* June 25, 1776.

[22] *Ibid.,* p. 652.

[23] *Ibid.,* p. 655 and p. 660.

[24] *Ibid.,* p. 663.

[25] *Ibid.,* p. 653.

ence and at the same time to stir up the patriotic fervor of the Associators. It said that the only design of their meeting was to put an end to their own power "by fixing upon a plan for calling a convention to form a government under the authority of the People." However, they had been compelled to take action on the resolution of Congress for calling out the militia because of the "sudden and unexpected separation of the assembly."[26] The people were then told that they were not only contending against the power of Great Britain and a tyrant king, but were also fighting for "permanent freedom, to be supported by a government which will be derived from yourselves, and which will have for its object not the enrolment of one man, or class of men only, but the safety, liberty and happiness of every individual in the community." The citizens were assured that it was in their power to immortalize their names by their "achievements with the events of the year 1776 . . . a year which we hope will be famed in the annals of history to the end of time, for establishing upon a lasting foundation the liberties of one-quarter of the globe." They were exhorted to remember that the honor of the colony was at stake; that the lives of their wives, children, and aged parents depended upon their exertions. "Remember the name of Pennsylvania. Think of your ancestors and of your posterity."[27] With this stirring appeal the sessions of the Conference came to an end.[28]

Thus the Conference, undoubtedly engineered by the Second Continental Congress, of which it was a subsidiary in many respects, fulfilled its purpose of calling a convention and effecting a separation from Great Britain.

---

[26] Refers to the adjournment of June 14. See *supra*, p. 134.

[27] *Proceedings*, pp. 44-5. Their thanks to the Philadelphia committee were expressed as follows: "*Resolved*, unanimously, That the thanks of this conference be given to the committee of this city and liberties of Philadelphia, &c., for their unwearied endeavours in the public service, and particularly for their patriotic exertions in carrying into execution the resolve of Congress of May 15th last, for suppressing all authority under the crown of Great Britain." *Pa. Arch.*, 2d ser., III, 665.

[28] After the Conference adjourned a dinner was given to the members at the Indian Queen Tavern, on Fourth Street. Among the many toasts were these: "Lasting dependence to the enemies of independence"; "A wise and

3. *The Constitutional Convention*

According to the plans of the Provincial Conference the election of members to the convention was held on July 8, beginning at ten o'clock. At noon on the same day the Declaration of Independence was read in the State House Yard[29] and then "proclaimed at each of the five Battalions."[30] It appears that the "patriots" had definitely planned to have the Declaration read at the very time the election was being held, hoping, no doubt, to exert an influence in favor of the Convention.[31]

By whom were the members of the Convention chosen? The Diaries in the Moravian Archives state: "From Philadelphia we learned that on Monday Independence was proclaimed from the State House, and that no one but violent partisans of the American cause had been elected to the Provincial Convention."[32] This, however, was to be expected, for with the rigid oaths imposed by the Conference and the excitement over the Declaration of Independence, it is altogether probable that only the patriots voted. Under these conditions the elections by no means represented the will of the legal electors, many of whom refrained from voting. In Northampton County, for example, the Moravians remained away from the polls and the Associators carried everything before them. Five Germans and three Irish farmers were elected as delegates.[33] That these men did not really represent

---

patriotic convention to Pennsylvania on the 15th of July." Scharf and Westcott, *op. cit.*, I, 312.

[29] Marshall's *Diary*, July 8; see also *Autobiography of Charles Biddle*, p. 86. Biddle says: "There were very few respectable people present." This is refuted by Marshall in his account (*Diary*, July 8). The *Pa. Gaz.* for July 10 says there were "many thousand spectators." See also *Pa. Packet* for July 8.

[30] Marshall's *Diary*, July 8.

[31] *Pa. Packet*, July 8. The Committee of Safety, on July 6, sent letters to the various county committees "enclosing a copy of the . . . Declaration, requesting the same to be published on *Monday* next at the places where the election of Delegates are to be held." Force, *American Arch.*, 5th ser., I, 1289.

[32] Entry for July 10 & 11, printed in the *Pa. Mag.*, XII, 389.

[33] Joseph M. Levering, *A History of Bethlehem*, p. 447. The Moravians were now denounced as Tories, and troops marching through Bethlehem were restrained with difficulty. *Ibid.*, p. 448.

the county may be inferred from the fact that two months earlier (May 1, 1776) James Allen, a conservative who opposed removing the instructions to the Pennsylvania delegates in Congress, had been elected a member of the Assembly by the overwhelming vote of 853 to 14.[34] No records are available of the number of votes cast throughout the state, but the total must have been very small.

The Convention opened its sessions in the West Room of the State House on July 15. Benjamin Franklin was unanimously chosen President, George Ross of Lancaster Vice-President, and John Morris and Jacob Garrigues Secretaries.[35] With great solemnity it was resolved that the Rev. Mr. William White, who later became the first Protestant Episcopal Bishop of Pennsylvania, "be requested to perform divine service to-morrow morning before this convention, that we may jointly offer up our prayers to Almighty God, to afford us his divine grace and assistance in the important and arduous task committed to us, and to offer our praises and thanksgivings for the manifold mercies and the peculiar interposition of his special providence, in behalf of these injured, oppressed and insulted United States."[36]

The rules of procedure, adopted July 18, are both interesting and illuminating, for they show the simple character of the men who composed the Convention. One rule was that "where any debate proves very tedious, and any *four* members rise and call for the question, the president shall put the same." No member was to interrupt another member when speaking; the use of "indecent or reflecting language" was forbidden, and no member was to "wilfully pervert the sense of what another member has said." None were to cross between "the chair and a speaking member," and the President was to have the right "to call to order, when a member may wander from the matter in debate."[37] A little later the Con-

---

[34] *Supra*, p. 102.

[35] *Proceedings*, p. 46.

[36] *Ibid.*, p. 47.

[37] The Minutes of the Convention may be found in Hazard's *Register*, IV, 193 *ff*; Force, *Am. Arch.*, 5th ser., II, 1-62; *Pa. Arch.*, 2d ser., III, 635 *ff* (ed.

vention on several occasions had to discuss the matter of
fines upon members for non-attendance.[38] Thomas Smith, a
member from Bedford County, wrote that a "motion was
made, without a blush, by a member, that whatever might require the consideration of the House might be printed before any resolve was passed upon it, for the use of members,
as several of them could read *print* better than writing."[39]

The main purpose of the Convention was to frame a constitution. At any time such a task calls for great ability and
talents of the highest order. But at this particular period, under the stress of martial feeling and bitter party strife, the
work of framing a fundamental organ of government required the services of men possessing not only a knowledge of
the principles of government, but also a wide practical political experience. The Convention was not composed of great
men. There were a few men of outstanding ability, but for
the most part the members were farmers and merchants, the
majority of whom were Associators. Many had been born
abroad, while some men refused to serve for that very reason.
For example, William Findley, a leader in the revolutionary
movement and a member of the first local committees formed,
refused to serve because he was not a native. His reason was
"that they ought not to put in the power of their enemies
either here or in Europe to say that they could not govern
themselves so far as even to form a constitution for their own
government without the assistance of strangers but lately
come to the country."[40]

The Rev. Francis Alison, in a letter dated Philadelphia,
August 20, 1776, said of this body: "They were mostly hon-

---

of 1875), and *Proceedings, op. cit.* The minutes were ordered to be published
weekly in both German and English. *Proceedings,* p. 49.

[38] *Vide Minutes* for Aug. 5, 17 & 26. On September 4 it was ordered that
a "Messenger be sent to Benjamin Bartholomew, Esq., an absent Member of
this House, to compel his attendance on his duty." It must be said, however,
that many members were on active military duty in New Jersey.

[39] Thomas Smith to St. Clair, *The St. Clair Papers,* ed. by Wm. H. Smith,
I, 373.

[40] *Pa. Mag.,* V, 442. For biographical sketches of members of the Convention see *Pa. Mag.,* III and IV.

est well meaning Country men, who are employed; but intirely unacquainted with such high matters . . . they seem
hardly equal to yᵉ Task to form a new plan of Government."[41]
Peter Grubb, an influential citizen of Lancaster, was not even
as complimentary as that, for he is reported to have referred
to the members of the Convention as "numsculs."[42] Thomas
Smith, one of the few members who had received a legal
training, said that "not a sixth part of us ever read a word
on the subject" of government. About three weeks after the
Convention opened its sessions, he wrote: "I believe we might
have at least prevented ourselves from being ridiculous in the
eyes of the world were it not for a few enthusiastic members
who are totally unacquainted with the principles of government. It is not only that their notions are original, but they
would go to the devil for popularity, and in order to acquire
it, they have embraced leveling principles, which . . . is a
fine method of succeeding."[43] It is evident that the democratic leaven was at work.

The one great man in the Convention was Franklin, but
he was frequently absent on account of his duties as a member
of Congress. It is not actually known what part he took in
framing the Constitution, but it is generally supposed that it
was very little.[44] Alexander Graydon said in his *Memoirs:*
"Doctor Franklin was . . . implicated in the production; and
either his participation in it, or approbation of it, was roundly
asserted by its fautors."[45] But Graydon remarked that he was
"told by a gentleman who acted with" Franklin "as Vice-
President, that he not only devolved upon him the whole
business of the department, but even declined the trouble of

---

[41] *Ibid.*, XXVIII, 379.

[42] Yeates Papers, (Hist. Soc. of Pa.). Sarah Yeates to her husband Jasper,
September 14, 1776.

[43] Burton A. Konkle, *Life and Times of Thomas Smith*, p. 75.

[44] *Life of Franklin*, Sparks ed., I, 408.

[45] P. 286. It has often been asserted that Franklin had some part in framing the constitution and was in favor of it because he opposed changing that
instrument in a paper written in 1789, entitled: "Queries and Remarks Respecting Alterations in the Constitution of Pennsylvania." *Writings*, Smyth ed.,
X, 54-60; see also *infra*, pp. 185-87, and Smyth, X, 472-73.

thinking. As to the Constitution, whose provisions it was sometimes necessary to consider, it did not appear to him, that he had ever read it; or if he had, that he deemed it worthy of remembering."[46] James Wilson, Pennsylvania's greatest jurist, was actively engaged in Congress, and not being a member of the Convention, had practically nothing to do with its work.[47]

Besides Franklin, the only other men known throughout the state were David Rittenhouse, the astronomer of Philadelphia,[48] and Colonel George Ross of Lancaster, the son of an Episcopal clergyman. The latter had received a classical education and had studied law. Engaging in politics, he had served in the Provincial Assembly from 1768 to 1775, save for the year 1772, and had been active in the whole revolutionary movement. Colonel James Smith, of York County, was another well-known member of the Convention. He was well informed, and had practised law. Like Ross, he had been a leader in the revolutionary movement. James Cannon, a native of Scotland, was slightly known through the state. He was a tutor of mathematics in the College of Philadelphia, had been active in forming the Association of that city and was the author of the "Cassandra" letters.

But perhaps the most active personality in forming the constitution was a man who was not even a member of the Convention. This was Judge George Bryan, a jurist of Philadelphia who had a particularly large following.[49] Since the Quakers, the conservatives, and the German secretarians opposed to war had little or nothing to do with the movement for a constitution, and since the great leaders of Pennsylvania like Wilson, Dickinson, Franklin, Morris and others were busily engaged in Congress or serving in the army, the Presbyterian influence was all-powerful. At the head of this

---

[46] *Memoirs*, pp. 286-87.

[47] Konkle, *Bryan*, p. 115.

[48] The biographer of Rittenhouse says that it is impossible to ascertain whether he had any influence on the deliberations of the Convention. *Memoirs of David Rittenhouse*, William Barton, ed., p. 262.

[49] Konkle, *Bryan*, ch. ix.

party was Judge Bryan. Alexander Graydon says in his *Memoirs* that the Constitution "was understood to have been principally the work of Mr. George Bryan, in conjunction with a Mr. Cannon, a schoolmaster; . . ."[50]

The work which confronted these men should not have been arduous, for there was a preponderant influence in favor of the old constitution. Therefore, there was not much to do so far as the constitution was concerned. The principal thing was to change the source of "authority" from the Proprietors and vest it in the people. But in spite of the apparent simplicity of the task the Convention did not finish its labors until September 28. The reason is evident.

a. WORK OF THE CONVENTION

After the brief preliminary work of organization the Convention started its momentous labors. Like many such bodies both before and since it spent much valuable time in drawing up a "Bill of Rights." The "Declaration of rights committee" consisted of twelve men, one from each delegation. While they were at work the Convention usurped all the powers of government, took all authority out of the hands of the old agents and carried on the executive and judicial as well as the legislative functions. The record of the very first day's business ends thus: "The convention then proceeded to the consideration of legislative business."[51] The next day's session finds the Convention engaged in the "consideration of legislative and executive business."[52]

That this action was a surprise to many people cannot be denied. John Morton, in a letter to Anthony Wayne, said that the Convention was doing "some things which people did not Expect as it was given out at the time of Choice they were only to form a new Government."[53] There were several reasons for this usurpation of power. In the first place, the

---

[50] Pp. 285-86.
[51] *Proceedings*, p. 47.
[52] *Ibid.*, p. 47.
[53] *Pa. Mag.*, XXXIX, 373.

members of the Convention considered themselves the true
representatives of the people—the sovereign power in the
state. Secondly, they looked upon the Assembly as a defunct
body by virtue of the resolution of Congress of May 15. The
Assembly was not even in session at this critical time; the
Provincial Conference had exercised governmental powers,
and the Convention was its successor. Lastly, the members
were faced with the very practical problem of defending their
homes against a threatened and impending invasion. The
British army had captured New York and was planning to
invade New Jersey. Forceful measures had to be taken, and
the logical body to act was the Convention—the representatives of the people who at that very moment were risking
their lives for their country. Furthermore, the assumption of
legislative power was but gradual and at the suggestion of
Congress. It seems to have been slowly and diffidently taken,
the first measures adopted being suggestions and recommendations rather than positive legislation.[54] Indeed, Congress
completely ignored the Assembly, directing all of its commu-
nications to the Convention. A letter was received from the
President of Congress on the first day's session desiring the
Convention to "take such measures as they may judge necessary and proper, for procuring as much lead, within that
Colony [state], as can be obtained for the supply of the flying
camp."[55] Two days later Congress resolved that its Secret Committee "be directed to apply to the convention of Pennsylvania, now sitting, and request them to appoint a select committee of their body, to confer with them on a matter of importance relating to their colony."[56] So cordial were the relations between the two bodies that a month later the Convention asked Congress for $100,000 "to be put into the

---

[54] *Vide* Reed, *op. cit.*, II, 20-1.

[55] *Journals of Congress*, Tuesday, July 16, 1776. On July 19 Congress asked
the convention "to hasten, with all possible expedition, the march of the
associators into New-Jersey, agreeable to a former request of Congress." *Journals of Congress.*

[56] *Journals of Congress*, July 17, 1776.

hands of the Council of Safety for the use of this State." Congress very graciously granted the sum desired.[57]

One of the first acts of the Convention was to vest the executive authority of the province in a Council of Safety until the new constitution should be put into operation. This was done on July 23, having been recommended by the Provincial Conference and approved by Benjamin Franklin. Thomas Wharton, Junior, who had manifested great ability as a member of the late Committee of Safety, was chosen President of this newly formed body.[58] It continued to exercise its functions until March 4, 1777, when the Supreme Executive Council, created by the Constitution, assumed control.[59]

It was rumored that British agents were inciting the Indians along the Pennsylvania frontiers. Whether the story was true or not made little difference, for the Indians were becoming restless. All too long had the pioneers suffered from inadequate protection because of the attitude of the Assembly. But now that the people themselves were in control of their affairs vigorous action was taken. Early in September the Convention allowed pay for two companies of militia on the western border to protect the citizens against attacks.[60] On September 14 the Convention, fearing an attack and stating that "there is too much Reason to apprehend that the Indians have been Encouraged by the Agents of his Britannic Majesty to fall on the Frontiers of these States," empowered the members of the Council of Safety of the frontier counties to "order or approve of the going out of such parts of the Associators as they may think necessary in case of an actual invasion. . . ."[61]

That there was a definite clash of economic interests in Pennsylvania is evident from the following ordinances of the

---

[57] *Ibid.*, August 26.

[58] *Pa. Mag.*, V, 431—"Thomas Wharton," by Anne H. Wharton. See Marshall, *Diary*, pp. 85-6, where the names of the Council are given. Marshall says that they were "a poor set for that important post at this time."

[59] *Infra*, pp. 243-44.

[60] Yeates Papers, (Hist. Soc. of Penna.), letter dated Sept. 7, 1776.

[61] *Ibid.*, extract from the Minutes.

Convention. On July 27, 1776, it called upon the sheriff of Philadelphia, William Dewees, to discharge from prison Colonel James Easton, confined "on actions of debt."[62] It declared that all persons within the state who had been imprisoned for debt, "or any criminal offence or offences, or practices against the present virtuous measures of the American States, or prisoners of war," be discharged.[63] Under an ordinance of August 1 the Continental bills of credit, as well as those "of the late Assembly," were made full "legal tender in all cases whatsoever within this State," and the death penalty was decreed for counterfeiting Continental money.[64] Thus the debtors in prison were freed and those who had escaped so far could now discharge their mortgages with cheap currency. By these measures the Convention made another class of people eternally grateful to it.

A few other acts of the Convention might be noted. On September 5 an ordinance was passed "declaring what shall be Treason, and for punishing the same, and other crimes and practices against the State."[65] A week later another ordinance was adopted for punishing persons guilty of opposing any of the measures of the United States for the "defense and support of freedom and independence."[66] Measures were also taken for more effectually collecting the arms of the non-Associators,[67] and expresses were at once dispatched to the counties and its enforcement began immediately.[68] Sometime later the Convention appointed a committee to confer with

---

[62] "Minutes," Force, *Am. Arch.*, 5th ser., II, 12.

[63] "Minutes," and *Pa. Gaz.*, Aug. 7, 1776. Commissioners were appointed for the several counties who had the power to hear and determine the cases of all persons in prison. On Sept. 13 an ordinance was passed "to compel Debtors, in certain cases, to give Security to their Creditors." This might seem to be a move in favor of creditors, but it should be noted that the sums involved were not to exceed five pounds, and "that such debtor is about to depart this State, with design to defraud his creditors."

[64] "Minutes," Force, pp. 15 and 16.

[65] *Ibid.*, and *Pa. Gaz.*, Sept. 11, 1776.

[66] "Minutes," September 12.

[67] *Pa. Gaz.*, Aug. 7. See *supra*, pp. 86-7.

[68] Pennsylvania Miscellaneous, V (Library of Congress).

the delegates of Virginia in Congress on the settlement of a temporary boundary between them.[69] Considering the purpose for which the Convention was called, this action does seem entirely uncalled for and unnecessary.

In this manner the Convention gradually assumed full powers of government. One ordinance inevitably suggested another and each was deemed necessary to meet a certain exigency or contingency. Such is true of most revolutionary bodies. The National Assembly in France, during the Revolution in that country a little over a decade later, usurped the powers of state until it held complete sway.

The Convention, of course, was fully cognizant of the opposition to its alleged usurpation of power, and on the last day's session appointed a committee to "draw up an address to the public, setting forth the reasons which induced this convention to make the several ordinances and resolves, which they have passed in the course of the sitting of this Convention."[70]

Before continuing the story of the Convention, it will be well to pause and consider its attitude towards the Declaration of Independence already proclaimed.

b. THE CONVENTION AND THE DECLARATION OF INDEPENDENCE

The members of the Convention were infuriated by the action of Pennsylvania's delegation in Congress respecting the Declaration of Independence. On July 1 Congress, in the Committee of the Whole, considered the resolution declaring independence and adopted it with but two dissenting votes

---

[69] It should be mentioned that this action was taken upon the instigation of the Virginia Delegates to Congress. On the very first day the Convention devoted to business the letter from the Virginia Delegates was read. Here again the Assembly was completely ignored. "Minutes," Force, p. 3, July 16. *Pa. Gaz.*, Sept. 26.

[70] *Journal of the House of Representatives of Pennsylvania*, I, 95-96. Another ordinance which seems entirely unnecessary was that "no Tavern-keepers or others take out any licences from the officers of the late Government of this State. Aug. 9.

—Pennsylvania and South Carolina. New York did not vote, not being empowered to do so. On that day Francis Lightfoot Lee wrote: ". . . tomorrow it will pass the house with the Concurrence of S. Carolina. The Pennsylvania delegates indulge their own wishes, tho they acknowledge what indeed everybody knows that they vote contrary to the earnest desires of the people . . ."[71] When the vote for independence was taken on July 2,[72] Pennsylvania's assent was given—not, however, by a majority of her delegates, but only by a majority of those present. Only five of the nine were in Congress at the time— Wilson, Franklin, Morton, Willing, and Humphreys—and of these five only three voted for independence.[73] On that eventful day[74] John Dickinson and Robert Morris were present but not voting; Andrew Allen and Edward Biddle were absent;[75] Willing and Humphreys voted against the said Declaration, while Franklin, Wilson, and Morton voted favorably.[76] Thomas Willing, an eminent lawyer who had studied law at the Inner Temple in London and who had been a Justice of

[71] Burnett, op. cit., I, 510.

[72] Journals of Congress, July 2, 1776. The declaration was: "Resolved, That these United Colonies are, and of right ought to be, free and independent states; that they are absolved from all allegiance to the British crown, and that all political connexion between them, and the state of Great-Britain, is, and ought to be, totally dissolved." See also John H. Hazelton, The Declaration of Independence—Its History, p. 166.

[73] Herbert Friedenwald, The Declaration of Independence, p. 129.

[74] John Adams, in a letter to his wife, written on July 3, says: "Yesterday, the greatest question was decided, which ever was debated in America, and a greater perhaps, never was nor will be decided among men. A Resolution was passed without one dissenting Colony 'that these United Colonies are, and of right ought to be, free and independent states, . . .'" Letters to his Wife, I, 124.

[75] Pennsylvania really had only seven representatives in Congress, for Allen was a British sympathizer and abandoned his seat, while Biddle took sick as a result of falling into the Schuylkill River on his way from Reading to Philadelphia and died during the session. Scharf and Westcott, op. cit., I, 317; Genealogy of the McKean Family with a biography of Thomas McKean, by Roberdeau Buchanan, p. 33. Thomas McKean, in the Freeman's Journal, June 16, 1817, said that Dickinson and Morris were present in Congress on July 2, but did not take their seats on that day.

[76] Of these three, Franklin was the only one who had been chosen in November, 1775, who voted for and later signed the Declaration voluntarily.

the Supreme Court of the Province of Pennsylvania, stated in his *Autobiography:*

I voted against this Declaration in Congress not only because I thought America at that time unequal to such a conflict as must ensue . . . , but chiefly because the Delegates of Pennsylvania were not then authorized by their instructions from the Assembly, or the voice of the People at large to join in such a vote.[77]

The Convention felt that Pennsylvania's vote for independence should be unanimous, so one of their first acts was to elect new delegates to Congress—not to fill unexpired terms, but to oust those who had voted against the Resolution of May 15 and the Declaration of Independence. On July 20 this new set of delegates was chosen. Franklin, Wilson, Morton, and Morris were reappointed,[78] and five new members were added—George Clymer, James Smith, George Ross, all members of the Convention, and Benjamin Rush and George Taylor.[79] It was only natural, therefore, that these men should favor independence.

Major General John Dickinson was justly indignant over

---

[77] *Pa. Mag.*, XLVI, 8; *Willing Letters and Papers*, p. xxxvii; *Willing's Autobiography*, p. 126. See *supra*, pp. 133-34.

[78] Morris was the only member of the delegation who had opposed independence to be returned by the Convention. He alone commanded sufficient popular confidence. "A Great Philadelphian, Robert Morris," Ellis P. Oberholtzer, in *Pa. Mag.*, XXVIII, 278. Morris, however, had not voted against independence, but absented himself from Congress in order that the vote of Pennsylvania might be cast favorably. Friedenwald, *op. cit.*, p. 140. In a letter to Joseph Reed on July 20 Morris said: "I did expect my conduct on this great question would have procured my dismission from the great council; but I find myself disappointed, for the convention has thought fit to return me in the new delegation, . . . " He said his interests prompted him to decline, yet he felt that duty called him to take part. Scharf and Westcott, *op. cit.*, I, 319. Benjamin Rush later wrote that Morris "was opposed to the *time* (not the act) of the declaration of independence, but he yielded to no man in his exertions to support it, . . ." *An Account of Sundry Incidences.* In a letter to General Gates written on October 27, 1776, Morris said that the framing of constitutions seemed to be the "present business of all America except the army. It is the fruit of a certain premature declaration which you know I always opposed."

[79] *Pa. Mag.*, XLVI, 9. For the vote on these new delegates see Marshall, *Diary*, July 20.

the proceedings of the Convention in ousting him from his seat in Congress, for he was then with the Army suffering the hardships of war. His feelings are shown in a statement he made years after:

I had not been ten days in camp at Elizabethtown when I was by my persecutors turned out of Congress. While I was exposing my person to every hazard, and lodging every night within half a mile ' of the enemy, the members of the Convention at Philadelphia, resting in quiet and safety, ignominiously voted me, as unworthy of my seat, out of the National Senate.[80]

The same day that the new delegates were selected, a committee composed of Matlack, Thomas Smith, James Cannon, David Rittenhouse, and John Bull was appointed to draft new instructions. These were adopted six days later. The delegates, while given broad powers, were strictly charged "not to agree to, or enter into any treaty of commerce or alliance with Great Britain, or any other foreign Power, but (on the part of America) as free and independent States." The question of a union was now being debated, so the delegates were ordered to use all means in their power to obtain unity and to work for a "just, equal and perpetual confederation."[81] The day before, on the twenty-fifth, the Convention unanimously approved the "declaration of Congress of the 4th" and declared "that we will support and maintain the freedom and independence of this and the other United States of America, at the utmost risk of our lives and fortunes."[82]

It was these delegates of the Convention who, on August 2, signed the Declaration of Independence as of July 4, although not appointed until the twentieth of that month. On July 19 the Secret Journal of Congress tells us that "the declaration passed on the 4th," was ordered to be "engrossed on parchment, with the title and style of—'The Unanimous Declaration of The Thirteen United States of America'; and that the same, when engrossed, be signed by every member of

---

[80] Stillé, Dickinson, p. 206.

[81] Pa. Eve. Post, Aug. 8, 1776.

[82] Proceedings, July 25.

Congress." Of the nine Pennsylvania signers of the Declaration only four were members of Congress when the famous document was adopted and one of them did not vote for it. Thus the majority were not selected by the legally constituted Assembly, but by the Revolutionary Convention—a body which actually had no power to alter the delegation. The Declaration of Independence, then, marked the end not only of the Royal power over the thirteen colonies but also of the charter government of William Penn.

C. CONTINUATION OF THE WORK OF THE CONVENTION

It was absolutely essential that the Convention maintain its supporters in control; to do so it simply set aside any existing regulations which might interfere with its domination of affairs. Although the terms of the Committees of Inspection and Observation were then expiring, the Convention decreed, on August 9, that no elections were to be held because the Associators, who composed a great majority of the electors, might be with the army. The present Committees were ordered to continue to exercise the duties of their offices until the militia returned.[83]

It was deemed necessary to have justices of the peace throughout the counties "under the authority of the people only, and deriving no power whatever from the late constitution," so the Convention passed a resolution on September 3 appointing the said justices for all the counties.[84] When inducted into office they had to renounce all allegiance to George the Third, oppose "the tyrannical proceedings of the King and Parliament of Great Britain," and swear that they would "support a Government in this State on the Authority of the People only."[85]

---

[83] *Pa. Gaz.*, Aug. 14; Marshall, *Diary*, Aug. 17. The Associators had been ordered into Jersey. Exceptions to this rule were made in the case of Cumberland, Bedford, Northumberland, and Westmoreland counties because their Associators had not been ordered to march.

[84] *Pa. Gaz.*, Sept. 4, 1776.

[85] *Pa. Eve. Post*, Sept. 5.

During the latter part of 1775 and the early days of 1776 the Associators had complained to the Assembly about the easy manner in which military duty could be evaded, and the extremely light burdens placed upon the non-Associators.[86] The Assembly did place a small tax on them,[87] but this was deemed insufficient. Turning its attention to this matter the Convention, on September 14, passed an "Ordinance *for rendering the Burthen of* Associators and Non-Associators, in the Defence of this State, as nearly equal *as may be*." It was ordered that "every Non-Associator, between the ages of sixteen and fifty years, shall pay, for and during the time of his continuing a Non-Associator, at the rate of Twenty Shillings for each and every month, to Commence from the publication of this Ordinance, and to continue until the end of the first session of the future Assembly of this State, unless the said Assembly shall, before that time, alter or repeal the same." The ordinance further stated that "every Non-Associator above the age of twenty-one years, shall pay, in addition to the aforesaid fine, at the rate of Four Shillings in the pound on the annual value of his estate as rated under the late laws of this State for raising provincial taxes," and that "nothing herein contained shall prevent or obstruct the levying, collecting and paying the fines heretofore set on Non-Associators by the late Assembly, but the same shall be collected under the same penalties, in the same manner. . . ."[88] The old Assembly, when it reconvened, declared the Ordinance illegal and resolved that "the said Sums ought not to be paid."[89]

While the Convention was thus exercising practically all governmental functions, it was, nevertheless, at work on a "Frame of Government." Much time was spent in the "Committee of the whole, in order to take into consideration some important matters relative to the proposed new frame of government."[90] No details of the proceedings concerning the

---

[86] See *supra*, pp. 85-6.
[87] *Supra*, 85; *Votes*, VI, 660-62.
[88] *Pa. Gaz.*, Sept. 18.
[89] *Pa. Eve. Post*, Sept. 26; *Votes*, VI, 764; *infra*, p. 167.
[90] *Vide Proceedings.*

Constitution are given in the records. They simply state on the several days that "the house resumed the consideration of the frame of government, and after some time adjourned.[91]

But why did the session of the Convention last so long? Even with the assumption of practically all the powers of government the work should have been finished long before it was. As already stated, the task before the Convention was not exceptionally difficult. Why, then, the long delay? The Associators, upon whom the Radicals depended for support, had been called to the front. Fearing, no doubt, that in the absence of so many Associators an election would spell defeat, the Radicals, according to James Allen, delayed the formation of a constitution—the work for which they had been elected —until they should be more confident of carrying the first election under it. In the meantime, of course, they kept the control of the state in their own hands.[92] Allen remarked: "In stead of immediately framing a new Government the Convention, unwilling to part with their power, continued exercising all power till the Voice of the people, i.e., the Whiggist part, obliged them to frame a Government & dissolve themselves; . . ."[93]

The growth of conservative ideas convinced the Radicals that unless they completed their work at once a counter-revolution might prevent them from doing it at all. Already signs of opposition were manifest. At this time the Moderates could have taken the lead because they had a considerable representation in the Convention, despite the manner of the elections. Had this group within the Convention, supported by the party leaders without, accepted independence and aided in the establishment of a new government, they might now have been able to control the Convention and secure a constitution in accordance with their ideas.[94]

<hr>

[91] *Proceedings*, p. 53 *et seq.*

[92] Lincoln, *op. cit.*, pp. 274-75.

[93] *Diary*, January 25, 1777.

[94] Lincoln, *op. cit.*, pp. 275-76. On July 25 Col. Matlack, Cannon, Col. Porter, Rittenhouse, Whitehill, and Col. B. Galbreath were added to the

Their attitude is expressed in the following letter of Charles Thomson to John Dickinson, dated August 16, 1776:

I know the rectitude of your heart & the honesty & uprightness of your intentions: but still I cannot help regretting, that by a perseverance which you were fully convinced was fruitless, you have thrown the affairs of this state into the hands of men totally unequal to them. I fondly hope & trust however that divine providence, which has hitherto so signally appeared in favour of our cause, will preserve you from danger and restore you not to "your books & fields," but to your country, to correct the errors, which I fear those "now bearing rule," will through ignorance—not intention—commit, in settling the form of government. . . .[95]

The few criticisms given by the moderate statesmen, and their opposition to the plan for a new constitution made the radical leaders more determined than ever to force their theories upon the people. Within the Convention sufficient votes could not be mustered to overthrow these men, supported as they were by almost solid delegations from most of the western counties.[96] Therefore the Left Wing was able to dominate affairs.

By the early part of September the Constitution was almost finished, and on Thursday, September 5, it was ordered that "the president, Mr. Rittenhouse and Mr. Vanhorn, be desired to revise the same, and make such alterations therein in method and stile, without affecting the sense, as they may think proper; and when that is done, to get 400 copies printed for public consideration."[97] On September 10 the proposed frame of government was published in twelve small folio pages.[98] It appeared in the *Pennsylvania Evening Post* on the same day, but not in the *Pennsylvania Gazette* until Septem-

committee for bringing in an essay for a frame of government. With the addition of these men to the Committee on the "Frame of Government," it became evident that the aggressive radical wing was in control of the Convention. Konkle, *Smith*, pp. 73-4.

[95] *Pa. Mag.*, XXXV, 500.
[96] Lincoln, *op. cit.*, p. 277.
[97] *Proceedings*, p. 52.
[98] Marshall's *Diary*, Sept. 11.

ber 18. A most violent debate started immediately and lasted well over a decade.

The action of the Convention in submitting the Constitution to the people for "consideration" can be looked upon as scarcely more than a gesture. It was not printed until the tenth, and did not appear in one of the leading newspapers until the eighteenth, while on the sixteenth the Convention "resumed the consideration of the frame of government"[99] and adopted it on the twenty-eighth. The difficulties of travel and communication at that time made it impossible for many people to have learned anything about it. The members of the Convention may have been sincere in their motives, but who knows? Thomas Paine said that the Convention ordered the Constitution "published, not as a thing established, but for the consideration of the whole people, their approbation or rejection, . . ." When the debate on the Constitution was resumed, Paine rather naïvely remarked that "as the general opinion of the people in approbation of it was then known, the constitution was signed, sealed, and proclaimed on the authority of the people; . . ."[100] Unfortunately, practically nothing is known of what transpired in the Convention concerning the constitution during the period from the sixteenth until its passage.[101] On the morning of the twenty-eighth a committee was appointed "to prepare a draft of a preamble to the declaration of rights and frame of government, and of the oaths of allegiance and office to be inserted in the said frame."[102] On the same day the *Proceedings* of the Convention

---

[99] *Proceedings*, p. 52. See the unsuccessful attempt to obtain a reconsideration of the single-chambered legislature on Sept. 16, *infra*, p. 185. This action was condemned by the meeting held on October 21 and 22 in the State House Yard. See the resolutions adopted, numbers 12 and 13. *Pa. Gaz.*, Oct. 23.

[100] Thomas Paine, *Writings*, (D. E. Wheeler, ed.), IV, 267-68. "On Constitutions."

[101] The author has been able to find only one serious discussion evoked during this period of "consideration," and this, naturally, was confined solely to the city of Philadelphia. It was the opposition to certain religious provisions which aroused the fears of some Philadelphia ministers. See *infra*, pp. 216-21.

[102] *Proceedings*, p. 53.

state: "The frame or plan of government and preamble, being now fairly engrossed, were deliberately read and compared at the table, and being bound up with the declaration of rights, were passed and confirmed unanimously, . . ."[103]

The next day the elections committee, consisting of Colonels Matlack and Thomas Smith, reported that the elections to the new Assembly should be held on November 5. Provisions were made for all the necessary officials, such as election judges, clerks, and inspectors, and also the following oath which every elector was required to take:

I ——— ————— do swear (or affirm) that I will be faithful and true to the commonwealth of Pennsylvania, and that I will not directly or indirectly do any act or thing prejudicial or injurious to the constitution or government thereof, as established by the convention.[104]

The Constitution was not submitted to a vote of the people but was proclaimed by the Convention. Upon a motion it was ordered that the President and every member of the Convention present sign the Constitution. After a few more resolutions directed toward putting it into effect and another giving a vote of thanks to the President, "the convention rose."[105] But contrary to the motion, all the members of the Convention did not affix their signatures. Of the ninety-six members, ninety-five appear to have been present when the signing took place, but twenty-three of these did not sign. It is interesting to note that of this number only five were from the frontier counties of Cumberland, Bedford, Westmoreland, Northumberland, Northampton, and Berks. No definite information is available as to why the members did not attach their signature. In the case of Owen Biddle, a member from the city of Philadelphia, it is known that on the days of the signing he sat in the Committee of Safety and was busy all day paying off the members of the Convention. One of his biographers says: "Whether in the hurry of business he

[103] *Ibid.*, p. 54.
[104] *Ibid.*, pp. 53-4.
[105] *Ibid.*, p. 66.

neglected signing, or was opposed to some of its provisions, cannot now be ascertained from any accessible documents."[106]

It is evident, however, that a dissenting party existed, and if the statement of the journal is correct—that the "frame or plan of government and preamble . . . passed unanimously . . ."—the explanation must be that those who opposed the constitution withdrew, as was the practice then, before the final voting and signing took place. From the very nature of the situation—the extra-legal call of the Provincial Conference to hold a Convention; the election of its members by a small majority of the voters; the usurpation of power by the Convention in transacting legislative, executive, and judicial business; and finally the Constitution itself—it was apparent that opposition would be aroused. Few people realized how difficult it would be to put the Constitution into effect. The opposition shook the old Quaker colony to its very depths, paralyzed the organs of government, and prepared the way for the coming of the enemy. The bitter quarrel over it ended only with the formation of a new constitution fourteen years later.[107]

4. The End of the Assembly

The Assembly led a precarious existence during the early days of June, 1776, as we have seen, and was able to muster a quorum only on several occasions. It finally despaired of accomplishing anything and on June 14, without a quorum, adjourned to meet again on the twenty-sixth day of August. This action was severely criticized. One writer in the *Pennsylvania Gazette* said that the Assembly, not having a quorum, "could only adjourn from day to day, . . . and not until an-

---

[106] Henry D. Biddle, "Owen Biddle," *Pa. Mag.*, XVI, 308. This, however, is not a very plausible excuse, for if any member, particularly one like Mr. Biddle who was actively engaged in official business, was in favor of the Constitution and wished to sign it, he certainly would have been given the opportunity to do so, especially under the stress of party feeling then existing. As we shall see in chapter VI, many members of the Convention took an active part in the battle against the Constitution.

[107] Constitution of 1790.

other sitting." The same writer further stated that it "deserted
the public trust in a time of the greatest danger and difficulty"
and through its "own act of desertion and cowardice have
laid the Provincial Conference under the necessity of taking
instant charge of affairs."[108] On the other hand, it must be
said that its incapacity to function was caused to a large extent
by the withdrawal of the extreme Whigs.

The Assembly met at the time specified, but only seventeen
members appeared. Many people felt that the Declaration of
Independence had put an end to the old government[109]
which few persons took seriously. James Allen, one of the
members, wrote: "It was a strange scene at the State House,
where the Congress, Assembly, Convention & Admiralty
Court were sitting, all at the same time."[110] But stranger was
the fact that fourteen members of the Assembly were likewise
members of the Convention.[111]

Having failed to obtain a quorum and having accomplished
nothing, the Assembly adjourned on the twenty-eighth to
meet again on September 23, after having ordered the clerk
to write to the absent members "requesting their attendance
at the Time of Adjournment."[112] At the time designated only
twenty-three members appeared. The next day the number
was increased to twenty-eight, and these in desperation decide to act without a quorum. Loyalty to the Governor demanded that his salary be paid, so by a vote of 16 to 12 it was
decided to grant him one thousand pounds for his support
"during the present year."[113] "Bad however as our Situation
was," Allen said, "we finished the year with some eclat, having paid the Governor & all other publick officers their full
Salaries, . . ."[114]

---

[108] *Pa. Gaz.*, June 26, 1776. "To the People."

[109] *Diary of James Allen,* Jan. 25, 1777.

[110] *Ibid.*

[111] It is interesting to note that nine of these fourteen had been elected
on May 1, 1776, as the additional representatives of the city of Philadelphia
and the western counties.

[112] *Votes,* VI, 743.

[113] *Ibid.,* p. 743.

[114] *Diary of James Allen,* entry for January 25, 1777.

The next few days the number of members kept dwindling. Realizing that the end had come the Assembly determined to reprove the Convention and denounce its proceedings. A member, whose name is not recorded in the journal, introduced a resolution which was carried by a majority of those present. It stated that "it is the sacred Right of Freemen to give and grant their own Money; and that all Taxes, levied without their Consent, are arbitrary and oppressive: . . .," and also that "the Convention have derived no Authority from the good people of *Pennsylvania* to levy Taxes and dispose of their Property . . ." It declared that the tax levied on the Non-associators "ought not to be paid," and that the Ordinance of the Convention empowering the "Justices of the Peace to imprison, for an indefinite Time, at their Discretion, all Persons whom they shall judge to be guilty of the offences therein specified, is, in the opinion of this House, a dangerous attack on the Liberties of the good People of *Pennsylvania,* and a Violation of their most sacred Rights; and therefore ought not to be considered as obligatory."[115] Allen somewhat exultantly notes in his *Diary* that the Assembly "passed 2 Resolves desiring our Constituents to disregard 2 Ordinances of the Convention and called them daringly arbitrary. . . ."[116]

The last act of the Assembly was to order Michael Hillegas,[117] the Provincial Treasurer, to "pay all such Certificates and Orders as have been heretofore drawn by the Assembly for the Salaries of public officers, and Services done the public; out of the Twenty-two Thousand Pounds issued by an Act of Assembly passed the Thirtieth of *September* last."[118] If the statement in Marshall's *Diary* is correct, the members

---

[115] *Votes,* VI, 764. This appeared in the *Pa. Eve. Post* on September 26 and in the *Pa. Gaz.* on October 2.

[116] Entry for January 25, 1777. The *Moravian Diary* for 1776, in noting briefly the end of the Assembly, refers to the vain resolutions of that body to ease the situation of the Non-associators. Levering, *op. cit.,* pp. 450-51.

[117] Michael Hillegas was also the treasurer of the United States, having been appointed by the Continental Congress in 1775. With George Clymer as his assistant he held that position until 1789. *Vide infra,* p. 236.

[118] *Votes,* VI, 764.

of the Assembly were apparently in an anxious state of mind, for he says: "The order was immediately drawn, signed by Morton,[119] Speaker, sent and the cash received."[120] Having paid the Governor and the public officers "The House then rose."[121]

There was nothing else left for it to do. All authority was in the hands of the Convention, which had been for the past two months carrying on the government of the state. The rule of the Eastern aristocracy was over; the last vestige of the Charter Government had now disappeared.

---

[119] This was John Morton who signed the Declaration of Independence. Apparently he was loyal to the Assembly, but what his attitude was towards the Convention the author has not been able to ascertain. *Vide infra*, p. 250.

[120] Entry for September 28.

[121] *Votes*, VI, 764.

V

THE CONSTITUTION OF 1776

THE hard and bitter struggle of the revolutionary group in Pennsylvania to form a new constitution and sever the bonds with the Proprietary interests had at last been rewarded. Another fetter from which the framers of the Constitution wished to free themselves was the rule of the aristocratic and conservative element in the colony. On the whole, the government of Pennsylvania was as democratic as the so-called "democracies" of the Puritan colonies in New England,[1] but a small class extremely jealous of its position controlled the Assembly by unfair property and geographic qualifications. At the same time a democratic spirit was making remarkable progress in Pennsylvania during the whole colonial period. The democratic leaven which threatened to destroy the privileges of this small coterie of Quakers and wealthy aristocracy was the spirit of the frontier and of the Scotch-Irish pioneers.

By the middle of the eighteenth century the province had passed out of the state of a politico-religious experiment[2] and had developed into a large and prosperous community. These new conditions produced a "steady democratizing process," without, however, arousing much conscious reflection.[3] It was not until the decade preceding the Revolution that there was any systematic discussion of the problems of political theory.

In resisting the laws of England the Colonists resorted to arguments of a constitutional nature. They said, for instance, that in taxing the American Colonies the British Parliment was resorting to measures not merely inexpedient and unjust, but actually contrary to the principles of the British Con-

---

[1] Merriam, Charles E., *American Political Theories*, p. 28.
[2] See Chapter 1.
[3] Merriam, *op. cit.*, p. 37.

stitution. Furthermore, they maintained that Parliment could not control them because they owed allegiance to the King only, from whom came their charters. In this argument, of course, the Colonists failed to recognize the change which had taken place in England during the century or more of their existence. Two kings, Charles I and James II, had been deposed. Parliament instead of the King had become supreme.

The Colonists tried to show that there was a difference between external and internal taxes, claiming that Parliament had the power to levy the former for the purposes of regulating trade, but not the latter. Again, they asserted that having all the rights of native-born English subjects they could be taxed only by their own representatives. The idea of "virtual representation"—meaning that a member of Parliament represented not only the few electors of his district but the best interests and wishes of the whole English people—was scorned by the Colonists. They maintained that only their own Assemblies truly represented them.

Such were the constitutional and legal arguments upon which opposition to the measures of the English Ministry was based. But revolutions are not created by constitutional and legal arguments alone. An appeal must be made to philosophical principles. The Colonial leaders quoted the very doctrines of the English when they revolted against the autocratic rule of their kings. The principles of "natural rights," the "contract" theory of government based upon the "consent of the governed," and the doctrine of "popular sovereignty" soon became the arguments of the Colonists.[4] These had received their classic formulation in the two *Treatises on Civil Government* written by John Locke. These ideas, well known to the leaders of American thought,[5] influenced the men of Pennsylvania when they met to frame their Constitution. Their work would be of the greatest importance, for the Pennsylvania Constitution would undoubtedly influence those of

[4] For an excellent discussion of the development of the idea of "natural rights," see Edward S. Corwin, "The 'Higher Law' Background of American Constitutional Law," *Harvard Law Rev.*, XLII, numbers 2 and 3.

[5] *Vide infra*, pp. 176-77.

other states yet to be framed.[6] A man from a neighboring state in a letter to a Philadelphia friend wrote:

In Pennsylvania you are now forming a new constitution; and I cannot but be extremely desirous, that it should be a good one, ... It is of more importance that such a constitution should be established in that, than perhaps in any other of these United States; from this and from its central situation it will be likely to give a complexion to the ideas of leading men from all parts, resorting thither, and consequently both to the present constitutions to be formed in the several states, to future proceedings therein, and particularly to the proceedings of Congress.[7]

Despite the discussions about theories of government and the numerous pamphlets issued at the time, the influence of the colonial charters must not be underestimated. These new state constitutions were really the outgrowth of the long-established colonial charters, and a distinct continuity is seen, even in Pennsylvania, where the breach with the past was especially wide.[8]

It has been previously stated that the work of the Pennsylvania Convention should not have been difficult. In a sense this is true, but two things must be borne in mind. First, the Convention assumed entire control of the government of the State, a tremendous task at a time of great political tension and war. Secondly, the framing of a constitution was of the utmost importance to the Colonists. They regarded their written constitutions with deep reverence and disdained the idea in Pope's oft-quoted couplet—*For forms of government let fools contest; Whate'er is best administer'd is best.*[9]

---

[6] Only N.H., S.Ca., Va. and N.J. had framed Constitutions so far. The Massachusetts General Court had already framed one but it was rejected by the people.

[7] *Pa. Eve. Post*, July 30, 1776.

[8] William C. Morey, "First State Constitutions," *Annals of the American Academy of Political and Social Science*, IV, (Sept., 1893). It should be noted that all the colonies which had bicameral legislatures retained them in their state constitutions, whereas Penna. and Georgia still clung to their old custom of a single house.

[9] Concerning Pope's idea John Adams wrote: "Nothing can be more fallacious than this. Nothing is more certain, from the history of nations and nature of man, than that some forms of government are better fitted for

In colonial eyes charters had a sacrosanct character.[10] They expressed clearly and definitely their rights as citizens and subjects. The people now called upon to formulate their own organic laws regarded the work momentous, even though they had before them the old constitutions and charters. The writing of new ones was difficult because important alterations had to be made to meet the new conditions.

Besides their own charter and the charters and constitutions of the other colonies,[11] the Pennsylvanians had before them several very important treatises or proposals for state governments. Early in 1776 John Adams' *Thoughts on Government* and Thomas Paine's *Common Sense* had appeared.[12] Of *Common Sense* Adams wrote:

Sensible men think there are some whims, some sophisms, some artful addresses to superstitious notions, some keen attempts upon the passions, in this pamphlet. But all agree there is a great deal of good sense delivered in clear, simple, concise and nervous style. His sentiments of the abilities of America, and of the difficulty of a reconciliation with Great Britain, are generally approved. But

---

being well administered than others." *Works*, IV, 193. James Wilson, in his lectures on law, stated: "The importance of a good constitution will, on reflection and examination, be easily conceived, deeply felt, and readily acknowledged. On the constitution will depend the beneficence, the wisdom, and energy, or the injustice, the folly, and the weakness of the government and laws." *Works, op. cit.*, I, 421—"Lectures on Law," 1790-91.

[10] Much of the "sacredness" of the colonial charters was due to the fact that the land titles depended upon them. Ninety percent of the colonists were farmers, hence it was not so much a matter of political theory that mattered, but the title to one's acres. The land hunger of the colonists cannot be exaggerated; it was to escape the feudal system of land tenure that brought many Europeans to these shores.

[11] The new constitution of New Jersey appeared in the *Pennsylvania Packet* on July 15, 1776, and in the *Pennsylvania Gazette* two days later. The constitution of Virginia was printed in the *Pennsylvania Gazette* on July 17, 1776.

[12] For Adams' *Thoughts on Government* see *Works*, IV, 193-200. For Paine's *Common Sense* see *The Political Writings of Thomas Paine*, 2 vols., New York, 1835. In the *Pennsylvania Journal* for Jan. 10, 1776, appeared the following: "This day was published, and is now selling by Robert Bell, in Third Street, (Phila.) price two shillings, 'Common Sense,' addressed to the inhabitants of North America." For an account of the opinions of the leading contemporaries of Paine and the controversy his pamphlet aroused, see Moncure D. Conway, *The Life of Thomas Paine*, I, ch. vi.

his notions and plans of continental government are not much applauded. Indeed this writer has a better hand in pulling down than building.[13]

In fact, Adams considered Paine's proposal for a form of government "as flowing from simple ignorance, and a mere desire to please the democratic party in Philadelphia. . . . I regretted," he said, "to see so foolish a plan recommended to the people of the United States, who were all waiting only for the countenance of Congress to institute their State governments. I dreaded the effect so popular a pamphlet might have among the people, and determined to do all in my power to counteract the effect of it."[14]

Adams proposed a bicameral legislature and a governor and other executive officials annually elected by the joint ballot of the legislature. The governor was to have extensive powers, including a veto on legislation, command of the armed forces and the appointment of subordinate officers and magistrates, subject to the consent of the upper chamber. Paine's proposal was less sound, but produced a profound impression by the force and lucidity of its radical ideas. Paine proposed a unicameral legislature to be elected annually. It was to be a large body representing the various parts of the commonwealth more equitably than had been the case under the old charter.[15] These views Adams combatted with great skill and force, but with the radicals of Pennsylvania Paine was exceedingly influential and the arguments of Adams had little effect.

Another proposal for a frame of government appeared in Pennsylvania in 1776, but its exact date is not known. From its very nature, however, we are led to believe it was printed

---

[13] Adams, *Letters to His Wife,* I, 90. March 19, 1776.

[14] In his "Autobiography" Adams tells how he found time to write his *Thoughts on Government* and states that "Matlack, Cannon, Young, and Paine, had influence enough, however, to get their plan adopted in substance in Georgia and Vermont, as well as Pennsylvania . . ." *Works,* II, 507-08.

[15] Inequalities in representation similar to those which existed in Pennsylvania were found also in Virginia and South Carolina.

before the Convention met or else during its sessions. This was *An Essay of a Frame of Government for Pennsylvania.*[16] It advocated vesting "the Supreme Legislature in three different bodies," on the ground that it would "give maturity and precision to acts of legislation, as also stability to the state, by preventing measures from being too much influenced by sudden passions." The legislature, however, was to be supreme. The executive branch was to be a plural body, like the one finally adopted, but was to have a share in legislation and was "not to be exposed to an annual vote of those who may wish to get into offices." The Senators and Councilors were to be chosen by lot. The *Essay* advocated a Governor with strictly limited powers; the idea of a strong governor was "too monarchical." Religious freedom was to be guaranteed. The judges of the Supreme Court were to "hold their commissions during good behavior." The latter proposal was earnestly advocated by many people in Pennsylvania, but "life" offices found no favor with the leaders in the Convention.

Another important discussion on government was a pamphlet printed in Philadelphia—*Four Letters on Interesting Subjects.*[17] The writer was not favorable to the theory of "checks and Balances," stating that the "notion of checking by having different houses, has but little weight with it, when inquired into, and in all cases it tends to embarrass and prolong business." It advocated a single chamber legislature, stating that the division of government into executive, legislative, and judicial bodies "is more a distinction of words than things." Another interesting suggestion was that a jury consist of twenty-five members, a majority of which would be able to return a verdict. Annual elections were favored and a suggestion, almost exactly like the one adopted, was

---

[16] *Printed by James Humphreys, Junior, Phila., M,DCCLXXVI,* signed *A. B.* This has been attributed to John Dickinson (See Harry A. Cushing, *American Historical Review,* I, 284). This is doubtful, but the present writer has been unable to determine its authorship.

[17] Printed by Styner and Cist, Philadelphia, 1776. The authorship is unknown.

made for preserving the Constitution. It stated that at "the expiration of every seven or any other number of years a *Provincial Jury* shall be elected, to enquire if any inroads have been made in the Constitution, and to have power to remove them; but not to make alterations, unless a clear majority of all the inhabitants shall so direct."

A similar provision was advocated by "Demophilus" in *The Genuine Principles of the Ancient Saxon, or English Constitution. . . . With some Observations on their peculiar fitness . . . for Pennsylvania.* He favored "a decennial meeting of delegates to examine the state of the constitution and conduct of the government . . . for keeping the constitution in health and vigor, by having an opportunity to see that it did not depart from its first principles."[18]

The people of Pennsylvania and the members of the Convention might have known certain other proposals from outside the State. One of these, advocating a unicameral legislature with great powers, was *The People the Best Governors; or a Plan of Government Founded on the just Principles of Natural Freedom.*[19] Another plan of government was written by Carter Braxton and printed in Philadelphia in 1776—*Address to the Convention——of Virginia; on the Subject of Government in general, and recommending a particular Form to their Consideration.*[20]

Thus the framers of the Pennsylvania Constitution had many plans and ideas for a government before them, in addition to their colonial charters and laws. Unlike the framers of the constitutions of New Hampshire, South Carolina, and

---

[18] Printed in Philadelphia, 1776, and sold by Robert Bell, on Third Street. The author stated that such a system "would be effectually holding the supreme power in its *only* safe repository, *the hands of the people.*"

[19] This was printed in 1776, but it does not indicate either the place of publication or the authorship. It was undoubtedly printed in N. H., but it is doubtful if it was known in Pennsylvania. It can be found in Frederick Chase, *History of Dartmouth College*, appendix. There is a brief discussion of it in the *Am. Hist. Rev.*, I, 284, by Harry A. Cushing.

[20] Since the Va. Convention met on May 6, 1776, and completed its work on June 29, this must have been printed before the Pa. Convention met, and was probably familiar to the members.

New Jersey, who considered their work as temporary, the men
of Pennsylvania desired to make a document of greater permanence.[21] The first two drawn, those of New Hampshire
and South Carolina, were so considered and consequently
were hastily made, while the New Jersey constitution was
looked upon in the same light.[22]

We are now in a position to examine the handiwork of
the Pennsylvania patriots who sat in Philadelphia from the
hot days of July until the end of September. As we might
expect, the injustices so long done to the frontier inhabitants
were rectified; the West repaid with a vengeance the long
neglect it had suffered at the hands of the East.

1. *The Preamble*

The *Declaration of Rights* and the *Plan or Frame of Government* were preceded by a *Preamble*. In this, as in the
Declaration of Rights, the influence of English political
thought is plainly discernible. The doctrines of John Locke,
the great expositor of the principles of the English revolution in 1688, formed the basis of the political thought of the
American Revolution. Of course few men in the Pennsylvania
Convention ever heard of Locke by name, but at this time
his ideas had been discussed by every important colonial
writer. Samuel Adams refers to him at one time as "the im-
mortal Locke," and at another as "one of the greatest men
that ever wrote."[23]

The theories of Locke and other writers, such as Harrington, Milton, Hume, Algernon Sidney, Montesquieu, and
Blackstone, had been given wide circulation by the time the
men of Pennsylvania met to draw up a constitution. The
Declaration of Rights of the Stamp Act Congress enumerated

[21] See Nevins, *op. cit.,* p. 176. It took the Pa. Convention longer than most
of the similar bodies to frame its constitution. See *ibid.,* p. 139, and *supra,*
chapter iv, pp. 151-65.

[22] Erdman, Charles R., Jr., *The New Jersey Constitution of 1776,* p. 46.

[23] Vernon L. Parrington, *The Colonial Mind,* p. 237; see also William S.
Carpenter, *The Development of American Political Thought,* pp. 18-19.

the cardinal doctrines of the Revolution, while the *Declaration of Rights* of 1774 and the various protests and state declarations had thoroughly popularized these political maxims.[24] The very first sentence of the *Preamble* is an epitome of these, for it states that "all government ought to be instituted and supported for the security and protection of the community" —the *social compact* theory. It mentions the "natural rights" of man, the doctrine of popular sovereignty, and the right of revolution, for it states that "whenever these great ends of government are not obtained, the people have a right by common consent to change it."[25]

The *Preamble* then enumerated the acts of the King and his ministers which precluded the citizens from enjoying their "natural rights," and declared, therefore, that "all allegiance and fealty to the said king" shall come to an end. Since the *Preamble* declared it necessary to have some proper form of government "founded on the authority of the people only, . . . the representatives of the freemen of Pennsylvania" had assembled to frame such a government.

2. *The Declaration of Rights*

The drafting of the *Declaration of Rights* should not have caused the members of the Convention much thought, for by this time these principles had received definite expression.[26] The *Declaration of Rights* of the Stamp Act Congress,

---

[24] John Adams, writing to Timothy Pickering in 1822, said: "As you justly observe, there is not an idea in it [Declaration of Independence] but what had been hackneyed in Congress for two years before. The substance of it is contained in the declaration of rights and the violation of those rights, in the Journals of Congress in 1774. . . ." Adams, *Works*, II, 514.

[25] The *Preamble* and the *Constitution* used in this study are found in the *Constitutions of Pennsylvania*, compiled by Fertig and Moore, Legislative Reference Bureau, Harrisburg, 1926.

[26] Besides Penna. the following states had Bills of Rights: Va., Md., N.C., Vt., Mass., and the N.H. Constitution of 1784. The hastily drawn constitution of 1776 in N. H. had none. See Poore, *Charters and Constitutions*. Thomas Paine wrote in 1805, "The Constitution of 1776 [meaning Penna.] was conformable to the Declaration of Independence and the Declaration of Rights . . ." *To the Citizens of Pennsylvania on the Proposal for Calling a Convention.* See also W. C. Webster, "A Comparative Study of the State Constitu-

the *Declaration of Rights* of 1774—which served as a model for all later state bills of rights—and the Declaration of Independence had already been drawn up.[27]

In May 1776 George Mason wrote the Virginia *Declaration of Rights,* the first state paper of that character to be adopted in America.[28] The Pennsylvania and Virginia documents are quite similar, both in form and content. In fact, as John Adams stated, the Pennsylvania Declaration is "taken almost verbatim from that of Virginia, which was made and published two or three months before that of Philadelphia was begun."[29]. While this is true, yet several important differences must be noted. Virginia, for example, forbade the requirement of excessive bail, the imposition of excessive fines, and the infliction of cruel and unusual punishments. The Pennsylvania Declaration fails to mention these points.[30]

The right of the people to "Assemble together to consult for their common good, to instruct their representatives, and to apply to the legislature for redress of grievances, by address, petition or remonstrance," was guaranteed in Pennsylvania, but a similar provision was lacking in the Virginia Declaration.[31] The right of emigration was stated in the Pennsylvania Declaration,[32] but is not found in the Virginia Bill of Rights.

---

tions of the American Revolution," *Annals of the Am. Acad. of Pol. and Soc. Science,* IX, 69.

[27] The *Declaration of Rights* "received the final assent of the convention" on Aug. 16, and was printed in the *Pa. Gaz.* on the 21st.

[28] Philip A. Bruce, *The Virginia Plutarch,* I, 222; Adams, *Works,* III, 220. Although the Virginia Bill of Rights was little more than a restatement of the great principles of English constitutional liberty as embodied in the Magna Charta, the Petition of Rights, and the Bill of Rights, yet it must be considered a notable victory for true democracy. Nevins, *op. cit.,* p. 146.

[29] *Works,* III, 220.

[30] However, the Penna. *Frame of Government* stated that "Excessive bail shall not be exacted for bailable offences; And all fines shall be moderate." Section 29. A clause similar to the one of Virginia was added to the constitution of 1790—Art. ix, sec. 13. All except Penna. and Vt. had similar provisions in their earlier constitutions.

[31] Sec. 16, Pa. *Declaration of Rights*—all except Va. and Md. had similar provisions.

[32] Section 15.

One striking provision in the Pennsylvania Declaration concerns *conscientious objectors*. One might expect the members of the Convention to be rather harsh with the pacific Quakers and the German sectarians opposed to bearing arms since they suffered from the policy of this class in the old Assembly. Yet their principles were recognized, for it was stated that no man "who is conscientiously scrupulous of bearing arms," can be "justly compelled thereto, if he will pay such equivalent."[33]

One other important difference should be noted. Virginia formulated the doctrine of the separation of the executive, legislative, and judicial powers, which, as we shall see later, was not favorably regarded in Pennsylvania.

a. RELIGIOUS LIBERTY

In the Constitution of Pennsylvania was found one of the first enactments of the principle of religious liberty on this continent.[34] Despite the tolerant spirit of William Penn, no Catholic could hold office in the province from 1693 to 1776, for every candidate for office had to swear that he did not believe in the doctrine of transubstantiation, that he regarded the invocation of the Virgin Mary and the saints as superstitious and the Popish Mass as idolatrous.[35] This oath excluded Roman Catholics from office, yet they had a right to live in the colony. The *Charter of Privileges* declared that no person or persons living in the province "who shall confess and acknowledge one Almighty God, the creator, upholder and ruler of the world . . . shall be in any case molested or

---

[33] Section 8; N. H. and Vt. were the only other constitutions of the time to contain similar provisions.

[34] Charles J. Stillé, "Religious Tests in Provincial Pennsylvania," *Pa. Mag.*, IX, 368.

[35] *Ibid.*, p. 377. This test was first imposed during the rule of Governor Fletcher and after Penn regained the colony the same requirements were continued. At a later date every prospective office-holder was compelled to declare his belief in the Athanasian definition of the Holy Trinity. Penn undoubtedly opposed these tests but he was powerless to act. They imposed civil disabilities on Catholics, Socinians or Unitarians, Jews and Infidels. No foreigner could be naturalized unless he was a Protestant. *Vide ibid.*, 377 ff.

prejudiced in his or their person or estate, because of his or their conscientious persuasion or practice."[36]

Section two of the *Declaration of Rights* stated that "all men' have a natural and unalienable right to worship Almighty God according to the dictates of their own consciences and understanding," and granted practically the same protection as that of Penn's *Charter of Privileges*.[37] Every member of the Assembly, however, had to subscribe to an oath professing faith in God and acknowledging the divine inspiration of the Old and New Testaments.[38] This provision was rather rigid, but a decided step in advance was made by providing that "no further or other religious tests shall ever hereafter be required of any civil officer or magistrate in this State."[39] This clause was inserted at the solicitation of Benjamin Franklin. In a letter written some years later he said that he thought the clause requiring Assemblymen to acknowledge the divine inspiration of the Scriptures "had better have been omitted." He stated that he "had opposed the clause; but, being overpowered by numbers, and fearing more might in future times be grafted on it, [he] prevailed to have the additional clause, 'that no further or more extended profession of faith should ever be enacted.' " In conclusion he said that "the evil of it was the less, as *no inhabitant,* nor any officer of government, except the members of Assembly, was obliged to make that declaration."[40]

Considering the times, the framers of the Constitution

---

[36] *Proceedings,* p. 32. Chapter II of the *Charter of Privileges* of 1701 stated: "And that all persons who also profess to believe in Jesus Christ, the Savior of the world, shall be capable (notwithstanding their other persuasions and practices in point of conscience and religion) to serve this government in any capacity, both legislatively and executively, . . ." The same provision is found in *The Laws Agreed Upon in England.*

[37] Section 2, *Dec. of Rights.*

[38] *Frame of Government,* sec. 10. This was also true in Del., Vt., and N.C. Practically the same oath had been required by the Provincial Conference for the members to the Convention.

[39] *Ibid.*

[40] Franklin's *Works,* Sparks ed., X, 134. Letter to a friend in England, written in Passy, August 21, 1784.

were very liberal in regard to religion. Besides Pennsylvania only Delaware and Rhode Island acknowledged the equality of all Protestant sects, and only Pennsylvania and Delaware extended equality to Catholics.

One additional clause under this heading might be mentioned. Section forty-five of the *Frame of Government* stated that "Laws for the encouragement of virtue and prevention of vice and immorality, shall be made and constantly kept in force," and that "all religious societies or bodies of men heretofore united or incorporated for the advancement of religion or learning, or for other pious and charitable purposes, shall be encouraged and protected in the enjoyment of the privileges, immunities and estates which they were accustomed to enjoy, or could of right have enjoyed, under the laws and former constitution of this state."[41]

b. FREEDOM OF SPEECH

Freedom of speech was guaranteed, but the provisions in both the *Declaration of Rights*[42] and the *Frame of Government*[43] were intended to preserve and not to extend this freedom. No person was exempted thereby from liability for slanderous or libelous words.[44] Nevertheless, this principle seems to have meant something, for there are many instances of its strong assertion. It made quite an impression on Schoepf, the German, in his travels through Pennsylvania, for he remarked that

Liberty of the press was one of the fundamental laws which the states included, expressly and emphatically, in the programmes of their new governments. It arouses the sympathies to see how often the Congress is mishandled in these sheets. The financier, Bob Morris, recently found himself slandered by an article in the *Independent Chronicle* and vigorously began process at law, but the public at large supported the printer and as free citizens

---

[41] For the bitter fight over the religious question, *vide infra*, p. 216.
[42] Section 12.
[43] Section 35.
[44] *Vide Respublica v. Oswald, 1 Dallas,* 319 (1788).

asserted their right to communicate to one another in this way their opinions and judgments regarding the conduct of public servants.[45]

Many other safeguards of the peoples' liberties were included, such as the inviolability of one's house and papers from seizure without a warrant,[46] trial by jury,[47] and the right of the people to bear arms.[48] Several important limitations on governmental power were missing. There was no prohibition of *ex post facto* laws or laws impairing the obligation of contract. Both of these provisions are found in the next constitution—that of 1790.[49] The *Laws Agreed Upon in England* provided for attainder working corruption of blood,[50] but the Constitution of 1776 was silent on this point, so no advance was made in this respect. The next Constitution, however, specifically stated "That no attainder shall work corruption of blood."[51] Section forty-six of the *Frame of Government* declared the *Declaration of Rights* "to be a part of the constitution . . . and ought never to be violated on any pretence whatever."

Although based upon existing documents, the *Declaration of Rights* was the true expression of the ideals of the American

---

[45] Schoepf, *op. cit.*, I, 87-88.

[46] Section 10.

[47] Sections 9 and 11.

[48] Section 13.

[49] Article ix, section 17.

[50] Sections 24 & 25. These provisions were a decided liberalization of the *Common Law* Doctrine. It is quite possible that the framers were not willing to abolish this because of the possibility of confiscating Tory property. There are many cases of attainder for treason to be found. *Vide Statutes at Large*, IX, X & XI. On March 8, 1780, an act was passed stating that "no attainder of treason to be had from and after the end of the present war between the United States of America and Great Britain, and the acknowledgement of the independency of the said United States by the King of Great Britain, shall extend to the disinheriting of any heir, nor to the prejudice of any person or persons other than the offender." *Statutes at Large*, X, 112. On September 15, 1786, an act amending the penal laws of the state declared that "no attainder hereafter shall work corruption of blood in any case, nor extend to the disinherison or prejudice of any person or persons other than the offender." *Ibid.*, XII, 281.

[51] Article ix, section 18.

Colonists, and the guarantees contained therein were the product of long and severe experience. With the exceptions already noted, and a few others of minor importance, this *Declaration* has remained practically unchanged until the present day.

3. *Frame of Government*

The Constitution was the hurried and necessarily imperfect work of actual revolution, framed by men with little knowledge of government, whose passions were heated and whose judgments were swayed by evanescent impulses and irritations.[52] It created, nevertheless, exactly what its authors desired—a *democratic* form of government. The Constitution established the most democratic state government in America at the time. Its main features, in so far as they became subjects of political discussion afterwards, were the unicameral legislature, and executive council, the abolition of property qualifications for voting, a Council of Censors, with the sole power of initiating amendments, and an ironclad oath of allegiance to the government thus created.

a. UNICAMERAL LEGISLATURE

The Constitution declared that the government of Pennsylvania should be vested in "an assembly of the representatives of the freemen" and a "president and council."[53] Only one legislative branch was constituted, for it was specified that the "supreme legislative power shall be vested in a house of representatives."[54] In adopting a unicameral system the

---

[52] A committee of the Convention published in the *Pa. Packet* of October 15, 1776, as an apology for one of their ordinances which was thought to be arbitrary and unjust, that it was passed when "the minds of the Convention were agitated, and their passions inflamed." No wonder a bitter fight ensued! It is not without reason, therefore, that "Brutus" referred to "the injustice, tyranny and cruelty of several of the ordinances of the Convention of this state, . . ." *Pa. Journal,* Oct. 2, 1776.

[53] Section 1.

[54] Section 2. Regardless of whether these new state constitutions were unicameral or bicameral, it should be emphasized that, as Prof. Corwin points out, "Throughout the Revolution the Blackstonian doctrine of 'legislative omnipotence' was in the ascendant." "Progress of Constitutional Theory,"

Convention simply followed a colonial precedent. Since 1701 there had been only one chamber.[55]

It might seem strange that this feature of the Constitution aroused so much agitation. The opposition was due mainly to the supreme power given to the Assembly. No governor could veto its laws and there was no "upper" house to check its action. Aside from the election of its members, the people controlled the Assembly in two ways. First, the proceedings had to be made public by printing the votes and transactions, and also by keeping the doors of the house open to "all persons who behave decently." Secondly, once in every seven years the community had the power to inquire into the whole conduct of the government.

In creating a single chamber the framers of the Constitution ran counter to the prevailing ideas of a legislative body. The only other unicameral legislatures were those of Vermont and Georgia.[56] John Adams, in his *Thoughts on Government,* said: "I think a people cannot be long free, nor ever happy, whose government is in one assembly. . . ." He ascribed to it "all the vices, follies, and frailties of an individual; subject to fits of humor, starts of passion, flights of enthusiasm . . . productive of hasty results and absurd judgments. . . ." Growing ambitious, it might "not hesitate to vote itself perpetual."[57]

To prevent "hasty results and absurd judgments," however, the Constitution provided that "all bills of public na-

---

Am. Hist. Rev., XXX, 517. Even in Virginia where the separation of powers was adopted, Jefferson, in his *Notes on Virginia,* bitterly assailed the convention of 1776 for having produced a concentration of powers in the legislative assembly, which answered to "precisely the definition of despotic government." *Writings,* Memorial ed., II, 160 *ff.* Quoted in Corwin's article, p. 519.

[55] See chapter i, p. 9.

[56] Georgia simply clung to her old custom of a single house, and Vt. was greatly influenced by Penna. The Vt. constitution was modeled after that of Penna., due chiefly to Thomas Young. He published an address on April 11, 1777, urging Vt. to declare for Independence and frame a Constitution. The Penna. sources of the Vt. Constitution are seen in *The Constitution of the State of Vermont,* etc., Brattleboro, 1891. See F. N. Thorpe, *Constitutional History of the American People,* I, 127.

[57] *Works,* IV, 195.

ture, shall be printed for the consideration of the people, before they are read in general assembly the last time for debate and amendment; and, except on occasions of sudden necessity, shall not be passed into laws until the next session of assembly; . . ."[58] This provision was of little practical value. Thomas Paine later wrote that it did not have the effect intended because "no given time was fixed for that consideration, nor any means for collecting its effects, nor were there then any public newspapers in the state but what were printed in Philadelphia, . . . thus a good and wise intention sunk into mere form, which is generally the case when the means are not adequate to the end."[59]

Since the unicameral feature of the Constitution aroused so much opposition it might be of interest to ascertain its supporters. This is difficult because the Convention was composed mainly of obscure men whose names have been forgotten and who did not write letters or keep diaries. Furthemore, the meager minutes contain nothing concerning the discussions of the constitution.

Opposition to a single chamber existed in the Convention itself, for on September 16, Mr. George Ross, seconded by Mr. Clymer, tried unsuccessfully to get a reconsideration of this question.[60] Thomas Paine, as we have seen, was in favor of a single chamber, and his influence with many members of the Convention was great. But Benjamin Franklin, the President of the Convention, probably exerted the deciding influence. One member, Timothy Matlack, wrote a few years later, "When the debate was nearly closed, Doctor Franklin was requested by the Convention to give his opinion on the point . . . and he declared it to be clearly and fully in favour of a

---

[58] Section 15.

[59] *The Political Writings of Thomas Paine,* "On the Proposal for Calling a Convention," I, 439-55.

[60] *Proceedings,* p. 52. "Resolved, That the further debate on the second section is precluded, because it was fully debated and determined before, as appears by the minutes of the 1st and 2d of August last." This is another proof that the action of the Convention in submitting the Constitution "for public consideration" was nothing more than a gesture. *Vide supra,* p. 163.

legislature to consist of a single branch, as being much the safest and best."[61] Respecting the propriety of two houses negativing each other, Franklin said that it was like putting one horse before a cart and one behind it, both pulling in opposite directions.[62] John Adams wrote to Francis Dana on August 16, 1776, "The Convention of Pennsylvania has voted for a single Assembly. Such is the force of habit; and what surprises me not a litle is, that the American philosopher should have so far accommodated himself to the custom of his countrymen as to be a zealous advocate of it."[63]

On the other hand, Dr. Benjamin Rush later wrote that Franklin's character was "lessened in the opinion of some people, by a supposition that he had a share in forming the constitution of Pennsylvania. It is true, he assented to it, but it is equally true, in a letter to general Wayne, & in conversation with Mr. John Morton, & myself, he strongly reprobated that part of the constitution which places the Supreme power of the state in the hands of a Single legislature."[64] The evidence is pretty clear, however, that Franklin did support this feature of the Constitution in the Convention and afterwards,[65] yet likely he was more interested in the great struggle with England than in the affairs of Pennsylvania. The widely circulated rumor naming him author of the Constitution arose because he carried a copy of it to France, shortly after the closing session of the Convention. In contradicting this report John Adams wrote that "it was not Franklin, but Timothy Matlack, James Cannon, Thomas Young, and

---

[61] *Pa. Gaz.,* March 31, 1779.

[62] *To the Citizens of Pennsylvania.* For another account of the above story *vide Works of Franklin,* (Sparks ed.), I, 409.

[63] Adams, *Works,* IX, 429.

[64] "Papers of Benjamin Rush," *Pa. Mag.,* XXIX, 29. Rush states that Franklin printed a paper in 1763 in which he supposes three branches preferable to two.

[65] *Vide supra,* note 45, p. 149. The vote in the Federal Convention for a Legislature of two branches "was agreed to without debate or dissent, except that of Pennsylvania, given probably from complaisance to Doc. Franklin who was understood to be partial to a single House of Legislation." *Documents,* etc., pp. 124-25.

Thomas Paine, who were the authors of it."[66] After discussing Franklin with M. Marbois, in Paris, Adams became a little piqued over the question and recorded in his *Diary* that it is believed that Franklin wrote all the American constitutions, whereas "He did not even make the constitution of Pennsylvania, bad as it is."[67]

In the minds of the political theorists of the day the purpose of an upper house was to prevent hasty legislation and check the lower and more popular body. The framers of the Pennsylvania Constitution were not at all desirous of checking the representatives of the people in their own assembly. Of "checks" they had had enough throughout the whole colonial period. The new Assembly, through the enlarged franchise, was the people's—and the people were supreme. John Adams probably came close to the truth when he wrote, "An apprehension, that the Proprietary and Quaker interest would prevail, to the election of characters disaffected to the American cause, finally preponderated against two legislative councils."[68]

b. PRINCIPLE OF REPRESENTATION

It required no seer to foretell upon what principle of representation the Convention would agree. On March 14, 1776, after years of patient waiting and agitation the Assembly added seventeen more members from the Western counties and the city of Philadelphia. With the Eastern party still in control the victory was nominal.[69] Furthemore, the franchise was still based on the amount of property owned.

A sign of what might occur is seen when the Provincial Conference decided to give each county equal representation in the Convention. The "people" were now to repay the East with a vengeance. The new Constitution provided that the Assembly which was to meet in November should be composed of six representatives from each county and six from the

---

[66] Adams, *Works,* IX, 623.

[67] *Ibid.,* III, 220.

[68] *Ibid.,* VI, 274.

[69] *Vide supra,* ch. i, pp. 38-9: ch. ii, p. 87; ch. iii, pp. 99-100.

city of Philadelphia. But this was nothing more than the old colonial basis of geographical representation, with a greater number of Assemblymen from the West and from the city of Philadelphia. The faults of such a system were obvious, so the principle of proportional representation was also adopted. Section seventeen of the Constitution stated that "representation in proportion to the number of taxable inhabitants is the only principle which can at all times secure liberty, and make the voice of a majority of the people the law of the land: . . ." The equal representation by counties was to last for two years only, when the Assembly should make out complete lists of taxable inhabitants "in the city and each county in the commonwealth respectively," and should "appoint a representative to each, in proportion to the number of taxables in such returns." An increase in population was provided for by a septennial reapportionment.

C. QUALIFICATIONS OF REPRESENTATIVES AND ELECTORS

The essentially democratic feature of the Constitution was the complete abolition of all property or financial qualifications, not only for the electorate but also for the elected. The feeling of the people about this triumph of democracy was shown in the press both before and during the meeting of the Convention. A writer in the *Evening Post* denounced financial qualifications for the suffrage as a "hurtful remnant of the feudal constitution. Why should these be made qualifications?," he asks. "Are not many, who have not these . . ., as fit to serve their country . . . as any that are worth money? This I think cannot be denied."[70] Another said that in order to secure perfection in government "all those who 'pay taxes should be entitled to the suffrages of the people,' . . . for to make a distinction between the rich and the poor for public honors, would be excluding perhaps the most useful and virtuous part of the community, . . ."[71]

---

[70] *Pa. Eve. Post,* July 30, 1776.
[71] *Ibid.,* Sept. 19, 1776. Letter signed "E." See *infra,* p. 190.

The *Declaration of Rights* stated that "all free men, having a sufficient evident common interest with and attachment to the community, have a right to elect officers, or to be elected into office." Giving definite expression to this idea, the Constitution enfranchised all "freemen of the full age of twenty-one years, having resided in this state for the space of one whole year next before the election of representatives, and paid public taxes during that time."[72] One slight concession was made to the holders of property, for the same section also stated that "sons of freeholders of the age of twenty-one years shall be entitled to vote although they have not paid taxes."

Instead of large property qualifications for the Assembly as most states had, Pennsylvania's Constitution stated that this body "shall consist of persons most noted for wisdom and virtue."[73] To prevent a monopoly of a seat in the House, it was provided that a representative serve no more than four years in seven.[74] Aside from Delaware, Pennsylvania alone in this period framed a constitution imposing no financial or property qualifications of any kind.[75]

An examination of some of the other constitutions regarding this question shows many striking differences and serves to emphasize the completeness of the democratic victory in Pennsylvania. New Jersey, a neighboring state, required a member of the Legislative Council to be a freeholder in the County in which he was chosen and be worth "at least one thousand pounds proclamation money, of real and personal estate, within the same county."[76] A member of the New Jersey Assembly was required to be in possession of 500 pounds in real and personal estate and every elector had to be worth 50 pounds.[77] The suffrage provision of New Hampshire was

---

[72] Section 6. Section 18 stated that no inhabitant was to have more than one vote.

[73] Section 7.

[74] Section 8.

[75] See below.

[76] Erdman, *op. cit.*, pp. 52-3. Constitution of 1776, Art. III.

[77] For a complete list of requirements of all the state constitutions of this period, see Morey, W. C., "First State Constitutions," *Annals of the Am. Acad. of Pol. and Soc. Science,* IV, 220-22.

about the same as Pennsylvania's, the voter being compelled to pay a poll tax; but to serve in the Legislature one had to possess an estate of 100 pounds in the town.

The qualifications for the governorship were even more stringent. In most of the states the governor had to be a free-holder, and in some instances the amount of the freeholder was fixed at a considerable sum. For example, in Massachusetts it was 1000 pounds, in Maryland 5000 pounds and in South Carolina 10,000 pounds.[78]

In no state were the leveling principles of democracy so thoroughly carried out as in Pennsylvania. The Declaration of Independence and the *Declaration of Rights* were not idle jests or fatuous asseverations; they meant exactly what they said. The spirit of the Convention is given in a caustic letter of Thomas Smith, one of its members, to his friend General Arthur St. Clair: "Our principle seems to be this: that any man, even the most illiterate, is as capable of any office as a person who has had the benefit of education; that education perverts the understanding, eradicates common honesty, and has been productive of all the evils that have happened in the world."[79]

In order to maintain the purity of the ballot it was pro-vided that "any elector, who shall receive any gift or reward for his vote, in meat, drink, monies, or otherwise, shall forfeit his right to elect for that time, and suffer such other penalties as future laws shall direct. And any person who shall directly or indirectly give, promise, or bestow any such rewards to be elected, shall be thereby rendered incapable to serve for the ensuing year."[80] The long struggle by the people for the control of their affairs was finally rewarded.

---

[78] See Miller, F. H., "Legal Qualifications for Office," *Annual Report of the Am. Hist. Assn.*, (1899) I.

[79] *The St. Clair Papers*, I, 373; see *infra*, pp. 208-11, and *supra*, p. 189. In this attitude one may find a remarkable parallel with, if not a direct influence of, the Romanticism which was then becoming rampant in France.

[80] Section 32.

d. ANNUAL ELECTIONS

To have annual elections was the one political dogma of the day held by the framers of the Pennsylvania Constitution. Section nine stated: "The members of the house of representatives shall be chosen annually by ballot, by the freemen of the Commonwealth, on the second Tuesday in October forever."

But this idea was not new to the people of Pennsylvania, for it was one of the political tenets of William Penn and is evidence of his democratic and tolerant spirit. It is altogether probable that very few of the framers ever heard of John Adams' maxim that "where annual elections end, there slavery begins."[81] Yet Pennsylvania Assemblies had been elected annually since the very inception of the colony. The *Proprietary Frame of Government* of 1682 stated that the freemen "shall yearly choose members to serve in a general assembly."[82] Likewise, the *Charter of Privileges* of 1701 decreed that "there shall be an Assembly yearly chosen,"[83] so it is evident that the members of the Convention had a strong colonial precedent to follow.

e. POWERS AND FUNCTIONS OF THE LEGISLATURE

The power given this unicameral legislature rather than the form evoked the bitter criticism in the period following the inauguration of the new Constitution. The Legislature was supreme. It had the power to choose its own speaker, its other officers, the treasurer of the state, and the representatives of the state in Congress; to "prepare bills and enact them into laws; judge of the elections and qualifications of" its members; expel a member; redress grievances; impeach state

---

[81] Adams, *Works*, IV, 205. So firmly was the doctrine of "annual elections" held in Massachusetts that the Constitution of the United States was ratified with difficulty because it departed from this principle in respect to the terms of Senators and Representatives in Congress.

[82] Section xiv.

[83] Section 2.

criminals and every state officer; grant charters of incorpora-
tion; and finally an "elastic clause" was added which said that
the Assembly "shall have all other powers necessary for the
legislature of a free state or commonwealth."[84] The only re-
striction placed upon these representatives of the sovereign
people was that "They shall have no power to add to, alter,
abolish, or infringe any part of" the constitution.[85]

Mention has already been made of the fact that the "doors
of the house in which the representatives of the freemen of
this state shall sit in general assembly, shall be and remain
open for the admission of all persons who behave decently,
except only when the welfare of this state may require the
doors to be shut."[86] The votes and proceedings of the Assembly were to be published, and all bills of a public nature were
to be printed "for the consideration of the people, . . ."[87] With
no veto power in the Council and with the nominal control
of public opinion the Assembly was practically supreme.

To maintain the freedom of criticism it was declared that
"The printing presses shall be free to every person who under-
takes to examine the proceedings of the legislature, or any
part of the government."[88]

In the early days of Athenian democracy the popular assembly was open to all citizens. In reality only those with
wealth and leisure could afford to attend. In the time of Peri-
cles pay was introduced, and only then was a real democracy
established. The thirty-sixth section of the Pennsylvania Constitution recognized this principle and vaguely stated:

As every freeman to preserve his independence, (if without a sufficient estate) ought to have some profession, calling, trade or farm,
whereby he may honestly subsist, there can be no necessity for, nor
use in establishing offices of profit, the usual effects of which are
dependence and servility unbecoming freemen, in the possessors

---

[84] Sections 9 and 11.
[85] Ibid.
[86] Section 13.
[87] See supra, pp. 184-85.
[88] Section 35.

and expectants; faction, contention, corruption, and disorder among the people. But if any man is called into public service to the prejudice of his private affairs, he has a right to a reasonable compensation: And whenever an office, through increase of fees or otherwise, becomes so profitable as to occasion many to apply for it, the profits ought to be lessened by the legislature.[89]

What this clause really means is difficult to say; it resembles a Delphic response. As John Adams wrote:

My first objection is, that it is not intelligible. It is impossible to discover what is meant by "offices of profit." Does it mean that there can be no necessity for, nor use in, annexing either salary, fees, or perquisites, to public offices? and that all who serve the public should have no pay from the public, but should subsist themselves and families out of their own fortunes, or their own labor in their private profession, calling, trade, or farm? This seems to be the sense of it, and in this sense it may make its court to the Quakers and Moravians, Dunkers, Mennonites, or other worthy people in Pennsylvania, that is to say, to their prejudices, . . .

Adams' second objection to the article is "that it is inconsistent. After seeming to require that officers should have no emoluments, it stumbles at its own absurdity, and adds" that they should. "And this is what I complain of in the article," he says, "that it diverts the attention, jealousy, and hatred of the people from the perquisites, patronage, and abuse, which is the evil, to the legal, honest profit of the office, which is a blessing."[90]

The Constitution which gave the Assembly supreme power alone limited it. And the people who made the Constitution were determined to rule. Their sacred document was to be preserved inviolate, for it was provided that every officer, "whether judicial, executive or military, in authority under this commonwealth," should take "the following oath or affirmation of allegiance . . . before he enters on the execution of" his duties:

---

[89] Section 36.

[90] Adams, *Works*, IX, 533-34; Letter to John Jebb, London, Aug. 21, 1785. See also other letters on the same subject to Jebb, *ibid.*, pp. 538 *ff* and 543 *ff*.

I . . . do swear (or affirm) that I will be true and faithful to the commonwealth of Pennsylvania: And that I will not directly or indirectly do any act or thing prejudicial or injurious to the constitution or government thereof, as established by the convention.[91]

Rigidly interpreted, this meant that no state official could either say anything in derogation of the Constitution, or endeavor in any way to alter or change its provisions. The storm aroused by this provision will be noted in the ensuing chapter.[92]

f. EXECUTIVE

The Constitution provided that "The supreme executive power shall be vested in a president and council."[93] The creation of a plural executive was due, no doubt, to the experiences of the people throughout the colonial period. The attempts of the Governor and his council to influence legislation and the Proprietary veto were well remembered. Consequently, they created this form of executive with no authority over the acts of the legislature. The powers of this Supreme Executive Council were confined to executing the laws.[94]

The members of this Council, one from the city of Philadelphia and one from each of the counties, were to be chosen by the electors to serve for three years.[95] The first councilors were to be elected in such a way that one-third of the number would retire annually. The reason is obvious.

By this mode of election and continual rotation, more men will be trained to public business, there will in every subsequent year be found in the council a number of persons acquainted with the pro-

---

[91] Section 40.

[92] See pp. 268-70.

[93] Section 3. The Vt. constitution created an executive board and N. H. had a council with a president. The latter had, however, little more power than the speaker of the House. Nevins, *op. cit.*, p. 90.

[94] White, *op. cit.*, intro., p. xxiii. This provision shows the reliance which these men placed upon the committee system.

[95] Provision was made for representing additional counties in the Council, should such be created. Section 19.

ceedings of the foregoing years, whereby the business will be more consistently conducted, and moreover the danger of Establishing an inconvenient Aristocracy will be effectually prevented.[96]

The framers were determined that no self-perpetuating, aristocratic bureaucracy be established. No member of the general assembly, delegate in congress, treasurer of the state or other similar officers were eligible to serve at the same time as councilor, and no person after holding the office for three successive years could be capable of serving in a like capacity until four years afterwards. By virtue of his office every councilor was a justice of the peace for the whole commonwealth.

It must not be supposed that the president of the council resembled the colonial governor or the governor in some of the other states. He had to be a member of the council and together with the vice-president was chosen annually "by the joint ballot of the general assembly and council."[97] He had few powers. Such influence as he exercised was due to his personality rather than to his position. He was really *primus inter pares*. The Constitution stated: "The president shall be the commander in chief of the forces of the state, but shall not command in person, except advised therto by the council, and then only so long as they shall approve thereof."[98] Obviously there was little chance for the president to become a military dictator.

The Council was to meet annually at the same time and place as the general assembly. Its powers were numerous and varied. All officers of the state not chosen by the people[99]

---

[96] Section 19. The provision in the Constitution of the United States respecting the election of senators was similar to this.

[97] Section 19. This was the only joint meeting of the two bodies. The term "president" was used in the N. H. constitution (1784), and also in that of S. C. (1776). The election of the president in Pennsylvania, however, was unique. In both Penna. and Georgia the vice-president was elected in the same manner as the president. Webster, *op. cit.*, p. 74.

[98] Section 20.

[99] Few officers were chosen by the people. Justices of the peace (section 30), sheriffs, and coroners (section 31), were the only ones so chosen.

or the assembly were to be appointed by the president—or in his absence the vice-president—and Council, five of whom were to constitute a quorum. It, therefore, appointed the attorney-general, the judges, naval and other officers, both civil and military. The Council was to communicate with other states; transact business with the state officers, civil and military, and prepare such business as appeared necessary to lay before the general assembly. It was also to have the power to "grant pardons, and remit fines, in all cases`whatsoever, except in cases of impeachment; and in cases of treason and murder, shall have power to grant reprieves, but not to pardon, until the end of the next session of assembly." Furthermore, it was "to take care that the laws be faithfully executed," and was to have the power to "call together the general assembly when necessary, before the day to which they shall stand adjourned."[100]

The power of impeachment was vested in the general assembly. All state officers were liable to be impeached, not only when in office, but curiously enough even after their resignation or removal for maladministration. The trial was to be held before the president, or vice-president, and the Council, who were to take "to their assistance for advice only, the justices of the supreme court."[101]

The powerful office of governor was gone and in its place was this plural executive, greatly limited in power, with no control over legislation. There was safety in numbers, the people thought, and as one contemporary writer put it: "A single man, however honest in general, is much more liable to biasses and prejudices than a body of men. . . ."[102]

g. THE JUDICIARY

Edmund Burke once said, "Whatever is supreme in a state, it ought to have, as much as possible, its judicial authority so constituted as not only to depend upon it, but in some

---

[100] Section 20.
[101] Sections 20 & 22.
[102] *Pa. Eve. Post,* July 30, 1776.

sort to balance it."[103] An independent judiciary is one of the most important branches of any government. It is the defender of the people's liberties, the safeguard against tyranny. Such was the aim of the men in the Convention; their purpose was almost accomplished.

The Constitution decreed that "The president, and in his absence the vice-president, with the council, five of whom shall be a quorum, shall have power to appoint and commissionate judges, . . ."[104] Thus the first principle of an independent judiciary was established, for the judges derived their power from the executive branch of the government and not from recurring elections.

This, however, is only one safeguard, for the Colonists had long ago learned that by controlling the salary of a judge he could be compelled to do their bidding. The independence of the Pennsylvania judiciary was further secured by being granted "fixed salaries."[105] This was different from the situation in New Jersey, where by the Constitution the salaries of the judges were dependent upon the Legislature, which could increase, decrease, or abolish them.[106]

The judicial term was seven years with the possibility of reappointment. Judges could be removed for misbehavior at any time by the general assembly. There had been much agitation for a judiciary holding office during good behavior, such as had been established in England in 1688. Many people recognized the dangers inherent in a limited term of office, but in the Convention the majority opposed life offices. Until 1776 judges held office at the pleasure of the Governor or Proprietary, which was virtually life tenure. The advocates of tenure during good behavior were disappointed

---

[103] *Reflections on the Revolution in France.*

[104] Section 20. Appointments were similarly made in Vt., Md., and Mass.

[105] Section 23. This is all the Constitution says about judicial remuneration. The term "fixed salaries" undoubtedly meant that the salaries should not be diminished during the term of office. *Vide* Art. 5, section 2 of the Constitution of 1790. The judges were forbidden to "take or receive fees or perquisites of any kind." Section 23.

[106] Erdman, *op. cit.*, p. 65.

with a term of seven years, but it was all that could be achieved under the trying circumstances and party antipathies which attended the meeting of the Convention.[107]

Two other provisions regarding the courts should be noted. Section twenty-four provided that

The Supreme Court, and the several Courts of Common Pleas of this Commonwealth, shall, besides the powers usually exercised by such courts, have the powers of a court of chancery, so far as relates to the perpetuating testimony, obtaining evidence from places not within this state, and the care of the persons and estates of those who are non compos mentis, and such other powers as may be found necessary by future general assemblies, not inconsistent with this constitution.

Section twenty-six provided that

Courts of sessions, common pleas, and orphans courts shall be held quarterly in each city and county; and the legislature shall have power to establish all such other courts as they may judge for the good of the inhabitants of the state. All courts shall be open, and justice shall be impartially administered without corruption or unnecessary delay: All their officers shall be paid an adequate but moderate compensation for their services: And if any officer shall take greater or other fees than the laws allow him, either directly or indirectly, it shall ever after disqualify him from holding any office in this state.

These provisions are clear and explicit. They give the legislature ample opportunity to develop the judicial system, but provide safeguards against encroachment by that body. They grant judges a fixed salary and attach severe penalties to the acceptance of any other fees.

Throughout the period of the Proprietary Government in Pennsylvania the English system of jurisprudence prevailed. This was continued, although in a slightly modified form, by

---

[107] See the article by the present writer, "A History of Judicial Tenure in Pennsylvania," *Dickinson Law Review*, XXXVIII, No. 3 (April, 1934), 168-183. Limited terms of office for judges were also found in the constitutions of Ga., N. J., and Vt.

the new Constitution.[108] The form of local government was not changed, so in this field there was no distinct difference between the province and the commonwealth.[109]

h. COUNCIL OF CENSORS

By far the most interesting and unique feature of the Constitution of 1776 was the establishment of a Council of Censors,[110] a body which was to be the guardian of the Constitution and of the rights of the people. The *Frame of Government* provided that, "in order that the freedom of the commonwealth may be preserved inviolate for ever," the freemen of each city and county should choose by ballot two persons to represent them in this Council of Censors. The first election was to take place in October 1783, and every seven years thereafter. When the men elected met in November they were "to enquire whether the constitution has been preserved inviolate in every part; and whether the legislative and executive branches of government have performed their duty as guardians of the people, or assumed to themselves, or exercised other or greater powers than they are intitled to by the constitution." They were also to inquire into the financial condition of the state and to see "whether the laws have been duly executed."

In order to carry out these duties, the Censors were to have the power "to send for persons, papers, and records," and were given the authority to "pass public censures, to order impeachments and to recommend to the legislature the repealing such laws as appear to them to have been enacted

---

[108] *Vide* "The Judiciary of Allegheny County," by J. W. F. White, in *Pa. Mag.*, VII, 143. The act of May 1722, which continued in force with slight amendments and some interruptions until after the Revolution, established and regulated the courts.

[109] "Local Self-Government in Pennsylvania," E. R. L. Gould, in *Pa. Mag.*, VI, 164.

[110] Section 47 deals exclusively with the Council of Censors. For a good account see "The Council of Censors," by Lewis H. Meader, in *Pa. Mag.*, XXII, 265-300. Meader traces the idea back to the early days of Greece and Rome.

contrary to the principles of the constitution." These powers were to be exercised for one year only from the day of their election.

A most important provision of any constitution is the amending clause. To make the process too easy is to invite rapid and inconsequential changes; to make it too difficult is to render the constitution too rigid and impede necessary alterations. The amending of the Pennsylvania Constitution was placed solely in the hands of this Council of Censors. They were to have the power "to call a convention to meet within two years after their sitting, if there appear to them an absolute necessity of amending any article of the Constitution which may be defective, explaining such as may be thought not clearly expressed, and of adding such as are necessary for the preservation of the rights and happiness of the people." However, no alteration could take place for seven years, no matter what occurred in the interim.

In order to give the people some voice regarding the question of their "rights and happiness," it was provided that the amendments proposed, or the articles to be added or abolished, were to be "promulgated at least six months before the day appointed for the election of such convention, for the previous consideration of the people, that they may have an opportunity of instructing their delegates on the subject."

This Council of Censors never accomplished the work for which it was created. It was to "enquire" and "also to enquire"; to "order" and "to recommend"; but nowhere do we find anything about the power of enforcing its findings or of compelling the legislature to act. Only one meeting was held, and that at a time of such tense party strife that practically nothing was accomplished.

Vermont copied this feature of the Pennsylvania Constitution, and there it worked better because the former state had a more homogeneous population and less violent party animosities. The New York *Council of Revision* was somewhat similar to the Pennsylvania and Vermont Council of Censors, although its composition and functions were different. Composed of the Governor, Chancellor, and three judges of the Supreme Court, or any two of the four acting with the Governor, it was to "revise all bills about to be passed into law by the legislature." It was intended as a check upon both the Governor and the Assembly.

Like most of the provisions of the Pennsylvania Constitution, the authorship of the Council of Censors is difficult to determine. It is probable that the leading part was taken by Judge Bryan,[111] supported in the Convention by Professor Cannon. An anonymous pamphlet written eight years later traces this to Cannon, the "fanatical school-master."[112] We have mentioned two other pamphlets published in Pennsylvania—*Four Letters on Interesting Subjects* and *The Genuine Principles of the Ancient Saxon, or English Constitutions*[113]—which proposed an idea almost exactly like the one adopted. It was designed chiefly to preserve the life of the Constitution, and of course was most virulently attacked by its opponents.

i. SEPARATION OF POWERS

The doctrine of the Separation of Powers found little favor with the framers of the Pennsylvania Constitution. The failure to define explicitly the powers and functions of the departments of government was due perhaps to an imperfect understanding of what the doctrine really meant. In the minds of most men of that day it connoted little more than a caution against plurality of office.[114] Furthermore, there was no great need for such a sharp distinction in Pennsylvania, as her provincial governors were not of the strong, arbitrary type such as Virginia had experienced.

Nevertheless, the hatred of the people for the proprietary governors led to a reaction against executive authority, which, as we have seen, resulted in the predominance of the legisla-

---

[111] Konkle, *Bryan*, p. 129.

[112] Nevins, *op. cit.*, p. 150.

[113] See *supra*, p. 175.

[114] Edward S. Corwin, "Progress of Constitutional Theory," *American Historical Review*, XXX. 516.

ture.[115] In the struggles of colonial times the citizens had learned to trust their legislature. Now they looked upon that body as the immediate representative of the sovereign people.[116] The most emphatic statement of the doctrine of the Separation of Powers among the new state constitutions of this time is found in the Massachusetts *Declaration of Rights*. The same principle was also endorsed by Maryland, North Carolina, Virginia,[117] and Georgia,[118] but the constitutions of Pennsylvania, New Jersey, New York, Delaware, South Carolina, and Vermont contain no specific statement of the principle, further than an occasional prohibition upon individuals holding more than one office.[119]

j. MISCELLANEOUS PROVISIONS
1. Education

Apart from the New England States, the general education of the people had made little progress in the colonies up to the Revolution. As a result, only a few of the first state constitutions contained provisions regarding education. In this field the constitutions of Massachusetts (1780) and New Hampshire (1784) were the most progressive,[120] although Pennsylvania's had fairly definite and specific provisions. Section forty-four provided: "A school or schools shall be established in each county by the legislature, for the convenient instruction of youth, with such salaries, to the masters paid by the

[115] Nevins says that "In no state did the Governor have a final veto upon legislation, and in only three did he have a partial veto power." *Op. cit.*, p. 166.

[116] This might seem contradictory to all that has previously been said, but it must be remembered that the Pennsylvania legislature did not represent the masses. Nevertheless, it was considered a safeguard against the Proprietary interests. In the Crown Colonies this trust or faith was much more marked.

[117] See Jefferson's criticism of the Virginia constitution, note 54, *supra*, pp. 183-84. While the principle was often stated, it generally meant very little.

[118] Webster, *op. cit.*, pp. 73-4.

[119] For these prohibitions in the Pennsylvania Constitution, see sections 7, 18, 23 and 40.

[120] Webster, *op. cit.*, pp. 89-90.

public, as may enable them to instruct youth at low prices:
And all useful learning shall be duly encouraged and pro-
moted in one or more universities." While the means for establishing a public school in each county are not clearly stated,
the fact that they are to be established is clear.

2. Imprisonment for Debt

The poorer classes had always opposed imprisonment for
debt, a practice brought from England. The sanitary conditions of the prisons in Pennsylvania were bad. In March 1772,
a time when many were imprisoned for debt, it was reported
that three prisoners had died from starvation.[121] The attempts made during the colonial period to bring relief to
this class had little effect. For example, the Act of 1730 for
the relief of insolvent debtors allowed a creditor to keep the
debtor in confinement upon the plea that he was not satisfied with his oath as to the delivery of all this property.[122]
When the Continental Congress assembled in Philadelphia,
debtors in the jail in that city petitioned Congress to direct
the various assemblies to devise methods to free all prisoners
for debt. But the President did not even read the petition,
"thinking it," as Richard Smith wrote, "coram non judice."[123]

To meet such a situation section twenty-eight of the Constitution provided that the "person of a debtor, where there
is not a strong presumption of fraud, shall not be continued
in prison, after delivering up, bona fide, all his estate real
and personal, for the use of his creditors in such manner as
shall be hereafter regulated by law."

A few other clauses were included in the Constitution,
such as one providing for naturalization, one giving the freedom to hunt and fish, and another for the encouragement
of public morals. Of course there was much that had no place
in an organic law, and much that, as we have pointed out,
was loosely drawn. The words "ought to be" instead of "shall

---

[121] Scharf and Westcott, *op. cit.*, I, 262.

[122] White, *op. cit.*, p. 163.

[123] "Diary," Saturday, Jan. 27 [1776]. Printed in Burnett, *op. cit.*, I, 331.

be" were used several times. As few members of the convention had any legal training, and only a small group had received any education or had read at all widely, these mistakes and errors are easily understood.

From this discussion it is evident that to attempt to adopt the Constitution, and then to govern the state under it, would arouse much opposition. The framers anticipated difficulties and strengthened their position by requiring of every state officer a very stringent oath—not to do anything prejudicial or injurious to the Constitution.

An exceedingly democratic Constitution had been framed, and the men who framed it were determined to see the product of their long labors preserved. But immediately the fight for its overthrow or revision began, and a veritable civil war ensued. Neighbors reviled neighbors; citizens forsook their citizenship, fleeing to more propitious soil, and in the internecine strife blood was spilled on the streets of Philadelphia.

VI

THE BATTLE OVER THE CONSTITUTION
AND THE ORGANIZATION OF
THE NEW GOVERNMENT

THE attempt to put the new Constitution into effect evoked one of the bitterest political struggles ever witnessed by an American State. Unfortunately it occurred when the British Army was at the very doors of Pennsylvania, paralyzing for a time not only her resistance to the foe but affecting as well the whole conduct of the Revolution. So critical were affairs in Pennsylvania that on two occasions Congress itself intervened to establish order. Vigorous action on the part of the state officials improved conditions temporarily, but the fight over the Constitution continued until 1790 when a new one was drafted.

Since the framers deliberately planned to efface all traces of the past, opposition was to be expected. Anything savoring of the control of the aristocratic and wealthy elements of the East was to be obliterated. Thomas Smith, a member of the Convention, wrote:

We are determined not to pay the least regard to the former Constitution of this Province, but to reject every thing therein that may be proposed, merely because it was part of the former Constitution. We are resolved to clear every part of the old rubbish out of the way and begin upon a clean foundation.[1]

Of course, the framers did not succeed in eradicating the past entirely. Some of the features of the old government, such as the unicameral legislature, were retained. Yet in

---

[1] Letter to Gen. Arthur St. Clair, *The St. Clair Papers,* I, 374. Persifor Frazer, writing to his wife, said that he thought "the convention were not politic in making so many alterations from the old establishment. . . ." *Pa. Mag.,* XXXI, 319.

many respects there was a distinct breach with the past. The new Constitution aroused violent opposition because it brought into power a class of people hitherto denied political privileges. Furthermore, the manner in which the Constitution was made and put into effect created much antagonism, and the form of government established stirred up bitter criticism.

1. *Opposition to the Framers and the New Rulers*

The antagonists of the new Constitution not only attacked the instrument itself but denounced the framers and the men to whom it gave power. We have noted that criticism followed the assumption by the Convention of legislative and executive functions.[2] The members of the Convention were neither well known nor adequately fitted for the great task before them.[3] This led to much fiery denunciation and not a little sarcastic ridicule. One critic said:

The other states have no such *leading* men—in their Conventions, as we have in *ours*—and what is more extraordinary, our leading men have never had much experience in public affairs . . . so vast and amazing is the genius of our leaders, that forming a frame of government, which in other parts of the world has been considered, when well executed, as one of the greatest efforts of the human mind, is nothing but mere Play to our statesmen. . . . Simplicity is the principle of our political leaders.[4]

This damned simplicity of their's will make us simple freemen—

---

[2] This opposition continued, for the important meeting held on Oct. 21 and 22 drew up a resolution saying that "the said Convention assumed and exercised powers with which they were not intrusted by the people." *Pa. Eve. Post,* Oct. 22, 1776. "Brutus," in the *Penna Journal,* in an article entitled "To the People of Pennsylvania," said: "I do not mean to take up your time in pointing out the injustice, tyranny and cruelty of several of the ordinances of the late Convention of this state, . . ." See *supra,* pp. 151-55.

[3] See *supra,* pp. 148-49.

[4] This is from the satirical dialogues running in the *Pa. Eve. Post* throughout Oct. and Nov., 1776, between "Orator Puff" and "Peter Early," or other characters. The dialogue given here is from the issue of Oct. 10. Christopher Marshall, in his *Diary* for Oct. 11, calls this "A severe Satire."

It all arose from so many plain country folks being in the Convention.[5]

The members of the Convention had their defenders. "Consideration," writing in the *Pennsylvania Gazette,* said that when the opponents could find no further fault with the new Constitution they began to revile its authors, concluding that it must be "a vile thing, because a certain Schoolmaster had a principal hand in forming it." He reminded them that Mr. Cannon was "a learned, sensible and disinterested Patriot," and mentioned, as none of the defenders failed to do, that Dr. Franklin and David Rittenhouse were members of the Convention. The writer states that the opponents do recall, however, that Colonel Matlack was a member, "but only to inform the true proprietors of dominion (the rich) that the fellow is an upstart and does not keep a chariot."[6] Another anonymous writer said that the Convention

. . . had scarcely met when your enemies [his letter is addressed "To the People"] began, in low whispers, at the corners of the streets, to traduce them. A regular established government under the authority of the people only would act with such vigour as to defeat all their diabolical machinations. This must not take place, for in a continuation of the unsettled state of our affairs depends their success. How shall this mighty work be effected? Why, the credit of the Convention must be ruined. "Stop every man you can with any propriety in the streets, and say something against the Convention to him. Let the presses teem with general censures on their proceedings, and reflections on their conduct . . . For if the new government is once set a going, we are undone." This is the

---

[5] "Orator Puff to John his friend, over a bottle of Madeira," *Pa. Eve. Post,* Oct. 19. Many people considered the "framers" as self-elected politicians.

[6] Oct. 30. The well-known anecdote concerning Matlack might be mentioned here. James Pemberton, a wealthy Quaker, noticing him girded with a sword, he being an Associator, asked: "What is that thing at thy side for?" Matlack replied, "That is to defend my property and my liberty"; to which Pemberton answered, "Why, Timothy, as for thy property, we know that thou hast none, and as for thy liberty thou owest that to me," he having relieved Matlack from imprisonment for debt. *Pennsylvania, Colonial and Federal,* Jenkins, p. 19. Dr. A. M. Stackhouse says it was Miers Fisher, not Pemberton, *Colonel Timothy Matlack,* p. 23.

language of our enemies at this time, as appears evident by their conduct.[7]

A further cause of opposition to the Constitution was its creation of an entirely new body of voters—and consequently rulers. The abolition of all suffrage qualifications brought into office a large class of men who formerly had nothing to do with the government—not even the right to vote. The change in rulers was thorough and complete. "It is a fact," said Franklin, "that the Irish emigrants and their children are now in possession of the government of Pennsylvania, by their majority in the Assembly, as well as of a great part of the territory; and I remember well the first ship that brought any of them over."[8]

To these men power was sweet, and they were determined to keep the authority in their own hands—hence the binding oaths not to "directly or indirectly do any act or thing prejudicial or injurious to the constitution or government" of the state "as established by the convention."[9] The moderates feared the rule of these new classes and strongly opposed them.

Those indebted to the Constitution for the right to vote became its enthusiastic supporters.[10] "Many . . . support it at all hazards," wrote Judge Yeates.[11] Alexander Graydon said that "as Whigism declined among the higher classes, it increased in the inferior; because they who composed them, thereby, obtained power and consequence, . . ."[12] Thomas Paine later remarked, with much exaggeration perhaps, that the Constitution "was the political bible of the State. Scarce a family was without it."[13]

These new rulers with little or no experience in the affairs of government were the target of criticisms from their

---

[7] "Cassius," in the *Pa. Eve. Post*, Oct. 8, 1776.
[8] Letter to William Strahan, Aug. 19, 1784, *Works*, Sparks ed., X, 131.
[9] Constitution, section 40.
[10] *Vide Pa. Mag.*, V, 433.
[11] Letter to Colonel Burd, *Letters and Papers*, p. 258.
[12] *Memoirs*, p. 285.
[13] Paine's *Writings*, Wheeler ed., IV, 269.

contemporaries. Persifor Frazer, with the army at Ticonderoga, wrote that he was "sorry so many novices are appointed in Pennsa at the head of affairs, none but men of the first Character for knowledge and probity shou'd now be at the helm. The Gale is boistrous [*sic*] and requires men of the best abilities to manage the Vessel and steer clear of rocks and shoals."[14] Dr. Benjamin Rush remarked that the new government was thought "by many people to be rather too much upon the democratical order, for liberty is as apt to degenerate into luxuriousness, as power is to become arbitrary."[15] Alexander Graydon said that "Power had fallen into low hands: . . ."[16] Robert Proud, the historian, wrote some caustic verse about the new ruling class, "On the Violation of Established and Lawful Order, Rule or Government ——Applied to the Present Times in Penns[a] in 1776:"[17]

> Of all the plagues, that scourge the human race,
> None can be worse, than *upstarts*, when in place;
> Their pow'r to shew, no action they forbear;
> They tyrannize o'er all, while all they fear;
> No savage rage, no rav'nous beast of prey,
> Exceeds the cruelty of Servile Sway! (1)
>   As if the foot to be the head inclin'd,
> Or body should aspire to rule the mind;
> As when the pow'r of fire, of air and flood,
> In proper bounds, support the common good;
> But when they break the bound, to them assign'd,
> They most pernicious are to human kind;
> So are those men, whose duty's to obey,
> When they usurp the rule, and bear the sway.

---

[14] *Pa. Mag.*, XXXI, 315. October 2, 1776.

[15] Letter to Anthony Wayne discussing the new Constitution. Printed in Charles J. Stillé, *Major-General Anthony Wayne and the Pennsylvania Line*, p. 40. Letter dated Sept. 24, 1776.

[16] *Memoirs*, pp. 283-84.

[17] Printed in *Pa. Mag.*, XIII, 435-36. Proud's notes are very interesting: "1—*Serville Sway*—That of servants, slaves, or lower ranks of people, when by *violence*, they usurp the power over their former masters and rulers, &c— . . . 2—Observe the order of the heavenly bodies. 3—Id est, devils, or rebels and destroyers; see Milton."

In order God has wisely rang'd the whole;
And animates that order, as the Soul:
In due gradation ev'ry rank must be,
Some high, some low, but all in their degree:
This law in ev'ry flock and herd we find,
In ev'ry living thing of ev'ry kind;
Their Chief precedes, as in the fields they stray;
The rest in *order* follow and obey.
Much more in men, this *order* ought to dwell,
As they in rank and reason do excel;
A state the nearest to the Bless'd above,
Where all degrees, in *beauteous order* move: (2)
Which those, who violate, are sure to be
The (3) tools of woeful infelicity!
Ev'n so are men, far worse than beasts of prey
When those *usurp the rule,* who should obey:
In self-security weak mortals find
The will of God is thus to scourge mankind. . . .

If one accepted the political dogma of the time as expressed in the Pennsylvania Declaration of Rights, that the people were sovereign, then there was no usurpation of power by the Convention. This view, held by many, is well expressed by an anonymous writer in the *Evening Post.* "To the Freemen of Pennsylvania," he said:

You have been very passionately addressed of late by several writers under the signatures of *F, Brutus, Camillus, Scipio,* &c. and everything which can alarm you against yourselves is conjured up. I wish to address you calmly, and to consult your reason, not your fears. You by great labour and assiduity obtained what you so long wished for, a Convention chosen by yourselves, to frame a government under your own authority.—They met and framed a government, and have therein derived every atom of power with which it is vested directly from you, and modelled it so that it not only returns at proper and stated periods into your hands again, but cannot be delegated so long into any one set of hands as to render it dangerous. . . .

The writer further stated that the gentry regarded the people "as their property, their beasts of burthen, born only to be ruled by these Lords of the Creation. . . ."[18] He said he had been told by them "that gentlemen would not submit to have power so much in the hands of the people. The people, say they, are not fit to be the guardians of their own rights! . . ."[19] Dr. William Shippen said that many of the men who heretofore had been at the head of affairs "in many instances behaved as though they thought they had a sort of fee simple" in their offices, and "might dispose of all places of Honour and Profit as pleased them best. . . ." He said he didn't wonder at their resentment of the change which "ousted" them, or at least brought them "down to a level with their fellow citizens. . . ."[20]

The attempt to seize the power from the former rulers, not the ignorance of the lower classes, was attacked. It is evident that this was a relentless class struggle; a determined fight between the big landowner and the propertyless class; a conflict of mechanics and artisans against bankers and wealthy aristocracy. These struggles were considered important in the debates on the Federal Constitution a decade later. James Madison very frankly stated then that the landowners and men of property "ought to be so constituted as to protect the minority of the opulent against the majority."[21]

Another writer shows that the members of the Convention were less greedy for power than was the case in some other states. "Other Conventions," he said, "either resolved themselves into Assemblies and undertook to appoint officers of State—though not appointed for that purpose; or sat until it took place.—Our Convention trusting to the virtue of their countrymen, on finishing their work dissolved themselves. . . ."[22]

The opponents of the Constitution made much of the argument that it "had never received the sanction or approba-

---

[18] *Vide* verse by Proud, *supra*, pp. 209-10. For another statement concerning the sovereignty of the people, *vide infra*, pp. 214-15.

[19] Oct. 15, 1776.

[20] *Pa. Mag.*, XLIV, 286.

[21] *Documents*, etc., p. 811.

[22] *Pa. Journal*, Oct. 9, 1776.

tion of the people."[23] A "Declaration of the Inhabitants of Cumberland County" stated, "we are of Opinion, that the Constitution formed by the Late Convention is Inconsistent with 'the Principles of free and good government, . . . It has never Received the Sanction of the good People of this state."[24] Since not a single state in the Union at this time submitted its constitution for popular vote, Pennsylvania's action was no exception.[25]

2. *Opposition to the Principles of the Constitution*

a. UNORGANIZED OPPOSITION

In the following discussion we shall endeavor to emphasize the opposition to the Constitution itself. In dealing with this question, however, it must be borne in mind that it is difficult to distinguish between opposition to the Constitution *per se* and *ad hominem* arguments against its framers and the manner in which they accomplished their work. Many of the Moderates and all of the Conservatives, supporters of the old charter, would have criticized any constitution. Much of the opposition, therefore, was purely partisan. As Judge Yeates wrote, "Many are determined to oppose it at all events, . . ."[26] A writer in the *Pennsylvania Journal* for October 16, 1776, said that the "resentment of the people . . . is so great and so general against the new form of government that the only question that now engages their attention, is, how they shall get rid of it."

The features of the Constitution which became the chief subjects of discussion were the unicameral legislature and

---

[23] *Pa. Gaz.*, Feb. 18, 1789. The writer also said that "it was forced upon the State by a few needy men, while the best men of the State were in the field opposing the enemies of their country." While the latter statement is true, it must be borne in mind that the common soldier and the associator were those who most ardently supported the new Constitution.

[24] MS, *Lamberton Scotch-Irish Coll.*, (Hist. Soc. of Pa.), II, no. 19.

[25] Nevins, *op. cit.*, p. 128.

[26] *Letters and Papers*, pp. 258-59.

the Supreme Executive Council, provisions concerning religion, the enlarged franchise, and the oaths required.[27]

1. Unicameral Legislature

In the chapter dealing with the work of the Convention we have seen the lack of unanimity in that body, hence opposition to the plan of the majority soon arose. The same was true on the outside. The fierce struggle over the Constitution probably began with the letter of "K" in the *Pennsylvania Packet* of September 24, which opposed the work of the radical leaders, and particularly denounced the single legislative assembly. It said that the Supreme Executive Council had nothing to do because all power was vested in the Assembly with the "most unbounded liberty and yet no barriers." "K" was immediately answered by "C" in the *Pennsylvania Evening Post* of September 26, with a defense of the Assembly, saying there "never was so many, nor such safe checks ever provided against the abuse of power in any legislature."[28] "Demophilus," in the *Pennsylvania Journal* of September 25, said he was "deeply affected to find the reluctance with which many of our principal people receive the plan of a single legislature." He himself was never "fully in the measure," but distrusting his own judgment, was con-

---

[27] Reed, *op. cit.*, II, 19. The Council of Censors was likewise severely criticized.

[28] "C" then enumerated the various checks, such as: a) doors of the Assembly were to be open; b) members were elected annually; c) even an unworthy man, continually elected by the people, is excluded at the end of four years; d) members of the Assembly were excluded from filling any executive department; e) the printing of the laws and referring them to the next succeeding session, thereby giving every man "an opportunity of judging of the propriety of enacting such law, and instructing his Representative accordingly, so that no law can ever pass against the sense of the people, nor be continued if its operation is contrary to their interests." As pointed out in chapter v (p. 185), Paine said this provision did not have the effect intended. Indeed, Paine later wrote, "The principal defect in the constitution . . . was, that it was subject, in practice, to too much precipitancy, but the ground work . . . was good." *The Political Writings of Thomas Paine*, I, 439-55.

tent to wait for some trial or experiment. "I now see," he said, "the very experiment will be mischievous if not fatal. . . . In no other question upon the proposed form are the friends of free and equal government so much divided." Alexander Graydon wrote that the Constitution was "severely reprobated by those, who thought checks and balances necessary to a legitimate distribution of the powers of government."[29]

"Casca" was rather bitter against the Convention because it "confounded a Bill of Rights—a Constitution—and laws together." Had it adopted such a distinction the "Counsel of Censors and Septennial Convention would have been unnecessary, and the state of Pennsylvania would not have been disgraced with a Frame of Government full of contradictions and absurdities."[30] This was a valid criticism,[31] and was likewise made by Dr. Benjamin Rush. In an excellent paper— *Observations upon the Present Government of Pennsylvania in Four Letters*[32]—he said that the "Bill of Rights confounded *natural* and *civil* rights in such manner as to produce endless confusion in society. It comprehends many things which belong to a Bill of Rights, and to Laws, and which form no part of a Constitution." Dr. Rush also opposed a single legislature.

The single chamber, on the other hand, had its supporters. One writer said, "To preserve government simple and free from improper controuls, they have vested the power of making laws in your immediate representatives [he is addressing the Freemen of Pennsylvania]; the men of your choice, who can have no interest independent of yours. This wise, this necessary, preservative against tyranny has given very great offense to some of our gentry, . . ."[33] Another writer said that the Convention "concluded justly that the power of government really resided in the body of the people, and

---

[29] *Memoirs*, p. 286.
[30] *Eve. Post*, Oct. 31, 1776.
[31] *Vide supra*, chapter v.
[32] Pub. by Styner & Cist, 1777.
[33] *Eve. Post*, Oct. 15, 1776.

considering we have no hereditary King nor Lords, whose prerogatives entitle them to negatives in their own right, a negative, or power of controuling the *united will* of the *whole community,* is not only *absurd* and *ridiculous,* but *highly dangerous.*"[34]

As the battle continued it became more severe. "Cassius," in the *Evening Post,* supported the Constitution against its denouncers and said that "F" has "told three as notorious lies as were ever uttered within the limits of one sentence." "Then comes Brutus," Cassius says, "who is so blinded with passion that he cannot give a genuine transcript of the oath of allegiance, . . ."[35] Edward Shippen, in a letter to Colonel Burd, wrote: "I say nothing about politics in letters. . . ."[36] Feeling at this time was tense. Since the radicals' hatred for the old ruling class was even more fierce than for the English enemy, it was wise to preserve a discreet silence. It was hard to distinguish between the Anti-Constitutionalists and the Loyalists who took shelter under their wing. This made it difficult to tell to what what extent one could criticize the Constitution.[37] General Arthur St. Clair, in a letter to James Wilson, said: "I am not sure if it may not be Treason to offer to find Fault with what our Convention has done, . . ."[38]

Soon people from other states entered into the controversy. A man in Maryland wrote to a friend in Pennsylvania that the frame of government which the Pennsylvanians established "has not only alarmed the friends of liberty and of America in your state, but also in this. The baneful influence of your weak counsels has extended beyond your state. It is the duty of every honest American to expose the absurdity and fatal consequences which will attend your state in particular, and America in general, by a submission to the gov-

---

[34] *Pa. Gaz.,* Mar. 26, 1777.

[35] *Eve. Post,* Oct. 8, 1776.

[36] *Letters and Papers,* p. 252.

[37] See Reed, *op. cit.,* II, 26.

[38] MS, (Hist. Soc. of Penna.), Oct. 21, 1776. St. Clair's description of the Constitution is interesting. He said it appeared to him "exactly like Voids description of Matter before the Creation."

ernment, or rather system of slavery, proposed by your late Convention."[39] Friends of the Constitution deeply resented this, and a reply in the very next issue of the same paper said: "This letter is rash and abusive and unlike the production of any of the Marylanders of distinction, who are remarkably polite in their address and behavior."[40]

2. Religion

It has previously been stated that the action of the Convention in submitting the Constitution to the people for consideration can be regarded as little more than a gesture. The only serious discussion evoked during this period of "consideration"[41] concerned religion.

The forty-seventh section of the first draft of the Constitution—the one appearing in the press—read as follows: "Laws for the encouragement of virtue and prevention of vice and immorality, shall be made and constantly kept in force, and provision shall be made for their due execution." The Reverend Henry Melchior Muhlenberg, senior minister of the united German Lutheran Congregations in Pennsylvania, from whose letter the following account is taken,[42] stated that on Monday, September 16, "The Provost of the College" came to him unexpectedly "and said that the condition of the Christian religion seemed in danger after independence had been declared and a new form of government was in process of formation; that no care at all had been taken to acquire even the outer ramparts. . . ." The Provost showed Rev. Muhlenberg a paragraph which he thought should be added to the forty-seventh section. The latter was pleased with the paragraph but believed they could do little about it. "What can despised preachers effect with a Rump Parliament?" he wrote. An informal gathering of a few of the

[39] *Eve. Post*, Oct. 24, 1776.
[40] *Ibid.*, Oct. 26.
[41] See *supra*, pp. 163-64.
[42] Letter dated "Providence, October 2, 1776," and printed in the *Pa. Mag.*, XXII, 129-31.

leading ministers was held to discuss the question, and Muhlenberg remarked at the meeting that "it now seems as if a Christian people were ruled by Jews, Turks, Spinozists, Deists, perverted naturalists." The ministers "were learned pillars," he said, "and would have much to answer for if they were now silent." The Reverend Dr. Alison[43] did not feel alarmed, saying that "it was of no consqeuence and it would be sufficient if the officials would only give testimony to the Supreme Being as creator and preserver of all things." This statement evoked some discussion, but the meeting accomplished nothing.

This group decided to meet again and to invite more protestant preachers. At a meeting the following day the Provost and Vice-Provost of the College and five ministers decided to request the Convention to annex to the forty-seventh section the paragraph which they had drawn up. One of their number was appointed to go to Dr. Franklin, the President of the Convention, "to ask permission to wait upon him." Franklin "condescendingly sent word," says Muhlenberg, "that he would come to us." He met with them and after being shown the said paragraph, promised to present it to the Convention. Rev. Muhlenberg discussed the matter with the Lutheran Church Council that afternoon. He was supported unanimously, so a petition to the Convention was drawn up and signed by him for the Lutheran congregation of the State and by the Rev. L. Weyberg on behalf of the Reformed. It was presented to the Convention on September 25, and after being read was ordered to lie on the table.[44] The petition asked the "Hon[ble] Convention to annect or add unto the 47th Section of the proposed Plan the following Words viz: 'and all religious Societies and Bodies of Men heretofore united and incorporated for the Advancement of Virtue and Learning and for other pious and charitable Purposes, shall be encouraged and protected in the Enjoyment of the Privileges, Immunities and Estates,

---

[43] For a previous mention of Dr. Alison, vide supra, p. 7, note 13.

[44] Proceedings, p. 53.

which they were accustomed to enjoy and might or could of Right have enjoyed under the Laws and former Constitution of this State.' " It closed by stating, "A Serious Attention to, and condescending compliance with our humble Petition' will rendre great Satisfaction, Security and Ease to all regular christian Societies and Denominations in this State and especially to your humble Petitioners. . . ."

The paragraph the ministers suggested was adopted, for section 45 of the final draft (corresponding to the forty-seventh section of the one which appeared in the press) contained their suggestion with only a few minor changes. The substitution of "religion" for "virtue" was the most important.

After the Constitution was proclaimed a sharp debate took place on article ten, which required every member of the Assembly to subscribe to an oath professing faith in one God, and acknowledging the divine inspiration of the Old and New Testaments.[45] "A Follower of Christ" said that this section "greatly affects the Christian religion and the salvation of souls." He maintained that the bars which William Penn's *Declaration of Rights* had created against "Deists, Jews, Mahomedans, and other enemies of Christ" had now been removed, and all such could sit in the House of Representatives.[46] He called upon the ministers to oppose the section and "secure to the people of Pennsylvania that inestimable blessing of the gospel of Christ," and stated that if "blasphemers of Christ and the holy blessed Trinity, despisers of Revelation and the holy bible, may be Legislators, Judges, Counsellors and Presidents in Pennsylvania, Wo unto the city! Wo unto the land."[47]

The same Rev. Henry M. Muhlenberg very early opposed the Constitution itself. He wrote, "The good, honest men who sit in conventions and the like [assemblies] may indeed

[45] See *supra*, pp. 179-81.

[46] Under Penn's *Declaration of Rights* Catholics could sit in the Assembly, but in 1705 an act was passed providing that thereafter only Protestants were eligible. *Statutes at Large*, II, 219.

[47] *Eve. Post*, Sept. 26, 1776.

be good fathers, citizens, mechanics, and even Christians but there are always among them cunning heads and perverse hearts, who, by false speech and art of disputing, outwit and entrap the simple-hearted ones, . . . " This interesting comment on conventions was followed by a febrile, sarcastic exhortation to the Christian people of Pennsylvania.

Up, up, you protestant congregations, strive, give up life and all else to retain the priceless freedom of conscience and you shall hereafter enjoy as a reward the freedom of conscience that you need believe in no Redeemer, no Spirit, no Word of God. If you only acknowledge a Superior Being with the mouth, you may assist in the government, moreover, you may deride, calumniate the enthusiasm and the old fashioned ideas concerning the Bible, a Savior of the world, the Spirit, and because the printing presses are to be free, place them on public exhibition and lead them in triumph. The law will protect you if you acknowledge a Superior Being. Where the Lord does not build the house, where the Lord does not watch over the city, if such incarnate spirits of elevated taste should succeed, there would very soon arise such grand, politic, free republics as flourished before the Flood in Sodom, and before the destruction of Jerusalem. . . .[48]

"Orator Puff" and "Peter Early" continue their dialogue on the subject of religion. "Peter" says:

Will not the people, and especially the clergy, be exceedingly alarmed to think in the midst of so dreadful a war, that we have, *by the public authority* of so great a state, passed such strongly implied censures of contempt on our holy religion, & *weakened the securities of it by law established,* while, at the same time, we are continually imploring the assistance of heaven in supplications and form of that religion. Is not this hypocrisy? The former qualification required by law was a positive, clear, direct, *"profession of the* christian faith," . . . How can we ask or expect success, while we thus deliberately, in the face of the whole world, are undermining the religion graciously delivered to us by Heaven, with such amazing circumstances of mercy? I tremble at the thought.[49]

---

[48] *Pa. Mag.,* XXII, 130-31. Letter dated Oct. 2, 1776.
[49] *Eve. Post,* Oct. 15, 1776.

Another writer asks, "Were the members of the Convention, Christians?" He thought that the "antient and approved test" was so "mangled" that "those who do not believe the *Christian* religion, may avail themselves of some such evasion or equivocation," and inquires whether the framers of the Constitution thought that "there were not *Christians* enough in *Pennsylvania* to fill the offices of State, who were willing to take the test of that antient and approved form?" In conclusion, he asks if it was not manifest "that the design of this attack on our religion was to lessen our reverence for it" and whether "any State on this continent . . . has treated the Christian religion with so much contempt as our Convention has done?"[50]

These examples suffice to show the heated discussion engendered by this question. The religious freedom which the Constitution granted was, of course, enthusiastically defended. One supporter, after the most burning denunciations and vituperations of its opponents, said to them: "You ransacked the Constitution through every page and paragraph, to find some real flaw in it that might expose it to contempt, but drove to the shameful shift of irritating religious spleen, your low art persuaded people that the *church,* and indeed our *land* was *in danger,* because the Athanasian Creed, Heidelberg Cathecism, Westminister Confession of Faith, or some other much esteemed *form of sound words* was not literally *transcribed* into our Constitution, and every man obliged to make solemn oath that he believed that formula before he could enjoy the rights of a citizen. . . ."[51]

---

[50] *Pa. Journal,* Oct. 16, 1776. The writer's pseudonym was "In hoc Signo vinces." As we have seen, the Pennsylvania Constitution was more liberal in regard to religion than most of the new constitutions. *Vide supra,* pp. 179-81.

[51] "Demophilus," in the *Pa. Gaz.,* March 19, 1777. In replying to "Phocion," "Demophilus" says: "Whether you are that proprietarian retainer—that compromising farmer—that procrastinating delegate, whose chilling breath backened all the measures of Congress, [probably refers to James Wilson] whether you are that piddling politician—that summer soldier [John Dickinson is undoubtedly referred to here]. . . ." etc. This shows the fierce personal attacks. John Adams two years before called Dickinson a "piddling Genius." *Supra,* p. 90.

"DETECTOR" wrote sarcastically that the "penetration" of the people of the West had not reached "so far as to discover that the vengeance of heaven might reasonably be expected to be poured down upon them for abetting a system in which the Christian Faith was treated with such disrespect as to omit inserting its most *mysterious* and disputable *credenda* into a test of qualification for civil offices. . . . "[52]

3. Opposition to the Oath

Aside from the question of religion, the most caustic fulminations were directed against the oaths to be taken by the electors and the elected. In order to secure the permanence of the Constitution and to fill all the offices with their own supporters, the framers enacted a series of oaths. These oaths were to be administered not only to every officer of government, but also to every elector at the polls. Those taking them swore that they would not "directly or indirectly do any act or thing prejudicial or injurious to the constitution, or government thereof, as established by the convention."[53]

"Brutus" denounced the oath in scathing terms. "Every man of sense in the state complains of" the imperfections of the Constitution, he said, "and yet in order to entitle himself to the privilege of an elector, he must swear or affirm that he will never 'directly' or 'indirectly' expose these imperfections, or propose an amendment of them. Remember, my countrymen," he concludes, "that slavery is a potion equally bitter, whether it comes to us thro' the hands of Lord North, Lord Howe, or My Lords the Members of the Convention."[54] John Adams, in a letter to his wife on October 4, 1776, said: "The proceedings of the late convention are not well liked by the best of the Whigs. Their constitution is reprobated, and the oath with which they endeavored to prop it . . . is

---

[52] *Eve. Post*, Nov. 12, 1776.

[53] Section 40. In the Constitution this applied only to officers of the government, but the Convention, on September 26, declared that "Every elector before his vote shall be received" had to take the same oath. *Proceedings*, pp. 53-4. See *supra*, pp. 193-94.

[54] *Pa. Journal*, October 2, 1776. A reply by "A Friend to Truth and the People" is found in the same paper for October 9.

execrated."[55] The mass meeting in Philadelphia on October 22 resolved: "That the conduct of the late Convention in prescribing oaths and affirmations, to be taken for the support of a Constitution [is] unprecedented on this continent." George Stevenson, chairman of the Committee of Inspection and Observation of Cumberland County, said that he thought the Design of the members of the late Convention when they enjoyn'd that Oath was to secure to themselves Seats in the next Assembly, my reason is this. Such only as approve of & take the Oath are entituled [sic] to Vote, such as like & swallow the Oath, of Consequence like and approve of the Makers of it, and will give them Seat in the House of Assembly. . . .[56]

"W" said in the *Pennsylvania Packet* on October 22, 1776, that Cromwell's action in placing "guards before the Parliament house with orders to suffer none of the members to enter" until they took a similar oath, should remove "from the oath of the Convention the reproach of novelty."

At the meetings in the various counties the vote on taking the oath was generally unfavorable. The Committee of Carlisle, for example, on October 8 resolved, "That they would not take that oath."[57] But at a later meeting of the County of Cumberland, held at the same place, "in pursuance of a letter of the Committee of Correspondence, requesting them to collect the sense of the inhabitants of their respective townships, concerning the oath," it appeared "that a great majority were satisfied with the oath and the constitution."[58]

The Council of Censors was likewise attacked. In one handbill it was referred to as "the political INQUISITION."[59]

---

[55] *Letters to his Wife*, I, 168-69. In the same letter Adams said: "We live in the age of political experiments. Among many that will fail, some I hope will succeed. Pennsylvania will be divided and weakened, and rendered much less vigorous in the cause by the wretched ideas of government which prevail in the minds of many people in it."

[56] *R. P.*, VI, no. 35.

[57] *Pa. Eve. Post*, Oct. 17, 1776.

[58] *Ibid.*, Oct. 29. Cumberland County was divided into 23 townships and at this meeting 18 were represented, 12 of which were satisfied with the Constitution and oath while 6 townships were not.

[59] Pennsylvania Broadsides, folio 144 (Library of Congress).

b. ORGANIZED OPPOSITION

These letters and addresses to the people continued in increasing numbers after the Constitution was adopted. Organized opposition to the Frame of Government did not begin, however, until the latter part of October. Christopher Marshall tells us that on October 17 he went to the Philosophical Hall in response to a printed invitation, "in order to consider a mode to set aside sundry improper and unconstitutional rules laid down by the late Convention, . . ."[60] At this meeting some amendments were agreed to "after sundry deliberate proposals, . . . and ordered immediately to be printed, with the reasons that induced this company to make such alterations, to be published immediately for the perusal and approbation of the whole State at large, . . ."[61] It was also agreed that a general town meeting be held the following Monday at the State House, "the proceedings of which [were] to be printed and immediately transmitted to all the Counties in the State. The whole of the meeting was conducted with great order and solemnity, and broke up past ten, in great union."[62]

The plans for the town meeting progressed rapidly, and on October 21 about fifteen hundred people assembled in the State House Yard, ostensibly to hold a debate on the Constitution. The real design of the conservative leaders was to prevent the Constitution from being put into effect, since the elections of Assemblymen and Councilors were near at hand. Colonel Bayard was chosen chairman and the meeting "proceeded to business, which was conducted with prudence and decency till dark." At this meeting the chief speakers against the Constitution were John Dickinson and Thomas McKean; its supporters were James Cannon, Timothy Matlack, Dr. Young, and Colonel Smith of York County.[63] The meeting continued the next morning when the resolutions

---

[60] *Diary.*
[61] *Ibid.*
[62] *Ibid.*
[63] Marshall's *Diary*, Oct. 21.

partially discussed the day before "were maturely considered" and "carried by a large majority."[64]

These resolutions denounced both the Convention and the Constitution in no uncertain terms. They said that the former exceeded its powers; "That the said Constitution *unnecessarily* deviates from all resemblance to the former government of this state, to which the people have been very accustomed"; that the people do not desire such *"strange innovations"*; that it differed not only "from that to which the people have been accustomed, but *in many important articles* from Every Government that has lately been established in *America* on the authority of the people— . . ." At this point an elaborate footnote, written by an expert pen, was added. It was a severe and succinct indictment of the Constitution, declaring:

1st. It established only a *single* legislative body. 2dly. It renders the *judicial* department dependent on that *single* legislative body, who may remove any judge from his office *without* trial, for anything they please to call "misbehavior." 3dly. It renders the executive dependent on that *single* legislative body; by whom alone the *executive* officers are to be paid for their services,—and by whom, from the great disproportion between the members of the Assembly and Council, the President and Vice-President must always be annually chosen,—besides, that every officer, *executive* or *judicial*, may be impeached *by the Assembly*, before six of the Council *thus dependent on the Assembly*, and be tried or condemned. 4thly. It erects no *Court of Appeals*, more necessary here than in some other States, as our Supreme Court may try causes in the first instance, and finally determine them, so that there is no mode settled for correcting their errors.

Returning to other objections the resolutions said that the "Constitution is confused, inconsistent, and dangerous"; that "the late Convention did not allow time to the people of this State to take into their consideration the proposed frame

---

[64] *Ibid.*, Oct. 22. One Anti-Constitutionalist wrote that "we had all the rich great men and the wise men, the lawyers and doctors on our side." *Pa. Gaz.*, November 13, 1776.

of government."[65] They deprecated the conduct of the Convention "in prescribing oaths and affirmations to be taken for the support of a constitution unprecedented on this continent," and said that at the election to be held on November fifth, the electors, as well as the Assemblymen elect, ought not to take the oath or affirmation "required by the ordinance of the late Convention." One of the resolutions declared that "the said Assembly ought to have full power to make such alterations and amendments in the Constitution aforesaid, as the said Assembly shall judge to be proper."[66] The true intent of the meeting was revealed in the last resolution, which stated that "no Counsellors ought to be chosen at the election to be held on the fifth day of November next."

The work of the meeting did not end with the drawing up of these resolutions. Together with letters and newspapers they were sent to the County Committees throughout the State to stir up opposition.[67]

At a meeting of citizens of Philadelphia held on November 2, 1776, in the Philosophical Society Hall, an address to the inhabitants was drawn up which denied the charges that they were "aiming to bring back the late royal and proprietary of this State," and declared that a "SEVEN YEARS familiarity with slavery may render us ever afterwards unfit to assert and maintain the privileges of freemen." The Address also stated that "There are more evils in our new frame of government than have been pointed out by the pen or tongue of any man."[68]

Thus the battle continued and was even more bitter when the time came to inaugurate the new government under the Constitution. To prevent this inauguration no efforts were spared by its opponents.

---

[65] See *supra*, pp. 163-64; 216.

[66] This was the 27th resolution. The 29th stated that the Assembly should submit such amendments to the people.

[67] *R. P.*, VI, no. 35. The resolutions appeared in the *Pa. Eve. Post* on Oct. 22; *Pa. Gaz.*, Oct. 23, and the *Pa. Packet* on Oct. 23.

[68] Pennsylvania Broadsides, folio 144 (Library of Congress).

3. *Organization of the New Government*

The Charter government of Pennsylvania was dead, but some people, believing in miracles, hoped for a resurrection. Reports came to Philadelphia that on October first, the old election day, elections for Assemblymen had been held in Chester and Bucks counties,[69] both of which were strongholds of the former rulers. The Council of Safety wrote Henry Wynkoop, of Bucks County, that it was "Informed that some evil minded persons disafected to the present Government have attempted to prevent its Establishement by supporting the late Government."[70] That these two were the only elections held is confirmed by John Adams who wrote, "The first day of October, the day appointed by the charter . . . for the annual election of Representatives, has passed away, and two counties only have chosen members, Bucks and Chester. The Assembly is therefore dead. . . ."[71]

Having failed in their attempts to revive the old government,[72] the opponents of the Constitution soon conceived of other plans to thwart the efforts of the "Constitutionalists." The elections under the new Constitution were to be held on Tuesday, November 5, which proved to be one of the most exciting election days in Pennsylvania's history. The opponents of the Constitution had three distinct plans: first, they determined to vote against all supporters of the Constitution as representatives in the Assembly; secondly, to persuade the voters to refuse to take the oaths required of electors; and thirdly, to cast no ballots for members of the Supreme Executive Council, but vote on the abstract question whether or not there should be Councilors. The underlying aim was to force a compromise upon the radicals by electing a sufficiently large number of the Assembly to prevent the im-

---

[69] Marshall, *Diary*, Oct. 4, 1776.

[70] *R. P.*, V, no. 36.

[71] *Letters to his wife*, I, 168-69. The "Moravian Archives" for October 1 stated: "To-day there was no election for assemblymen." Printed in the *Pa. Mag.*, XII, 391.

[72] It is exceedingly doubtful if these attempts were taken at all seriously.

mediate execution of the Constitution. If possible, they were to call a convention to prepare another form of government or revise the new Constitution, publish the results of their work and dissolve. In this manner, as one writer declared, "Before Christmas at farthest, a new government can be formed."[73]

With these ends in view meetings were held in Philadelphia and throughout the State. As early as October 25 a meeting of the Northern and Southern Districts of Philadelphia County was held at Camping Town, "to consider how to carry on the elections."[74] In Philadelphia the movement started on October 31 with a meeting at the Coffee House to "appoint Inspectors and to think of six suitable persons to represent" the city in the Assembly.[75] Its proceedings were referred to a larger assemblage to be held the following evening. So few attended this meeting that it was decided to postpone "the full discussion of affairs" until the next evening.[76]

On November second "a large [and] respectable number of citizens" met at the Philosophical Hall and drew up the ticket of the Anti-Constitutional party. Their nominees were George Clymer, Robert Morris, John Cadwalader, John Bayard, Michael Shubart, and Joseph Parker.[77] It was decided to draw up the proceedings of the meeting and "have them printed in handbills and distributed through the City before or on the Election Day, . . ."[78] The Constitutional party chose their candidates and were likewise active.

At the same time similar meetings were being held in the counties. The situation in Cumberland County is illustrative. The resolutions of the gathering of October 22, received

---

[73] *Pa. Journal,* October 16, 1776. For a further discussion of these plans see Reed, *op. cit.,* II, 22; Oberholtzer, *Robert Morris,* pp. 23-4; Marshall, *Diary,* Nov. 8; and Lincoln, *op. cit.,* p. 284.

[74] Marshall, *Diary,* p. 99.

[75] *Ibid.,* p. 100.

[76] *Ibid.,* p. 101. The meeting of Oct. 22 had, of course, already decided that no councilors were to be elected.

[77] *Ibid.,* pp. 101-02.

[78] *Ibid.,* p. 102. See *supra,* p. 225, for extracts from the handbill.

there on the twenty-seventh, were transcribed by George Stevenson, chairman of the County Committee, and sent by him, together with a newspaper and a few words from himself to the different parts of the County.[79] A meeting was held and the ticket selected, but Stevenson was not too optimistic, for he wrote that "the Town of Carlisle will furnish near twenty Votes, and I believe no more, for And^w. McKee (who will swallow the Oath, if there were as many Fish-Hooks in it as there are Letters) is appointed Inspector of the Town, therefore a non-juror can't give a Ticket." Not a single opponent of the Constitution was elected from Cumberland County.[80]

In some cases the elections were controlled by the Associators who made voting difficult for non-Associators and for those who refused to take the oath. None of the Moravians from Bethlehem attended the election in November for Inspectors because it was understood that the Associators would hold the election "according to battalions," and neither non-Associators nor non-jurors would be permitted to vote.[81]

The Constitutionalists, as might have been expected, carried most of the western counties and elected both Assemblymen and Councilors.[82] In Philadelphia the story was different. Christopher Marshall, one of the election judges, tells us that he went to the State House about nine in the morning and remained there until near two the following morning, "where all matters in general were conducted with great harmony and concord in the house; two or three small buffetings, I heard about the door in the street, but soon went over." The whole Anti-Constitutional ticket was victorious, and by a vote of 406 to 211 it was decided that no Councilors be elected.[83] In Philadelphia County the vote on the above ques-

[79] R. P., VI, no. 35. Letter to James Wilson, Nov. 4, 1776.

[80] Ibid. The ticket which Stevenson predicted would win was selected by the Stony Ridge Convention. Every man on the ticket was chosen.

[81] Levering, op. cit., pp. 450-51.

[82] Pa. Eve. Post, Nov. 12, 1776.

[83] Marshall, Diary, Nov. 5. The votes for the assemblymen were as follows: Parker, 682; Clymer, 413; Robert Morris, 410; Samuel Morris, Jr., 407—

tion was 370 to 133.[84] In both the city and county elections it was stated that electors omitted to take the oath prescribed by the Constitution.[85] Under these conditions it is not surprising that the total vote was small. "Phocion," writing in the *Pennsylvania Journal*,[86] said that out of an electorate of 50.000 or 60,000 in the state, not more than 2,500 voted. A "Declaration of the Inhabitants of Cumberland County" stated:

Those who Assume the title of "the Representatives of the Freemen of the Commonwealth of Pennsylvania" [referring to the new Assembly] are not in our Judgment entitled to that Character, because they were not elected by a Tenth part of the Freemen of the State, and Because the Freedom of Election was most Injuriously Violated by an Arbitrary and Unreasonable Oath.[87]

No exact figures are available, but it is true that the vote was not large, for even some Whigs declined to vote. As Allen recorded in his *Diary*, the Constitution "split the Whigs to pieces, the majority disliking the frame & therefore not voting for the new Assembly, which was of course chosen by very few."[88]

The Conservatives, victorious in Philadelphia, held a public meeting at the State House. Instructions to the city's representatives, previously drawn up by a group of men, were read by Dr. Benjamin Rush. The people expressed their approval by raising their hands. The representatives were asked to use their "utmost influence to prevent the execution" of the Constitution and to demand its prompt revision.[89] De-

---

John Cadwalader withdrew as a candidate in favor of his cousin Samuel Morris; Bayard, 397; and Shubart, 393. Joseph Parker appears to have been chosen by both parties. The defeated candidates were: Rittenhouse, 278; Matlack, 268; Jonathan B. Smith, 273; Jacob Schriner, 269; and Thomas Wharton, Jr., 268.

[84] *Ibid.*, Nov. 6. See letter of George Ross, Library of Congress, Mss. Div., Penna. Misc. Box no. 7.

[85] *Pa. Packet*, May 27, 1777; *Diary of James Allen*, Jan. 25, 1777.

[86] March 12, 1777.

[87] MS, *Lamberton Scotch-Irish Coll.*, II, no. 19 (Hist. Soc. of Pa.).

[88] Jan. 25, 1777.

[89] Marshall, *Diary*, Nov. 8.

spite the Conservative victory in Philadelphia the radicals by carrying most of the western counties dominated the new Assembly which met on Thursday, November 28. Of the seventy-two members, twenty-six had been in the Convention and thirteen had served in the Provincial Conference.[90]

There was, however, a determined minority, powerful enough to prevent a quorum and to dictate its own terms. Led by John Dickinson, Robert Morris, and George Clymer this minority "threatened to leave the rest if they proceeded to business, . . ."[91] At this crisis John Dickinson made a proposal to extricate the Assembly from its embarrassment. He proposed that the minority

Consent to the choice of a Speaker, sit with the other members, and pass such acts as the public affairs may require; provided that the other members, the majority, will agree to call a free Convention for a full and fair representation of the freemen of Pennsylvania, to meet on or before the ———— day of January next, for the purpose of revising the Constitution framed by the late Convention, and making such alterations and amendments therein as shall by them be thought proper, and making such ordinances as the circumstances of affairs may render necessary: provided that no part of said Constitution be carried into execution by this Assembly, and provided that this Assembly be dissolved before the meeting of the Convention.[92]

a. BRITISH INVASION

News had already been received of the British invasion of New Jersey, so the factions laid aside their quarrels long enough to elect John Jacobs, of Chester County, Speaker, and Michael Hillegas, Treasurer, but refused to call a convention as Dickinson and his followers requested. Consequently, he and his friends withdrew from the Assembly.[93] After the

---

[90] Six served in both bodies. See *Journals of the House of Representatives of the Commonwealth of Pennsylvania* (hereafter referred to as *Journals*), I, 34-5 and 97-8.

[91] Allen, *Diary*, Jan. 25, 1777.

[92] Stillé, *Life of Dickinson*, pp. 208-09.

[93] Dickinson shortly afterwards received a letter from Dr. Rush in which he said: "While I disapprove most heartily of the coalition of parties in the

followers of Dickinson left, a quorum could seldom be mustered because some of the delegates had never taken their seats. With the Supreme Executive Council unorganized, the government was in a state of paralysis.[94] The Council of Safety continued to act as the executive head of the government.[95] It was stirred to activity in the middle of November when word was received that General Howe was moving across New Jersey toward Philadelphia. On November 25 Congress requested the Council of Safety to call out immediately "all the associators in the city of Philadelphia, and its liberties, and in the counties of Philadelphia, Chester, Bucks, and Northampton."[96] On December 2 Congress again requested the Council of Safety to "send off expresses immediately to those counties who have been desired to send forth their associators, urging them forthwith to march out, to oppose the hasty advance of the enemy."[97] It is apparent from these requests of Congress that the situation was serious; new armies had to be raised immediately. Would the "mob," as they were called, turn out again, when the "better people" sat at home in idleness and luxury? A crisis had, indeed, been reached. Stirring appeals to the Associators appeared in the press. "Hampden," in the *Evening Post,* wrote:

The time is at last come in which the salvation of this country depends upon the exertions of the individuals of this state. The enemy have collected all their strength, and are determined, if possible, to spend this winter in Philadelphia. For Heaven's sake

---

Assembly, I cannot help lamenting that you have left the House upon the account of it. The members from Westmoreland and Bedford will turn the scale in our favor as soon as they come to town, and we shall have a convention and a consistent legislature in spite of all their cunning and malice. . . ." Quoted in Stillé, *op. cit.,* p. 211.

[94] George Stevenson, of Carlisle, lamented the fact that Pennsylvania did not have a "full and free representative body." *R. P.,* IX, no. 25.

[95] Wm. Leas, chairman of the York County Committee, writing to the Council of Safety in Dec., 1776, said: "Your Board is now the only Body in the Province that has the most General Approbation of the People. . . ." *R. P.,* VII, no. 96.

[96] *Journals of Congress.*

[97] *Ibid.*

let all disputes about frames of government subside for the present, or we shall be obliged to receive a government from the sword of a proud and successful enemy.[98]

But such appeals had little effect. "Great pains were taken to get the militia out, but in vain; but few were prevailed on to turn out."[99] In spite of the demands of Congress few troops were mustered. On December 9 Congress again urged the Council of Safety "to march what troops they can collect, armed and provided in the best possible manner," to join the army under General Washington.[100] Again the response was small. The radicals had won their battle and were little concerned by the British invasion. The Chairman of the York County Committee told the Council of Safety that "Several men Friendly to the Cause of Liberty are on their March to the Metropolis. But we are sorry to say, many, too many are so lost to Virtue and love of Liberty as to refuse Marching; Notwithstanding all the persuasions and admonitions that have been used to them."[101] George Stevenson wrote from Carlisle that some had gone to defend the state, but "a greater Number, even of the Inhabitants of this County . . . have tarried at home and minded their own private Affairs as unconcern'd as if there was the most profound Peace in the Country, . . ."[102] The Council of Safety was informed that "many of the principal Associators of Col. Hunter's Battalion of Berks County, refuse to march, to join General Washington's army at this Important Crisis, . . . and proceeded even to dare to enforce the resolve of this Council upon them:— . . ."[103] Washington himself, writing from Bucks

---

[98] Nov. 28, 1776.

[99] *Examination of Joseph Galloway*, p. 15. See the exhortations to the citizens to turn out in Pennsylvania Broadsides 144, December, 1776 (Library of Congress).

[100] *Journals of Congress.*

[101] *R. P.*, VII, no. 96.

[102] Letter to James Wilson, Jan. 30, 1777, *R. P.*, IX, no. 25.

[103] *Pa. Arch.*, 4th ser., III, 623. The Council resolved "that Col. Hunter was to collect the well affected, seize the ringleaders of the defection, and send them under guard to Philadelphia." Jan. 18, 1777.

County on December 15 to the Council of Safety, said: "The Spirit of Disaffection that appears in this County, deserves your serious Attention. Instead of giving any Assistance in repelling the Enemy, the Militia have not only refused to obey your general Summons and that of their commanding Officers, but I am told exult at the Approach of the Enemy and our late Misfortunes."[104] Even though paid in advance, almost a whole Lancaster County Battalion commanded by Peter Grubb took their guns and went home instead of marching into New Jersey.[105]

In the face of this languor, even desertion, it is somewhat surprising that by New Year's evening several thousand of the Pennsylvania Militia under General Cadwalader had joined Washington at Trenton,[106] and later had fought in the battle of Princeton where the valiant General Mercer of Philadelphia was killed.

The Council of Safety knew the situation exactly, for in a "Representation to the House of Assembly" it said:

The people are disgusted at the Inconveniences, hardships and Losses which they suffered in their late Service, while Non associators were permitted to remain at home in the peaceable Enjoyment of their professions, and many of them increasing their Wealth by grasping the Trade of the absent Associators, whose patriotic Exertions have been Sneered at, and their hardships & fatigues, and the distresses of their families, insultingly made a jest of . . . It has been Proposed to call out the Battalions of the City and Liberties tomorrow morning, but under these circumstances, with the hardships of a Winter Campaign and the dread

---

[104] MS, (Hist. Soc. of Pa.). Washington said that for such people to have arms was dangerous. He advised the Council to deprive them of their arms, saying that if they thought fit to empower him to do so, he would "undertake to have it done as speedily and effectually as possible." The Council gave him the power.

[105] Information given to the Convention, Sept. 12. Force, *Am. Arch.*, 5th ser., II, 38. While the Convention was sitting news came that the Pennsylvania soldiers on duty in New Jersey were rebellious. Several letters were received from John Dickinson complaining of the "uneasiness" and "desertion." A commission was sent to make an investigation.

[106] T. J. Wertenbaker, *The American People—A History*, pp. 76-7.

of their leaving their Families to perish from the want of the necessaries of Life, what can we Expect from the Class of Men, who live from day to day on the product of their Industry— Mechanicks, Tenants & Laborers, of which to the Scandal of Men in more easy circumstances the Associators of this State are chiefly composed?[107]

Apparently these charges were not exaggerated. Two years before, John Adams wrote that there was "uneasiness among some of the members [of Congress] concerning a contract with Willing and Morris for powder, by which the House, without any risk at all, will make a clear profit of twelve thousand pounds at least."[108] On November 26, 1776, Congress was informed that some persons in the city of Philadelphia, "governed by principles inimical to the cause of America, and with views of avarice and extortion, have monopolized and engrossed shoes, stockings, and other necessaries for the army, whilst the soldiers of the Continent, fighting for the liberties of their country, are exposed to the injuries of the weather, at this inclement season." Congress recommended that the Assembly "adopt such immediate measures for remedying this evil, as their wisdom shall suggest to be adequate to the present purpose, and for preventing like pernicious practices in future."[109]

Thus aroused by Congress and by the people of Pennsylvania, the Assembly resolved on November 29 to "take imidi-

---

[107] *R. P.*, VI, no. 59. The Council proposed that a fine be levied on all able-bodied men from 16 to 50 who refused to enter the service when called upon to do so, and that "reasonable assessment be made on the Estates of those above that age . . ." General Armstrong wrote, "A farther agrievance is with great injustice complained of that many persons above the Age of fifty-three, possess considerable, some of them large property, yet have been under no obligation & contributed nothing—Some few females also are wealthy, should not property defend itself in some form or other? . . ." MS, (Hist. Soc. of Pa.).

[108] *Works*, "Debates in Congress," II, 448 *ff*. See vote of thanks of the Committee of Privates of Philadelphia to the Committee of Inspection on April 2, 1776, "for the steps they have taken to prevent the monopolizing, and too high price of goods. . . ." *Pa. Eve. Post*, April 4, 1776.

[109] *Journals of Congress*, Nov. 26, 1776.

ate [*sic*] Measures to make effectual the Provisions of the late House of Assembly, respecting the collection of Fines imposed by that House on all Non associators,"[110] and that it would "as soon as possible, enact a Militia Law, and take such other Measures as will put the defence of this State on a just and equitable footing—so as to encourage those worthy Associators who freely and virtuously, step forth in the defence of their Country."[111] But nothing was done about the monopolists or profiteers.

From the last of November until news came of Washington's victories at Trenton and Princeton, Philadelphia was in a state of confusion and excitement. Marshall wrote in his *Diary* on December 10: "Our people in confusion, of all ranks, sending all their goods out of town into the country." At a meeting of "Real Whigs" on December 1 it was unanimously agreed to recommend to the Council of Safety that business in Philadelphia and its vicinity end after 12 o'clock the next day, and all stores and shops be shut "in order that the Battalions may be more readily completed and forwarded to join General Washington."[112] On December 2 the Council of Safety resolved "that all the Shops in this City be shut up, that the Schools be broke up and the inhabitants engaged solely in providing for the defence of this City at this time of extreme danger."[113]

To obtain a quorum in the House now became impossible because many Assemblymen were needed to order out the Associators and to prepare the battalions for Howe's advance.[114] Since the state government could not function with-

---

[110] *Vide supra*, pp. 85-6.

[111] *R. P.*, VI, no. 71. A list of the totals of the fines laid on the non-associators in Berks County, given on July 7, 1777, was 2,901 pounds. *Ibid.*, XIII, no. 50.

[112] *Ibid.*, VIII, no. 1. They further resolved that in the present emergency, and until a militia law be enacted, the Council of Safety order out every person between the age of 16 and 50 "for the defence of this State." They also recommended that taxes be laid on all those who do not bear arms.

[113] *Ibid.*, VII, no. 6. *Vide Col. Rec.*, XI, 26.

[114] *Journals*, December 14, 1776.

out a quorum Congress intervened, Philadelphia was placed under martial law, and General Putnam was "constituted chief ruler in this province."[115] On December 12 he issued a Proclamation requesting the inhabitants "not to appear in the streets after ten o'clock at night, as he has given orders to the picquet guard to arrest and confine all persons who may be found in the streets after that hour."[116] Word was also sent to the Assembly that if it did "not agree to act," the Congress "wou'd take the Government of Pennsylvania into their own hands."[117]

Congress itself became alarmed, and on December 12 requested James Wilson to notify the Assembly and the Council of Safety that it was moving to Baltimore.[118] Congress moved there so precipitously that Michael Hillegas, Treasurer of Pennsylvania and also of the United States, left with all the state funds and account books. The Speaker of the House requested the "treasury board of congress to detain the said treasury, till this house have time to call on him and receive the funds now in his hands belonging to this state." This move failed, however, because Congress and the Treasury

---

[115] Marshall, *Diary*, Dec. 8, 1776. *Journals of Congress*, Dec. 10. On the same day that General Putnam was given wide powers "to make the proper defences for the protection and security of" Philadelphia, Congress also ordered General Mifflin to make a tour of the counties of Pennsylvania "to arouse the freemen thereof, to the immediate defence of this city and county," and requested the Assembly to appoint a committee "to make the said tour with General Mifflin, in order to assist him in this good and necessary work." The Assembly did so on December 11th, appointing fourteen men.

[116] Marshall, *Diary, Appendix E.*

[117] *Diary of James Allen*, Jan. 25, 1777. Of course Congress did not actually make such a statement, but by reading their resolutions of December 10th one can readily see that they intimated as much. "A Citizen," writing in the *Eve. Post* on Dec. 7 suggested that a dictator be appointed "for three or six months, with full powers to exert the strength of the state in any way he should think proper against our enemies." He further stated that the present "langour" is due to "placing so *little* power in the hands of the executive branch of government," which is "a most *essential* and fundamental fault in all our new constitutions."

[118] Congress had already decided on December 9 that in case it should be under the necessity of moving from Philadelphia it would adjourn to Baltimore. *Vide Journals of Congress.*

Board couldn't tarry, so a committee had to be sent to Baltimore to get the State's funds. Not until January 18, 1777,
could the Speaker announce "that the *treasury* is now brought
into town . . ."[119]

After the departure of Congress the Assembly dispersed.
From December 14 until January 13 no meetings were
held.[120] Aside from the military dictatorship set up by
Congress, the Council of Safety was now the sole authority.
On December 23 Thomas Wharton, its president, addressed an appeal to the people to exert their utmost influence to prevent the threatened invasion and "to come forth
to the assistance of our worthy General Washington, and our
invaded brethren in the Jersies: . . ."[121] An appeal from
Reading on December 18 touched every human emotion.
To "Friends and Fellow Countrymen" it said that "all is lost
without vigorous Exertions of all the Power & Strength of
this State," and then talked about "Debauching your Wives
& Daughters" and "The ravished Maiden—The buffeted
hoary Head . . . their God & your God call on you to drive
from this once happy Land these bold & Impious Invaders
of our Place."[122]

It is evident that the situation was serious and, as usually
happens under such circumstances, private rights were violated. On January 22, 1777, the Council of Safety directed
that the militia be quartered "upon the Non-Associators who
have not served in this winter's campaign."[123] James Allen re-

---

[119] *Journals*, December 11 & 13, 1776; January 18, 1777.

[120] *Ibid.*, Jan. 13, 1777. A number met and adjourned from day to day,
however. As previously mentioned, many members were on active duty with
the army. When the House did reconvene the Speaker was requested to
write to Timothy Matlack, the clerk, to return immediately from the army
to attend "his office here." *Ibid.*, Jan. 16. Colonel Eckhart requested leave of
absence because he had promised his battalion to accompany them to camp.
The House declared that it could not "at this time dispense with his services," and ordered that he "have a copy of this minute to justify him for
not complying with the aforesaid promise to his battalion." *Ibid.*, Jan. 14,
1777.

[121] *Pa. Eve. Post*, Dec. 28, 1776.

[122] Pennsylvania Miscellaneous MSS, 1776. (Library of Congress.)

[123] *Pa. Eve. Post*, Jan. 25, 1777.

marked, "This province is now Governed by the Council of Safety, who by their Resolves continue to oppress the Non-associators & have put the execution of their decrees & the whole dispensation of Justice into the hands of the field-officers of the several battalions."[124]

It is undeniable that much of the apathy of Pennsylvania towards the war was due to the struggle over the Constitution. And this struggle weakened the resistance expected of Pennsylvania in halting the advance of the British. Brigadier General John Lacey, discussing the refusal of John Cadwalader and Samuel Meredith to accept appointments as brigadier generals,[125] said they "had leaged [sic] themselves with the party hostile to the New Constitution, determined to oppose all measures used to carry it into operation—Their enmity to it was so great, they intirely overlooked the fatal effects their opposition might produce in distroying the general Cause of Independence. . . . "[126] Even the "scarcity of salt," said a circular letter to the Council of Safety, "has furnished the enemies of America with too good an occasion to create uneasiness in the minds of many who have credited their false insinuations and artful tales, calculated to destroy all confidence in this Council and the persons intrusted with the management of our publick affairs."[127] Some people very ingeniously, as one writer observed, ascribed "the high price of beef and mutton to the Constitution, but whether," he asks, "they mean the constitution of the *state,* or of the *stomach,* is not fully defined. However, this I know, that good temper is

---

[124] *Diary,* Jan. 25, 1777. Allen wrote on June 6, 1777, that the "rights of property are no longer preserved, impressing waggons, horses, blankets &c is done by inferior officers for their own convenience."

[125] *Vide Pa. Eve. Post,* May 17, 1777.

[126] *Pa. Mag.,* XXVI, 104. Lacey said that they very unwisely judged this to be the proper time to reform the Constitution "while the Enemy was at our Gates—indeed Among us, . . . for we had a formidable Enemy in the numerous Tories . . . who ketched at this opposition, and fand the Flame they had so auspiciously began Among the Wigs themselves as they conceived, and which they hailed as a happy Omen of their sertain tryumph and victory."

[127] *Pa. Arch.,* 2d ser., I, 648-49.

absolutely necessary in restoring health and strength to either."[128]

Lacey, in his *Memoirs,* says that all was peace and harmony when he left Pennsylvania in the summer of 1776, but upon his return in December he "soon discovered a radical change had taken place in the Political sentiments" of his neighbors and acquaintances. The people "appeared all hostile to each other, Whig & Tory in a state little better [than] open Enemies. . . . I had almost begun to doubt," he says, "whether I had not mistaken my Native Country for that of an Enemies —The Hostility of the Tories was so great to Indipendence, [*sic*] that nothing but cowardice alone prevented their Taking up arms and openly declaring themselves in favour of and joining the British Army."[129] The home of Lacey was Bucks County, a hotbed of Toryism.[130]

But these conditions were found not only in Philadelphia and Bucks counties. Farther west the situation was the same. Colonel Thomas Hartley writing from York to James Wilson on December 22, 1776, said:

Col.[1] Ross and you told me when at Philad[a] that I would find a great Change in the County—your observations were but too true. . . . The disaffected have spared no Pains to improve on those unlucky events. The Committee from mismanagement have lost their authority—there are no Justices—no Law—every one seems to do what he listeth—I am surprized that there are not more Murders & Robberies committed for these ever flourish in anarchy and Confusion. . . .[131]

In January George Stevenson wrote from Carlisle that the inhabitants of Cumberland County had "distilled nearly all the Rye, and now . . . they are beginning to distil Wheat, because Whiskey is now sold at" a higher price than the grain would bring. He said that "if this Destruction of Wheat

---

[128] *Pa. Eve. Post,* May 20, 1777.

[129] *Pa. Mag.,* XXVI, 102.

[130] *Vide Pennsylvania Scrap Book, Bucks County,* (State Library, Harrisburg), I, 65-9; 82-3.

[131] Ms., Gratz Coll. (Hist. Soc. of Pa.). See also *R. P.,* VII, no. 96.

is not stop'd [sic], it will raise the Price of Forage, increase the present scarcity of Beef and Pork, enhance the Price of Bread, and occasion some Degree of Famine, at least the Expence of maintaining our Army will be greatly increased, to the Damage of the united States, not a little. 'Tis said some Farmers have thrash'd their Wheat & mixed it with Rye, to elude the Force of any Act which may be made to prevent distiling [sic] Wheat."[132] Distilling wheat must have been widespread, for Washington wrote he was informed that some "of the Southern States have already passed Acts prohibiting the distilling of unreasonable Quantities of Wheat and other Grain into Whiskey, and I hope Pennsylvania will do the same."[133]

James Allen became exceedingly wroth at the existing conditions, for he said that to "describe the present state of the Province . . . would require a Volume. It may be divided into 2 classes of men, viz. Those that plunder and those that are plundered. No justice has been administered, no crimes punished for 9 months. All power is in the hands of the associators, who are under no subordination to their officers . . . Private friendships are broken off, & the most insignificant now lord it with impunity & without discretion over the most respectable characters. . . ."[134] Such was the critical state of affairs in Pennsylvania during the latter part of that eventful year 1776. Revolutions are glorious only when successful, and success was far distant at that time. The "mob" was triumphant, and those who had controlled the affairs of the State for years were now at the mercy of those who "plundered" —that is, those who had previously been "plundered."

4. Completion of the Organization of the Government

The victories of Washington at Trenton and Princeton greatly ameliorated the bitterness of the party strife in Pennsylvania, so the discussion over the *Frame of Government*

---

[132] *R. P.*, IX, no. 25.
[133] *The Writings of George Washington*, John C. Fitzpatrick *ed.*, VII, 250.
[134] *Diary*, Jan. 25, 1777.

subsided somewhat. Military news now began to occupy a prominent place in the newspapers. Allen recorded in his *Diary* that the "alarm of taking Philad[a] being over matters are returning to the old channel."[135] The sessions of the Assembly were resumed when some of the absenting members returned. On January 14 David Rittenhouse, whose sterling integrity and numerous public services were bound to inspire confidence, was unanimously chosen treasurer to succeed Michael Hillegas. This position he held for the next twelve years.[136]

But not all of the Assemblymen returned. John Dickinson, George Gray, and Thomas Potts, representatives of Philadelphia County, refused their seats. Special writs were issued for an election to be held on February 14 to fill the county's quota, and to choose a representative in the Council. Thomas Wharton, Jr. was selected for the latter position. A week later George Bryan was elected councilor for the City of Philadelphia. The change of sentiment in this action is evident, for the same city in the November elections had decided by a two-thirds majority that no councilors be elected.[137]

In the meantime the vengeance of the Assembly had fallen most heavily upon its delegates in Congress who had opposed the Constitution. With the exception of Benjamin Franklin and Robert Morris the whole delegation was removed on February 5 and staunch supporters of the Constitution ap-

---

[135] *Ibid.*, Feb. 17, 1777.

[136] *Memoirs and Life of David Rittenhouse*, Barton, p. 264. Barton erroneously states that Rittenhouse was chosen the first state treasurer, forgetting that Hillegas was the first incumbent. It is interesting to note that Rittenhouse had been defeated in Philadelphia for a seat in the Assembly in the November election. Timothy Matlack, who likewise suffered defeat, had already been chosen clerk of the House. Both had served in the Convention.

[137] *Vide supra*, p. 228. Robert Morris had been chosen a member of the Assembly in November. Upon his election to Congress his seat was, according to the Constitution, declared vacant by the Speaker. His place had to be filled at this election. These elections were denounced by "Aristides" as unconstitutional. He said that Dickinson, Gray, and Potts "are not said to be dead, to have resigned, to be disqualified, or to be absent." He observed that the election "ordered for choosing also 'one fit person to represent the

pointed.[138] Allen noted in his *Diary* that "The reason for leaving out so many old members, it is said, is that the new light Presbyterian Party have the ascendant in Assembly. . . ."[139] This action was indeed unfortunate, for Congress was deprived of the services of such eminent men as Benjamin Rush and George Ross. Dr. Rush wrote:

During the preceding Autumn I had joined Mr. Dickinson and several other of the most enlightened Whigs in Pennsylvania in public testimony against the constitution. . . . This act had destroyed my popularity with the Assembly that had convened to legislate under that Constitution. I remained in Congress until their next meeting at which time I was left out of their delegation.[140]

This action of the Assembly aroused bitter comment, and, of course, lowered still further its prestige in the minds of many. General Arthur St. Clair, in a letter to James Wilson, said:

I had heard, and heard it with very great Disgust that our Assembly had left you out of the Nomination to Congress, but a little Reflection cured me, for, considering what a contemptible dis-

---

freemen of the said county in the Executive Council'" was "a double deviation—one from the sentiments of the freemen of the county, a majority of whom at the general election voted that there should be *no Counsellors*, the other from the Constitution." *Pa. Eve. Post*, June 5, 1777.

[138] Those chosen on February 5 were Franklin, Morris, Roberdeau, Jonathan B. Smith, and William Moore. The last named declined to serve the next day, so the Assembly agreed to elect a member in his place, and also to add one more to its delegation. This action was probably taken because of the furor aroused by leaving out James Wilson and George Clymer. The new elections were held on February 22 and both these men were then reelected. They had been named by the Convention on July 20, 1776. *Vide Journals*, pp. 108-14; *Journals of Congress;* Burnett, *op. cit.*, II, lxi-lxvii; *supra*, pp. 157-58.

Wilson was quite surprised at his election, and wrote Robert Morris on February 28: "What in the Name of Wonder has induced the Assembly to re-appoint me?" (Burnett, II, lxvi.) Although Morris opposed the Constitution, his importance was such that he could not tactfully be omitted from the Pennsylvania delegation. This was probably the reason for Wilson's final reappointment also.

[139] February 17, 1777.

[140] *An Account of Sundry Incidents*, etc., p. 99.

jointed Body that is, 'tis in some Measure disgraceful to be of their Choice.[141]

a. ORGANIZATION OF THE SUPREME EXECUTIVE COUNCIL

With the election of Thomas Wharton and George Bryan as Councilors, the number of men who were willing to serve enabled the Supreme Executive Council to organize at last. It met on March 4,[142] and at once entered the Assembly to hold a joint session for the election of officers.[143] Thomas Wharton was elected President and George Bryan Vice-President.[144] The selection of Wharton was an admirable one, for he was a conservative, and a candidate whom men of conflicting views would unite to support.[145] Furthermore, he had wide executive experience as a member of the Committee of Safety from June 30, 1775, to July 22, 1776, and as President of the Council of Safety throughout its whole history— from July 24, 1776, to March 13, 1777. George Bryan, the Vice-President, was the powerful political leader of Philadelphia and one of the important figures in framing the Constitution.

The inauguration took place at noon on March 5,[146] "in

---

[141] MS., (Hist. Soc. of Pa.), dated *Morris Town*, March 19, 1777. Referring to Wilson's later election to Congress, St. Clair said: "You are not of their Choice but have been appointed Through Necessity, an acknowledgement of their own Folly and your Superiority."

[142] Only six members were present, however. *Vide* "Minutes of Supreme Executive Council," *Col. Rec.*, XI, 173.

[143] Section 19 of the Constitution.

[144] *Pa. Eve. Post*, Mar. 4, 1777; *Col. Rec.*, XI, 173.

[145] Wharton had opposed the Constitution, for in a letter to Arthur St. Clair written soon after it was adopted, he said: "True it is, there are many faults which I hope one day to see removed; but it is true that, if the Government should at this time be overset, it would be attended with the worst consequences, not only to this State, but to the whole continent in the opposition we are making to Great Britain. If a better frame of government should be adopted, such a one as would please a much greater majority than the present one, I should be very happy in seeing it brought about; and any gentlemen that should be thought by the public qualified to take my seat, should have my hearty voice for it . . ." *Pa. Mag.*, V, 436.

[146] On this day only seven members of the Council were present. *Col. Rec.*, XI, 174.

the presence of a vast concourse of people, who expressed the highest satisfaction on the occasion, by unanimous shouts of acclamation."[147] Thirteen Hessian cannon captured at Princeton fired the salute. After the inauguration the Assembly gave a banquet at the City Tavern to which members of Congress were invited.[148] It was a day of great pomp, and a fitting climax to the efforts of those who had struggled from the early summer of 1776 to establish for Pennsylvania a free and independent government.

It was now thought that the resources of the State could be mobilized to carry on the war. John Evans, a member of the Council from Chester County, wrote Thomas Wharton that "it must give real pleasure to every friend of Liberty & virtue, to behold the dawn of a free and Independent Government, rising out of the Ashes of one that was likely to sap from us all that was worthy a freemans enjoyment. . . ."[149] John Adams wrote, "The Assembly of Pennsylvania is also sitting . . . and are gradually acquiring the confidence of the people, and opposition has subsided."[150] An anonymous writer in the *Evening Post* said, "At present our affairs begin to put on a more favorable appearance. Law and justice may be restored before the spirits of the people are quite debauched, and we may still return into good order without any great exercise of severity, which is rarely the case where men have been long without civil government. . . ."[151] "Good order without any great exercise of severity" was established, and is an early example of the essential humanity, restraint, and tolerance—or perhaps it may be apathy—of the American people. A later example is to be found in the days following the Civil War and the violent political campaigns of later years. During this bitter struggle in Pennsylvania no bloody proscriptions occurred, such as took place in the days of

[147] *Pa. Eve. Post*, Mar. 6, 1777; for further accounts see *ibid.*, and *Pa. Gazette*, March 12.

[148] Scharf and Westcott, *op. cit.*, I, 338.

[149] MS, (Historical Society of Pennsylvania).

[150] *Works*, IX, 451. Letter dated Baltimore, Feb. 3, 1777.

[151] "Philerene," March 18, 1777.

Marius, Sulla, and Anthony in Rome; in the days of Judge Jeffreys in England; in the Reign of Terror in France; or in the liberal uprisings throughout Europe in the nineteenth century.[152]

Since reconvening, the Assembly had been very active and passed legislation to open the courts and to hold elections for justices of the peace. One law was enacted "declaring all offices void excepting the Trustees of the loan office."[153] The Assembly likewise passed a law "enforcing the Continental Currency and the Bills of Credit emitted by Resolves of the late Assembly making them a legal tender."[154]

But it must not be supposed that all opposition to the Constitution and the government had ceased; far from it! A large part of the people never recognized the new government, and many refused to serve under it. Mention has already been made of the refusal of Messrs. Cadwaldader and Meredith to accept commissions as brigadier generals from the Assembly, and the refusal of John Dickinson and his followers to serve in that body. Another important instance of the same thing is the case of Joseph Reed. Although it was known that he was opposed to the dominant party and disliked the Constitution, he was unanimously chosen the first Chief Justice by the Executive Council on March 20, 1777. In his letter to the Council declining the office he said in part:

So far as an individual may be allowed to express his concern, I cannot but lament that the Constitution has not provided a more adequate and earlier mode of improving what is right, and amending what is wrong. If there be any radical weakness of authority proceeding from the Constitution, if, in any respects, it opposes the genius, temper, or habits of the governed, I fear, unless a

---

[152] Many Europeans have often marveled at the tranquillity and calmness with which the people of the United States accept the results of a most fiery and violent political campaign. *Vide* Lecky's *American Revolution*, ed. by J. A. Woodburn, pp. 131-32.

[153] Allen, *Diary*, Feb. 17, 1777.

[154] Marshall, *Diary*, Feb. 4, 1777; *Journals*, Jan. 29, 1777. See letter of Gen. Washington to the Pa. Council of Safety, Jan. 29, 1777. *Writings of George Washington*, Fitzpatrick ed., VII, 79.

remedy can be provided, in less than seven years, Government will sink into a spiritless languor, or expire in a sudden convulsion. . . . With this sentiment, I feel an insuperable difficulty to enter into an engagement of the most solemn nature, leading to the support and confirmation of an entire system of government, which I cannot wholly approve. . . .[155]

This feeling must have been widespread among many of the leading men of the state, for Thomas Wharton shortly after his election to the presidency of the Council said: "I feel myself very inadequate to the station I am in; but some that were fit for it have either withdrawn themselves entirely, or are opposing the Government. . . ."[156]

This calm was merely on the surface, a lull before another storm. After the fear of Howe's invasion had abated somewhat the opposition forces renewed their attacks not only against the Constitution but also against the way in which it was being administered. A writer in the *Pennsylvania Gazette* on March 26, 1777, said: "Sorry am I to see that rancorous contest concerning the Constitution . . . revived with all the asperity it first commenced." "The party who believe the government to be a good one is too inconsiderable to be noticed," wrote Benjamin Rush.[157] The renewed struggle began on March 5, 1777—the very day of the inauguration of the Supreme Executive Council. On that day the Assembly received a petition from Attorney Robert Galbraith, of Bedford, praying that he be given the offices of Prothonotary, Recorder of Deeds, and Register of Wills for the said county, then held by Thomas Smith.[158] This was the first warning that Smith was to be punished for his opposition to the Constitution. Several members of the Assembly from Bedford County remonstrated against any such action. Three days later the

---

[155] Reed, *op. cit.*, I, 300-02. He was with the army of General Washington at the time and this may have had something to do with his refusal to accept the office. When he later accepted the office of President of the Council he was bitterly criticized.

[156] *Pa. Mag.*, V, 436. Letter to General St. Clair.

[157] *Observations on the present Government of Pennsylvania*, pp. 20-1.

[158] *Journals*, p. 124. *Vide Pa. Eve. Post*, Mar. 15, 1777.

Constitutionalists presented a counter-remonstrance asking for a new election of representatives from Bedford. The opponents of the Constitution were so powerful there that the Assembly ordered "seventy copies of the Constitution of this Commonwealth be procured, sent up and dispersed among the inhabitants of the county of Bedford."[159]

Galbraith received the appointment and demanded of Smith the "Books, Records, and other Papers and Seals of Office of the office of Prothonotary, Register of Wills, Recorder of Deeds, and Clerk of the Orphan's Court for the County of Bedford."[160] These Smith refused to surrender,[161] so the Supreme Executive Council ordered: "That the said Thomas Smith, Esq'r, be Arrested and Confined in the Gaol of the said County of Bedford, according to Law."[162] Smith was finally taken into custody by the sheriff, whereupon "he delivered up the Records, Seals, &c. . . ."[163] Galbraith soon afterwards wrote President Wharton that he had "been at Bedford and opened the Courts without any opposition, . . ." and that the "generality of the People in Bedford County are well disposed to the Constitution, and a little Time I am persuaded will put matters upon good footing. . . ."[164]

b. ORGANIZATION OF PARTIES

As might have been expected, these discordant groups soon began to crystallize into two political parties.[165] "Party spirit in Pennsylvania," wrote Graydon, "had . . . taken a consistency, and the politicians were divided into Constitutionalists and Republicans."[166] The radicals, paradoxically, took

---

[159] *Journals*, March 20, 1777. For the remonstrance of the several Bedford members see *ibid.*, March 17.

[160] *Pa. Arch.*, 1st ser., V, 638.

[161] *Ibid.*, p. 730.

[162] *Col. Rec.*, XI, 373.

[163] *Pa. Arch.*, 1st ser., VI, 238.

[164] *R. P.*, XVI, no. 39. Oct. 31, 1777; *Pa. Arch.*, 1st. ser., V, 730.

[165] *Vide* S. B. Harding, "Party Struggles over the first Pennsylvania Constitution," *Annual Report of the American Historical Association for 1894.* (Washington, 1895), pp. 382-84.

[166] *Memoirs*, p. 331.

the name of Constitutionalists, while their opponents styled themselves Republicans.[167] The former were naturally the supporters of the Constitution and the government organized under it. Their chief leaders were George Bryan, the Vice-President and later the President; Timothy Matlack, the clerk of the Assembly, and Franklin and Rittenhouse. Their strength lay in the outlying districts where these Philadelphia leaders were ably supported by Robert Whitehill, John Smilie, and William Findley. The Republicans opposed the Constitution, its framers and the party now in control. "Many of the First Characters in the State," wrote John Lacey, "out of a dislike of some of the Sections of this Constitution . . . it . . . being too loose and Democratic . . . exhibited a most formidable opposition. . . ."[168]

It was indeed a "formidable opposition," for among the leaders were such men as Robert Morris, James Wilson, Dr. Benjamin Rush, George Clymer, and Thomas Mifflin. Alexander Graydon, himself a lawyer, tells us that "there was an agreement, or at least an understanding, among the lawyers, who were generally on the republican side, neither to practice or accept of any office under the Constitution, which, in that case, they would be bound, by oath, to support. . . ."[169]

As the situation became more accute the Whig Society, a group of the Constitutionalists, held a meeting on March 18 and prepared an address to the people to be published

---

[167] Graydon said, "The term republicans was embraced, as recognizing the principles of the revolution, and as indicative perhaps of tenents, which admitted the utility of modifications and restraints, in a system resting on the broad base of general suffrage and popular sovereignty. The word *democrat* was not yet much in use, neither was the distinction established between a democrat and a republican, . . ." *Ibid*, p. 331.

[168] "Memoirs," *Pa. Mag.*, XXVI, 104. Lacey said they "called themselves the Nobility and better sort of People."

[169] *Memoirs*, p. 332. Graydon continues by saying: "But the constitutionalists had a Roland for their Oliver. They had prothonotaryships, attorney-generalships, chief justiceships, and what not to dispose of. Patriots have their price, 'tis said; and persons were found to accept these, some of whom, indeed, had cautiously avoided committing themselves by the promulgation of rash anathemas."

in all the papers in the state, both English and German. This address told the people that in view of the conditions in Pennsylvania everything depended upon unanimity.

A noisy and ill-natured wrangling, about the designs of the framers or opposers of the Constitution, can answer no other purpose than to injure and disgrace us . . . An enemy is at our gates, an enemy is within our doors; without government, laws, and civil magistrates, we can neither draw forth our military strength to oppose the one, nor exert our civil power to suppress the other.

Referring to the battle in the press and the pamphlet warfare begun anew, the message concluded:

Our only apology for this address is the alarming tendency of a few publications, which, whatever merit they might have had in a season of general tranquillity, we cannot omit informing you we now look upon as very ill-timed at least, and whatever may be asserted, by no means [represent] the present sense of the Whig Society in this city.[170]

This exacerbation of party strife again threw the state into turmoil and disruption. James Wilson, in a letter to General St. Clair on March 24, 1777, said: "Pennsylvania is in the greatest confusion: . . . The very critical situation of public affairs is of much advantage to the Assembly and their friends."[171] In Lancaster County conditions were extremely bad. A riot had occurred there, and Christian Wertz testified before the Supreme Executive Council that his life and property were no longer safe. The Council requested William Atlee, Chairman of the Lancaster Committee, to grant Mr. Wertz "such relief as the nature of his case will admit until Justices of the Peace be properly Commissioned to keep the Peace. . . ."[172] A number of freeholders and inhabitants of the borough of Lancaster sent a petition to the Assembly and the Council, setting forth the great inconveniences under which they labored for want of magistrates and

---

[170] *Pa. Gaz.*, Mar. 26, 1777. Signed by Charles Willson Peale, Chairman.

[171] *St. Clair Papers*, I, 392.

[172] *R. P.*, X, no. 43, March 25, 1777. *Pa. Arch.*, 1st ser., V, 266—here the name is spelled "Wirtz."

other borough officers.[173] About this time Judge Yeates, of
Lancaster, wrote a most despairing letter to Colonel Burd in
which he said:

I have not time nor patience to mention in how many instances
the Assembly has infringed the *inviolable* frame of government, or
to point out the impropriety of some late appointments; it is sufficient to say that the late steps give infinite dissatisfaction to the
men of property and understanding. The Clamors of the Red-Hot
Patriots Have Subsided into Easy Places and Offices of Profit! The
posts of mere TRUST go a begging! No one can be found to accept *them!* Whenever I reflect on the times, I am seized with the
blue devils. I walk about the room in a sweat, look at my family,
and wish them and myself out of the way of vexation. . . .[174]

Benjamin Rush later wrote of John Morton, a member of
Congress from Pennsylvania who had voted for the Declaration of Independence, that "His hatred to the new constitution of Pennsylvania, and his anticipation of its evils were
such, as to bring on a political hypochondriasis which it was
said put an end to his life a year or two after the declaration
of independence."[175]

These views were not merely those of ardent partisans or
political hypochondriacs. James Lang, for example, wrote to
the Council from Lancaster that "Every means of Depreciat-
ing the paper Currency" of the state were practised there,
and that "Toryism [was] holding up its head with impunity. . . . The Menonists Refuse to sell their Produce unless for hard cash . . . [and] will carry it home again Sooner
than sell it for Congress Currency."[176] Lieutenant Bartrem
Galbraith wrote that the "want of Magistrates in Lancaster is
the Greatest loss I'm at . . . I alone with a few Individuals,
am become the Butt of the whole County. I have had many
threatenings but paid no attention, & unless something
spirited is don [*sic*] I know not whether I may be safe, as they

---

[173] Mombert, *Hist. of Lanc. Co.*, p. 264.
[174] *Letters and Papers*, pp. 258-59.
[175] *An Account of Sundry Incidents*, etc.
[176] *R. P.*, XIII, no. 27.

have began [*sic*] with so much violence. . . ."[177] William Duer wrote that here "toryism, or rather treason, stalks triumphant; the credit of our money is sapp'd by the arts and advances of the malignants, and monopolists (?), and such is the desperate situation of affairs that nothing but desperate remedies can restore these people to reason and virtue."[178] From Cumberland County Colonel John Armstrong wrote President Wharton that "The greatest opposition by much that I have heard to the present Governm[t] happens to be in this County, where temper hath had too great a lead of reason, . . ."[179] From the same county William Thompson wrote to James Wilson on April 14, 1777, as follows:

The Sensible and vertious [*sic*] part of this County, have since you left us, been indeavoring to set this Villanous Constitution aside, and we had great reason to believe we should have been successful, had not Blaine brought up & reported that two thirds of the People below liked and would support the Constitution, and said it would be inforced by fixed Bayonets.

He refers to the "Damed Constitution," and says that Blaine "must have made some very valuable Contact with the Rascals that call themselves the Executive Council."[180] General Washington despairingly wrote General Schuyler that the "disaffection in Pennsylvania, which I fear is much beyond anything you have conceived, and the depression of the people of this State, render a strong support necessary to prevent a systematical submission; besides, the loss of Philadelphia would prove a very great injury, as we draw from thence almost all our supplies."[181] Early in March Congress returned to Philadelphia from Baltimore and John Adams found the city "a dull place, in comparison of what it was. More than one half of the inhabitants have removed into the country,

---

[177] *Ibid.*, no. 21. Letter to "Governor" Wharton, Lancaster, June 20, 1777.
[178] Letter to John Jay, Philadelphia, May 28, 1777. *Jay Papers*, I, 137-39.
[179] *Pa. Arch.*, 1st ser., V, 324.
[180] Ms. (Historical Society of Pennsylvania).
[181] *Life of Washington*, Sparks ed., IV, 360. See also Fitzpatrick, *Writings of George Washington*, VII, 36, 319.

as it was their wisdom to do. The remainder are chiefly
Quakers, as dull as beetles. From these neither good is to be
expected nor evil to be apprehended. They are a kind of
neutral tribe, or the race of the insipids. . . ."[182]

Such conditions were exactly what the Republicans wanted,
for their chances of securing alterations in the Constitution
—or even a new one—were in direct proportion to the amount
of disorder which existed. But a second time General Howe
upset their plans. Early in April an invasion of Pennsylvania
appeared imminent and, the Assembly having adjourned,
Congress threatened to intervene. On April 14 Congress declared:

WHEREAS The State of Pennsylvania is threatened with an immediate invasion, and from the adjournment of the legislative and
executive authority of the commonwealth,[183] it is impracticable to
carry into immediate execution, many measures of the utmost
importance, not only to the safety of this commonwealth, but likewise to the general welfare of the United States, *Resolved,* That
it is the indispensable duty of Congress, to watch over all matters,
the neglect of which may, in its consequences, deeply affect the
welfare of the United States, till such a time as the legislative and
executive authorities of the commonwealth of Pensylvania, can
resume the (regular) exercise of their different functions.[184]

The President of the Executive Council was requested to
call together the legislative and executive authority of the
state. A committee of three from Congress was appointed to
confer with the President of the Council and such other
members of that body who could be convened, together with
the Pennsylvania Board of War, to agree upon "the mode of

---

[182] Adams, *Letters to his Wife,* I, 194.

[183] The Council adjourned on April 10 and did not meet again until
May 6. (*Col. Rec.,* XI 203-06). This adjournment of the Executive Council
was strongly condemned. In a "Memorial" to the Council it was stated that
"Your Memorialists" saw "with surprise your Executive Council adjourn
themselves in a manner unprecedented by such bodies in any country, and
at a time when the exertions of some supreme authority were of the utmost
importance to the safety of the state." *Pa. Eve. Post,* May 17, 1777.

[184] *Journals of Congress,* April 14, 1777.

authority which they shall conceive most eligible to be exercised, during the recess of the house of assembly and the council. . . ." These various groups met in conference and decided that "the Executive Authority of the Common-Wealth of Pennsylvania is incapable of any exertion, adequate to the present crisis, . . ."[185]

Thus the efforts of the opponents of the Constitution were again thwarted by the intervention of Congress. "If a regular system was formed between General Howe and the friends of our Constitution," James Wilson wrote, "his motions could not have been better timed for them than they have been in two different instances. When an opposition has been twice set on foot, and has twice proceeded so far as to become formidable, he has twice, by his marches toward Delaware, procured a cessation. The Assembly have twice taken advantage of it to promote *their own* purposes, though those in the opposition generously, and like true patriots, have suspended it, while the approach of the enemy was dreaded. . . ."[186]

The heated fight over the Constitution continued and consumed the energies of the people in violent partisan strife at a time when every exertion was needed to overthrow the forces of Great Britain. The legion of Loyalists in Pennsylvania were thus able to find shelter under the aegis of the Anti-Constitutionalists, and bred suspicion and ill-feeling among the people, public men, and soldiers, thereby vitiating the state's participation in the Revolution. This statement is not meant to minimize the part Pennsylvania played—which was great indeed—but merely to show that only a fraction of her potential forces were ever mobilized. A *Memorial* presented to the Assembly in May 1777 said that the "natural strength and resources [of Pennsylvania] are such as, if properly col-

---

[185] *Pa. Arch.*, 1st ser., V, 311.

[186] James Wilson to General Arthur St. Clair, July 3, 1777. *St. Clair Papers*, I, 417. In the same letter Wilson said, however, that "to a man, the citizens of Philadelphia agreed to suspend their disputes about the Constitution and to join unanimously in every measure proper for repelling the enemy and defending the State."

lected and employed, would alone be sufficient to repel the present force which threatens us with an invasion."[187] The same idea is expressed in a letter of Colonel Thomas Hartley, written in Morristown on July 5, 1777. He said that General Conway was obliged to lead a few hundred men when "he is capable of commanding thousands. The Deficiency owing to the indolence of the Rulers in Pennsylv^a. . . ."[188]

The "Rulers" had achieved their aims and were not much interested in continuing the war. They had no grievances against England; they owed no debts to British merchants from which a successful war might free them.[189] They merely wanted to govern themselves. Their position was precarious and every nerve had to be strained to maintain it. No risk could be taken by sending large forces against the British. Democracy had achieved its goal. Thus it was that the battle for a new or revised constitution started almost simultaneously with the completion of the work of the Convention and ended only when the *Frame of Government* of 1776 was destroyed and a new Constitution was written in 1790.

---

[187] *Pa. Eve. Post,* May 17, 1777. Interrogated in England in 1775 Richard Penn said he thought there were 60,000 men in Pennsylvania fit to bear arms. *Pa. Mag.,* XXV, 137.

[188] MS, Gratz Collection, (Hist. Soc. of Penna.).

[189] *Vide* the situation in Virginia in this connection. Isaac S. Harrell, *Loyalism in Virginia* (Duke Univ. Press, 1926). George Mason wrote to Patrick Henry that the question was frequently heard in conversation: "If we are now to pay the debts due to the British merchants what have we been fighting for all this while?" Quoted in *ibid.,* p. 130.

CONCLUSION

TWO great themes in American history are the influence of immigration and the frontier upon the life and institutions of the country. Both these factors, which stimulated the development of a democratic spirit, are clearly seen in the study of the revolutionary movement in Pennsylvania and the framing of the first State Constitution. Penn's desire to build a flourishing and prosperous colony led him to encourage an artificial immigration, so that by the year 1755 almost half of the population was foreign-born. But this does not tell the whole story, for only about one-third of the total population was of English stock. The rest, Scotch-Irish and German, had little in common with the English Quakers. It was natural that these people of foreign birth or ancestry should contest the conservative rule of the Quakers. This struggle began in the early days of Pennsylvania's history and reached its climax in 1776 with the formation of the democratic Constitution.

The tendency of the frontier was to make the radicals and dissenters even more radical, and to convert the conservatives who settled there. Thus there developed on the frontier of Pennsylvania a thoroughly democratic spirit intolerant of the cautious and conservative policies of wealthy and aristocratic people living in peace and quiet in the East. We have traced the development of this opposition throughout the long period of colonial wars and have seen the suffering of the frontiersmen because of inadequate defense. After a long and angry struggle the revolt of the American colonies from the Mother Country afforded these people the desired opportunity to throw off the yoke of Eastern domination and to establish a more democratic form of government. Contrary to accepted belief, the revolutionists in Pennsylvania had far greater grievances against the rule of the Eastern aristocracy than against the policies of the English ministry. By joining in the movement for independence, they saw a golden opportunity to gain for themselves the control of affairs. The hatred felt by the Patriots for the Tories was perhaps less than their antipathy for the Anti-Constitutionalists.

The same conditions which prevailed among the frontiersmen were likewise found in the city of Philadelphia. Here, too, thousands of workers, artisans, and mechanics were denied the right to participate in the government. And why? Simply because they did not possess a certain amount of property or receive a specified income. The democratic spirit was developing in the minds of these people just as surely and determinedly as it was among the inhabitants of the frontier. As James Madison pointed out in Number Ten of the *Federalist:* ". . . the most common and durable source of factions has been the various and unequal distribution of property. Those who hold and those who are without property have ever formed distinct interests in society. Those who are creditors, and those who are debtors, fall under a like discrimination." Those who held property in Philadelphia controlled the government, while those who did not had no part whatever in the affairs of state. As a result, the disfranchised elements in the East were just as eager as the frontiersmen to overthrow the established order and create a government in which they would have a voice.

The leadership for this revolutionary movement came from the city of Philadelphia. Here there were greater opportunities for consultations, meetings, and gatherings of various kinds than in the sparsely settled communities of the West. Much was happening in Philadelphia and the leaders took part in every important event. Without the guidance and direction of such Philadelphians as Franklin, Bryan, Cannon, and Matlack it is doubtful if the old charter of William Penn would have been destroyed. When these men were unable to triumph by their own efforts they gained powerful allies among the more radical members of Congress. This alliance with Congress proved to be of great importance.

Again, the dissension in Pennsylvania vitally affected the course of the war with Great Britain. Only a small proportion of the available man-power was ever enlisted in the struggle against the English. The old idea that the year 1776 was a period of almost universal patriotic enthusiasm had no foundation in fact. Students of the American Revolution are thoroughly familiar with the urgent requests of General Washington for troops[1] and the inability of Congress to supply them. We now see quite clearly how the fight over the new Constitution of Pennsylvania rent the state asunder, preventing her from making the expected opposition to England. Armies are composed of the masses; those who die on the fields of battle are the so-called "common people." The great fortunes of war are made by those who stay at home and manufacture the supplies for the armies and gain monopolies of the essentials of life. Such was the case during the World War, and such was the case during the American Revolution. The "common people" in Pennsylvania had just achieved a remarkable political triumph—they had framed a Constitution according to their own views and had gained the right to control their own affairs. The first real democratic government in America had been established. But the opposition of those deposed from power was great. It was dangerous for the masses to march off to the firing-line and leave these dispossessed classes, which refused to bear arms, at home where they could easily regain the control of government. Consequently, the masses refused to enlist and the badly needed armies could not be raised. Even when the British were at the very doors of Pennsylvania troops could not be recruited. "Great pains were taken to get the militia out, but in vain; . . . few were prevailed on to turn out."[2] There was apathy almost everywhere in the colony. Even among the

---

[1] For example, on October 13, 1777, he wrote: "It gives me pain to repeat so often the wants of the army, & nothing would induce me to it but the most urgent necessity." *Pa. Arch.*, 1st ser., V, 669. *Writings of George Washington*, Fitzpatrick (ed.), VII, 319.

[2] *Examination of Joseph Galloway*, p. 15.

frontiersmen of Cumberland County many people "tarried at home and minded their own private Affairs as uncon- cern'd as if there was the most profound Peace in the Coun- try."[3] Of course the Associators would not march to the front

... while Non-associators were permitted to remain at home in the peaceable Enjoyment of their professions, and many of them in- creasing their Wealth by grasping the Trade of the absent Asso- ciators, whose patriotic Exertions have been sneered at, and their hardships & fatigues, and the distresses of their families, insultingly made a jest of . . .[4]

As we have pointed out, most of the apathy of the people of Pennsylvania to the war was due to the struggle over the Constitution. Party feeling was so intense that a large body of men refused to enlist simply because by so doing they would better the fortunes of those in control and would strengthen the hated frame of government. It is probably true, as General Lacey said, that some in this class entirely "overlooked the fatal effects their opposition [to the Con- stitution] might produce in distroying [sic] the general Cause of Independence."[5] John Adams wrote that Pennsylvania will be "rendered much less vigorous in the cause by the wretched ideas of government which prevail in the minds of many people in it."[6] In many instances the people were more interested in the new government than in the contest they were waging with England.

The struggle obviously was based on economic interests. It was a conflict between the merchants, bankers, and com- mercial groups of the East and the debtor agrarian population of the West; between the property holders and employers and the propertyless mechanics and artisans of Philadelphia. It was the beginning of a struggle which was to come to frui- tion in the formation of the Constitution of the United States

---

[3] *R. P.*, IX, no. 25; see *supra*, p. 232.
[4] *Ibid.*, no. 59; see *supra*, p. 233.
[5] *Pa. Mag.*, XXVI, 104.
[6] John Adams, *Letters to his Wife*, I, 168-69.

eleven years later and which is still a major problem in America.

What permanent influence did the establishing of the Constitution of 1776 have upon the subsequent history of Pennsylvania? The adoption of the Federal Constitution in 1789 strengthened the hands of the party in Pennsylvania opposed to the state Constitution[7] and finally enabled them, after a struggle of fourteen years, to call a convention to revise the frame of government. The Constitution of 1790 was quite different from that of 1776. In fact, it was exceedingly reactionary and undid much of the work of the early framers. In the new Constitution the legislative, executive, and judicial powers were distinguished and defined according to the now classic American method. Provision was made for a governor, an assembly, and a senate. A judiciary serving during good behavior was also established—an idea strongly opposed in the Convention of 1776 as entirely too aristocratic. The new Constitution was, in fact, in almost every respect a copy of the Federal Constitution.

But the democratic spirit which had won a triumphant victory in 1776 was not dead. The life tenure of the judges became the subject of a vitriolic attack, culminating in a series of impeachment proceedings against the judges. The Whiskey Rebellion of 1794 in Western Pennsylvania was likewise a manifestation of the democratic spirit and a sign of the opposition of the Westerners, mostly Scotch-Irish, to the stern rule of the Federalist party. The House-Tax, or Fries' Rebellion in 1799 was an indication of the same spirit among the Germans in the eastern counties of Bucks, Montgomery, and Northampton. In spite of later changes in the Constitution, the Declaration of Rights of 1776 remained practically unchanged to the present day and exerted a permanent influence upon the political thought of Pennsylvania.

---

[7] *Vide* McMaster and Stone, *Pennsylvania and the Federal Constitution.*

BIBLIOGRAPHY

IN THE preparation of this study the writer has relied mainly upon the colonial press of Pennsylvania, both for its newspapers and its controversial pamphlets, and the manuscript letters of the actors in the drama of democracy in Pennsylvania. Many letters are here printed for the first time. But as has been mentioned, little is known about the actual proceedings of the Constitutional Convention because most of its members were farmers and artisans and not great letter writers. However, this source is invaluable, for it gives us an intimate glimpse into the real thought and feeling of the time.

The more important newspapers are as follows: *The Pennsylvania Gazette,* established December 24, 1728; published by Franklin and Meredith, 1729-32; by Franklin alone from 1732 to 1748; by Franklin and Hall, 1748-66; by David Hall, February-May, 1766, and by Hall and Sellers after May, 1766. The paper was suspended from November 29, 1776 to February 5, 1777. *The Pennsylvania Journal,* established by William Bradford on December 2, 1742. Published by William and Thomas Bradford from 1766 to 1793, except during its period of suspension from November 27, 1776 to January 29, 1777, and during the period of the British occupancy of Philadelphia from September, 1777, to 1778. *The Pennsylvania Packet,* established October 28, 1771, by John Dunlap. It was suspended from November 26 to December 18, 1776. Moved to Lancaster in 1777 and remained there until July, 1778. *The Pennsylvania Evening Post,* established January 24, 1775, by Benjamin Towne and published by him until about 1784. The title was changed in 1781. As late as 1777 the *Evening Post* was a radical paper, advocating national independence and a new state government. But when the British captured Philadelphia the editor changed sides and was proscribed by the state authorities. In 1778, after publicly recanting his British sympathies, the continuation of his paper was permitted. The paper had numerous suspensions from September 23, 1777 to 1778. *The Pennsylvania Ledger* established January 28, 1775, by James Humphreys,

Jr., as a Tory paper, was forced to suspend from November 30, 1776 to October 10, 1777. It stopped publication with the issue of May 23, 1778, just prior to the evacuation of Philadelphia by British troops. During the period covered by this study there were no newspapers published in Pennsylvania outside of Philadelphia.

The manuscript material has been found largely in the excellent collections of the Historical Society of Pennsylvania, the collection of Revolutionary Papers in the Archives Division of the Pennsylvania State Library, and the following collections in the Manuscript Division of the Library of Congress: Pennsylvania Miscellaneous MSS, Pennsylvania Broadsides (folio 144), The Franklin Papers, Miscellaneous, I, the Charles Thomson Papers, I, and the Edward Shippen Papers, 1727-1783. Among the manuscript collections of the Historical Society of Pennsylvania the following were particularly rich in material for the topics we have discussed: Peters MSS, Yeates MSS, Gratz MSS, and the Miscellaneous MSS in the York County Papers. Much of the pamphlet literature is cited in Charles R. Hildeburn, *A Century of printing. The issues of the press in Pennsylvania, 1685-1784* (Philadelphia, 1885-86); Charles Evans, *American Bibliography, 1689-1820.* 10 vols. (Chicago, 1903-29); and Joseph Sabin, *Dictionary of Books Relating to America from its Discovery to the Present Time* (New York, 1868-date).

Mention should also be made of the *American Historical Review,* and especially the *Pennsylvania Magazine of History and Biography* published by the Historical Society of Pennsylvania, of which fifty-eight volumes have appeared to date (1934). It is rich in source material and also contains many excellent articles dealing with the period under discussion by well-known authorities. No attempt will be made to cite these articles here, as most of them have already been given in the references.

In the following list there has been no attempt to make an exhaustive bibliography. Only those works which have been used in the preparation of this study are given.

PRIMARY SOURCES

1. *Official Documents*

Votes and Proceedings of the House of Representatives of the Province of Pennsylvania, 1682-1776. 6 vols. Philadelphia, 1752-76. These have since been printed in the 8th series of the *Pennsylvania Archives.* No dates

of meetings are given, however, thus greatly impairing their usefulness.
Journals of the House of Representatives of the Commonwealth of Pennsylvania, 1776-81, with the Proceedings of the several Committees and Conventions before and at the Commencement of the American Revolution. Michael Hillegas, ed., Phiadelphia, 1782.

The Acts of the General Assembly of the Commonwealth of Pennsylvania, 1777-81, with an Appendix containing the "Laws now in Force passed betweend September 30, 1775, and the Revolution." Philadelphia, 1782.

Proceedings Relative to Calling the Conventions of 1776 and 1790, etc. Harrisburg, 1825.

Constitutions of Pennsylvania, compiled by Fertig and Moore, Legislative Reference Bureau. Harrisburg, 1926. It is doubtful if the original Constitution of 1776, preserved in the Archives Division of the State Library at Harrisburg, was used in this compilation, for many discrepancies have been noted by the present writer.

The Statutes at Large of Pennsylvania, 1682-1801. Compiled by James T. Mitchell and Henry Flanders. Harrisburg, 1896 and subsequent dates.

Federal and State Constitutions, Colonial Charters, and Other Organic Laws, etc., ed. by Francis N. Thorpe, 5 vols., Washington, (Government Printing Office), 1909.

Federal and State Constitutions, Colonial Charters, &c. 2 vols., ed. by Ben: Perley Poore. Washington, 1877.

Laws of the Commonwealth, ed. by Dallas. 4 vols., Philadelphia and Lancaster, 1797-1804.

Laws of Pennsylvania, ed. by J. Bioren. 8 vols. Philadelphia, 1803-08.

Laws of Pennsylvania, ed. by Smith. 10 vols. Philadelphia, 1810-44.

The Pennsylvania Archives. Series I, 12 v. Philadelphia, 1852-6; Series II, 19 v., Harrisburg, 1874-90. (Another edition, 1879-90); The edition used was that of 1874-90, volume iii being published in 1875; Series III, 30 v. Harrisburg, 1894-1900; Series IV, 12 v. (Papers of the Governors). Harrisburg, 1900-02; Series V, 8 v. Harrisburg, 1906; Series VI, 15 v. Harrisburg, 1906-7; Series VII, 5 v. (Index to 6th series). Harrisburg, 1914; Series VIII, 4 v. Harrisburg, 1931; Series IX, 6 v. (Executive Minutes). Harrisburg, 1931. (See *American Historical Association Report,* 1900. v. 2. Washington, 1901. "Report of the Public Archives Commission," pp. 267-278.)

Colonial Records, 16 vols. Harrisburg, 1851-53.

Minutes of the Provincial Council of Pennsylvania from the organization to the termination of the proprietary government, 10 v. Harrisburg, 1851-52. (This is included in the *Colonial Records*). Volume X contains the minutes of the Committee of Safety from June 30, 1775, to November 12, 1776. (The Council of Safety superseded the Committee on July 24, 1776. Vol. XI contains its proceedings.)

Minutes of the Supreme Executive Council, 6 vols. Harrisburg, 1852-3 (These are volumes 11 to 16 of the *Colonial Records*).

American Archives, ed. by Peter Force, 4th and 5th series. Washington, 1837-53.

Journals of the Continental Congress. Philadelphia, 1800. Also Library of Congress edition, Washington, 1904-date.

Minutes of the Yearly Meeting of the Friends in Philadelphia, 1755.
Documents Relative to the Colonial History of New York. New York, 1856-58.
New Jersey Archives. 1st series, vol x.
Register of Pennsylvania, Samuel Hazard, ed., 16 vols., Philadelphia, 1828-35.
Penn MSS. *Charters and Frames of Government.* (Hist. Society of Penna.)
　　　　Official Correspondence. vols. i, ii, iii. (Hist. Society of Penna.)
　　　　Letter Books. 12 vols. (Hist. Society of Penna.)
Correspondence between William Penn and James Logan, 2 vols. *Memoirs of the Historical Society of Pennsylvania,* vols. 9 and 10. Philadelphia, 1870 and 1872.
Documents Illustrative of the Formation of the Union of the American States. Washington, Government Printing Office, 1927.

2. *Personal Writings*

Adams, John. *Works, with a Life of the Author,* ed. by Charles Francis Adams, 10 vols., Boston, 1850-56.
Adams, John. *Letters addressed to his Wife,* ed. by Charles Francis Adams. 4 vols., Boston, 1841.
Allen, James. *Diary.* Ms. in the Historical Society of Pennsylvania. (Part of this diary has been printed in the *Pennsylvania Magazine of History and Biography,* vol. ix.)
Allen, William. *Extracts from William Allen's Letter Book,* ed. by L. B. Walker. Pottsville, Pa., 1897.
Biddle, Charles. *Autobiography.* Philadelphia, 1883.
Franklin, Benjamin. *Works, . . . with Notes and a Life of the Author,* ed. by Jared Sparks, 10 vols., Boston, 1836-40.
　　　　Writings, ed. by A. H. Smyth, 10 vols., New York, 1905-7.
Galloway, Joseph. *A Candid Examination,* etc. New York, 1775. Reprinted in London, 1780.
Galloway, Joseph. *The Examination of Joseph Galloway, Esq., Before the House of Commons, . . .* London (J. Wilkie), 1779.
Graydon, Alexander. *Memoirs of His Own Times,* ed. by John S. Littell, Philadelphia, 1846.
Jay, John. *The Correspondence and Papers of John Jay,* 4 vols., New York, 1890-93.
Lee, Charles. "Papers," *New York Historical Society, Collections,* 4v., New York, 1871-74.
Letters of the Members of the Continental Congress, ed. by Edmund C. Burnett, 3 vols., Washington, 1923.
Letters and Papers relating Chiefly to the Provincial History of Pennsylvania, ed. by Thomas M. Balch, Philadelphia, 1855. (Sometimes erroneously called the "Shippen Papers.")
Marshall, Christopher. *Extracts from the Diary of Christopher Marshall.* (Called by him a "Rememberencer"), ed. by William Duane, Philadelphia, 1849, and Albany, 1877.
Muhlenberg, Rev. Henry Melchior. "Extracts from the Journal of Henry M. Muhlenberg," *Collections of the Historical Society of Pennsylvania,* Philadelphia, 1853.

Paine, Thomas. *Writings*, ed. by D. E. Wheeler, 10 vols., New York, 1908.
    The Political Writings of Thomas Paine, 2 vols., New York, 1835.
Reed, Joseph. "Narrative," *Thomson Papers, New York Historical Society Collections*, 1878. New York, 1879.
Rush, Benjamin. *Essays*. Philadelphia, 1798.
    An Account of Sundry Incidents in the Life of Benjamin Rush, Written by Himself. (Printed in *Benjamin Rush —a Memorial*, by Louis Biddle, 1905.)
St. Clair. Arthur. *The St. Clair Papers*, ed. by William H. Smith, 2 vols. Cincinnati, 1882.
Schoepf, Dr. J. D. *Travels in the Confederation* (1783-84), 2 vols., Philadelphia, 1911.
Smith, Wm. *A Brief State of the Province of Pennsylvania*. London, 1755.
Stiles, Ezra. *Itineraries and Correspondence*, ed. by F. B. Dexter, New Haven, 1916.
Thomson, Charles. "The Thomson Papers, letter to William H. Drayton," *New York Historical Society Collections, 1878*. New York, 1879.
"Warren-Adams Letters," vol. i, *Massachusetts Historical Society Collections*, vol. 72, 1917.
Washington, George. *The Writings of George Washington*, ed. by John C. Fitzpatrick, Washington, Government Printing Office, 11 vols. to Feb., 1934, 1931-date.
Washington, George. *Writings*, etc. Ed. by Jared Sparks. 12 vols. Boston, 1837.
    Writings. Ed. by W. C. Ford. 14 vols. New York, 1889.
Willing, Thomas. *Willing Letters and Papers*, ed. by Thomas W. Balch. Philadelphia, 1922.
Wilson, James. *Works*. 3 vols., Philadelphia, 1804.
Witherspoon, John. *The Dominion of Providence over the Passions of Men.* To which is added *An Address to the Natives of Scotland residing in America.* (Preached at Princeton on May 17, 1776.) Philadelphia, 1776.

SECONDARY WORKS

Albert, George D. *History of the County of Westmoreland*. Philadelphia, 1882.
Aldrich, P. E. "John Locke in America," *American Antiquarian Society Proceedings*, 1879.
Armor, William C. *Lives of the Governors of Pennsylvania*. Philadelphia, 1873.
Austin, James T. *The Life of Elbridge Gerry*. 2 vols. Boston, 1828.
Barton, William. *Memoirs of David Rittenhouse*. Philadelphia, 1813.
Beveridge, Albert J. *Life of John Marshall*. 4 vols., Boston, 1916-19.
Biddle, Louis. *Benjamin Rush—A Memorial*. Philadelphia, 1905.
Bishop, Cortland F. "History of Elections in the American Colonies," *Columbia Univ. Studies in History, Economics and Public Law*, vol. iii. New York, 1893.
Bolles, Albert S. *Pennsylvania: Province and State*. 2 vols. Philadelphia and New York, 1899.
Buchanan, Roberdeau. *Genealogy of the McKean Family with a biography of Thomas McKean*. Lancaster, 1890.

Carpenter, W. S. *Democracy and Representation.* Princeton, 1925.
> *The Development of American Political Thought.* Princeton, 1930.

Conway, Moncure D. *Life of Thomas Paine.* 2 vols. New York, 1893.

Corwin, E. S. "The Progress of Constitutional Theory," *American Historical Review,* XXX.
> "The 'Higher Law' Background of American Constitutional Law," *Harvard Law Review,* XLII, nos. 2 & 3.

Cribbs, George A. *The Frontier Policy of Pennsylvania.* Pittsburgh, 1919.

Cushing, Harry A. "The People the Best Governors," *American Historical Review,* I.

Dealey, J. Q. *The Growth of American State Constitutions.* Boston, 1915.

Dickerson, Oliver M. *American Colonial Government.* Cleveland, 1912.

Erdman, C. R. Jr. *The New Jersey Constitution of 1776.* Princeton, 1929.

Ford, P. L. "The First Pennsylvania Constitution," *Political Science Quarterly,* X.

Friedenwald, Herbert. *The Declaration of Independence.* New York, 1904.

Gordon, Thomas F. *History of Pennsylvania.* Philadelphia, 1829.

Greene, Evarts B. "The Provincial Governor," *Harvard Historical Studies,* VII. Cambridge, 1898.

Harding, Samuel B. "Party Struggles over the first Pennsylvania Constitution," *Annual Report of the American Historical Association for 1894.* Washington, 1895.

Hazelton, John H. *The Declaration of Independence—Its History.* New York, 1906.

Harrell, Isaac. *Loyalism in Virginia.* Duke Univ. Press, 1926.

History of Northumberland County. Philadelphia, 1876.

History of Bedford, Somerset, and Franklin Counties. Chicago, 1884.

Jenkins, Howard M., ed. *Pennsylvania, Colonial and Federal.* 2 vols. Philadelphia, 1903.

Knauss, James O. *Social Conditions among the Pennsylvania Germans in the 18th Century.* Lancaster, 1922.

Konkle, Burton A. *George Bryan and the Constitution of Pennsylvania—1731-1791.* Philadelphia, 1922.
> *The Life and Times of Thomas Smith.* Phila., 1904.

Levering, Joseph M. *A History of Bethlehem.* Bethlehem, 1903.

Lincoln, Charles H. *The Revolutionary Movement in Pennsylvania.* Publications of the University of Pennsylvania. Phila., 1901.

McMaster, John B., and Stone, Frederick D. *Pennsylvania and the Federal Constitution.* Lancaster, 1888.

Merriam, Charles E. *A History of American Political Theories.* New York, 1926.

McKinley, Albert E. *The Suffrage Franchise in the Thirteen English Colonies in America.* Boston, 1905.

Miller, F. H. "Legal Qualifications for Office," *Annual Report of the American Historical Assn., 1899.* vol. 1.

Mombert, J. I. *Authentic History of Lancaster County in the state of Pennsylvania.* Lancaster, 1869.

Montgomery, M. L. *History of Berks County in the Revolution.* Reading, 1894.

Morey, William C. "First State Constitution," *Annals of the American Academy of Political and Social Science.* vol. iv, September, 1893.

Nevins, Allan. *The American States During and After the Revolution.* New York, 1927.

Oberholtzer, Ellis P. *Robert Morris—Patriot and Financier.* New York, 1903.

Parrington, Vernon L. *The Colonial Mind.* New York, 1927.

Proud, Robert. *History of Pennsylvania.* 2 vols. Phila., 1797-8.

Reed, William B. *Life and Correspondence of Joseph Reed.* 2 vols., Philadelphia, 1847.

Root, Winfred T. *The Relations of Pennsylvania with the British Government.* New York, 1912.

Sachse, Julius F. "Pennsylvania: The German Influence in its Settlement and Development," *The Proceedings of the Pennsylvania German Society,* VII (1897).

Scharf, J. Thomas, and Westcott, Thompson. *A History of Philadelphia.* 3 vols., Philadelphia, 1884.

Selsam, J. Paul. "A History of Judicial Tenure in Pennsylvania," *The Dickinson Law Review,* XXXVIII, no. 3, 1934.

Sharpless, Isaac. *A Quaker Experiment in Government.* Philadelphia, 1898. (See also other works by Sharpless on the Quakers.)

Shepherd, William R. "A History of Proprietary Government in Pennsylvania," *Columbia University Studies in History, Economics and Public Law,* VI. New York, 1896.

Siebert, Wilbur H. *The Loyalists of Pennsylvania.* Columbus, 1920.

Smith, Horace W. *Life and Correspondence of the Rev. William Smith, D. D.* 2 vols., Philadelphia, 1879-80.

Smith, W. R. "Sectionalism in Pennsylvania During the Revolution," *Political Science Quarterly,* XXIV, 1908.

Stackhouse, A. M. *Col. Timothy Matlack—Patriot and Soldier.* (Privately printed, 1910.)

Stillé, Charles J. "The Life and Times of John Dickinson," *Memoirs of the Historical Society of Pennsylvania,* XIII. Philadelphia, 1891.
    Major-General Anthony Wayne and the Pennsylvania Line in the Continental Army. Phila., 1893.

Thorpe, Francis N. *A Constitutional History of the American People.* 2 vols., New York, 1898.

Webster, W. C. "A Comparative Study of the State Constitutions of the American Revolution," *Annals of the American Academy of Political and Social Science,* IX.

Wertenbaker, Thomas J. *The American People: a History.* New York, 1926.

White, Thomas R. *Commentaries on the Constitution of Pennsylvania.* Philadelphia, 1907.

INDEX

Adams, John, 114; arrival in Philadelphia, 61; influence of Continental Congress, 65-6; change after Lexington, 77-8; position on conciliation, 1775, 89-90; Quaker attitude to independence, 93; exhortation to independence, 110-1, 113 *notes*, 70, 71; on vote for independence, 156 *note;* on Alexander Pope, 171 *note* 9; *Thoughts on Government*, 172-83; opinion of *Common Sense*, 172-3; on unicameral system, 184, 186; on annual elections, 191; objections to salary clause of Constitution, 193; on opposition to Constitution and oath, 221-2; on new confidence in Pennsylvania, 244; on powder contract, 234; on dullness of Philadelphia, 251-2; effect of Constitution on people, 258.

Adams, Samuel, 110.

Admiralty Court, 166.

Alison, Rev. Francis, 7, 148, 217.

Allen, Andrew, 91-2, 101-2, 112, 156.

Allen, James, 77, 85, effect of non-allegiance resolution, 115; on change in Continental Congress instructions, 133; member of Assembly, 147; gives reasons for long session of Convention, 161; on meetings in State House, 166; on last acts of Assembly, 167; split in Whigs, 229; on arbitrary actions of Council of Safety, 238; on conditions in latter part of 1776, 240; on ascendency of new parties, 242; on resumption of public affairs, 241.

Allen, William, Chief Justice, 97.

Amboy, 87.

Amendment, of Constitution, 200.

Anti-constitutional party, 227.

Aristocrats, 209-11; *see also*, Tories, Whigs, right wing, Proprietary interests.

Arms, right to bear, 182.

Armstrong, John, 251.

Arndt, Jacob, 80.

Assembly, Provincial, growth in power, 9-10; control of the purse, 10-5; taxation of Proprietors' estates, 15-8; on provincial defense, 18-31; representation unequal, 31-9; action on Stamp Act, 45-6; message to Boston, 52-3; votes for Continental Congress, 59; entertains Congress, 63; approves first acts of Congress, 64; appoints delegates to 2nd Congress, 65, 73-4; firm attitude, 72; rejects conciliation plan of Parliament, 73; votes for association and supplies after Lexington, 78, 79; lenient treatment of non-associators, 80-1; organizes militia from Associators, 83-4; arms of non-associators collected, 87; refused appointment of generals, 88-9; attitude on conciliation and independence, 89-93; readjusts representation, 97, 99-100; refuses to rescind instructions, 100; warning on overthrow, 107; Philadelphia citizens protest, 117-8; difficulties, 129-31; Committee on Continental Congress resolves, 130; blind course, 131; resolutions of Provincial Conference on, 137; electorate same as for Convention, 138; inability to meet needs, 142; ignored by Congress, 152; attitude toward Indian depredations, 153; bills of credit legal tender, 154; majority delegates for convention not selected by, 159; meeting of new, 164; difficulties and adjournment, 165; 2nd adjournment through lack of quorum, 166;